PAPER TRAILS

FROM TREES TO TRASH – THE TRUE COST OF PAPER

PAPER TRAILS

FROM TREES TO TRASH – THE TRUE COST OF PAPER

MANDY HAGGITH

Published by Virgin Books 2008

2 4 6 8 10 9 7 5 3 1

First published in Great Britain in 2008 by
Virgin Books
Random House
Thames Wharf Studios
Rainville Road
London, W6 9HA

www.rbooks.co.uk

Addresses for companies within The Random House Group Limited can be found at:
www.randomhouse.co.uk/offices.htm

The Random House Group Limited Reg. No. 954009

A CIP catalogue record for this book
is available from the British Library.

ISBN 9780753513293

Typeset in Palatino by Palimpsest Book Production Limited,
Grangemouth, Stirlingshire

The paper and board used on this book are 100% recycled.
The manufacturing process conforms to the regulations of the country of origin.
The Random House paper procurement policy can be found at
www.rbooks.co.uk/environment
Printed and bound in Great Britain by CPI Mackays, Chatham ME5 8TD

For people all over the world with forest livelihoods and homes,
and to Bill for sharing his with me.

rustle of leaves:
good books and toilet rolls
felling ancient trees

CONTENTS

PREFACE

Trees are amazing. They breathe in sunshine and animal-fumes and weave them into cellulose fibres tough enough to stand in a hurricane. We humans, creative and peculiar as we are, have found ways to melt them down and spin them into tissue, board and literature. But at what cost?

Forests regulate our climate by storing carbon; they create rain, clean rivers and protect freshwater supplies; they contain the vast bulk of the world's biodiversity and are the source of a cornucopia of useful materials, medicines, textiles, timber and food. Forests are also important because, contrary to popular perception, they are not uninhabited places; they are all cultural landscapes. Every forest in the world is or was someone's home. Any forest tale is really a human story.

I am one of those lucky enough to live in the woods. In late winter, I stand under the biggest holly tree, breathing in the air beneath it then puffing it back out dragon-style. I have mixed the oxygen distilled by the tree with carbon so my plume of steam is part carbon dioxide. The holly tree will absorb it and pass it back again, decarbonated, as pure oxygen. So do all the trees of the world, and so do all the other plants making up the forest ecosystems: climbers such as the honeysuckle, so eager for spring that it is showing leaves already; ferns that now lie crumpled and brown, timing their total disintegration for some distant May morning when they will begin to unfurl new leaves from violin-head scrolls; mosses and lichens, upholstering every rock and tree stump they can find with cushions and mattresses; tender herbs and flowers, such as the primroses, wood sorrel and violets, starting to poke optimistic fronds from among the litter of last year's greenery.

Here is where breathable air is made, inside these leafy lungs. I inhale deeply, thankful to the holly, and I marvel at its resilience. It is a strange, triangular shape, carved on one side by exposure to the south-west, the direction of the prevailing winds, which glide or gallop in from the Atlantic ocean just a few hundred metres away. They sculpt everything that grows in their wake as effectively as motorised hedge-cutters.

Last night, the forest roared and danced like a crazed audience at a stadium rock concert, as a storm force 11 blasted in, gusting at close to 120 km (75 miles) per hour. The trees here must face such ferocity each winter and as the climate changes, they will have to endure worse and more frequent storms. They duck and dive, wave and wiggle, and although occasionally one snaps or tears or falls over, their elasticity and strength is quite extraordinary. They operate as a huddle, sheltering each other in their throng, but unlike penguins in Antarctica, they can't take turns to be on the outside. Those that are, like this holly, are carved in lasting memorial to the storms they have weathered.

When the trees are still, however, their trunks seem unshakable. I squeeze the bark of a birch tree: it feels hard as marble, solid and immovable. Their secret is wood, the complex structure inside their bark. Each year it grows another invisible layer, ring by ring. It is made out of the carbon that the trees have stripped from the air and the water that they suck out of the earth, with the alchemy called photosynthesis. Green leaves sauté carbon dioxide and water in sunshine to produce sugars, which trickle down into the tree to be, eventually, transformed into wood.

The trunk of a tree is a huge system of tubes called xylem, like a bundle of straws, for drawing water up from the ground. Wrapped around the outside is a thin layer of tubes, called phloem, which transports sweet juice down from the leaves to the rest of the plant. All the xylem and phloem tubes are a single cell wide, and their walls are made of a simple carbon-based substance called cellulose, strings of which form tough fibres. As the xylem in the centre of the tree grows old, it hardens with a sticky substance, called lignin, into what is known as heartwood. As the phloem ages it becomes bark. So cells that begin life as sappy vessels end it as tough, weight-bearing timber, or as poet Kathleen Raine put it, trees 'bear the weight of sky and cloud / Upon the fountain of their veins'.

This book is a gathering of stories about what happens when trees are made into paper. Except where I state otherwise, these stories are the result of a journey I made in the first half of 2006 from my home in Scotland overland to Sumatra, Indonesia, and then across North America. The purpose of this trip was to see where all the paper we use in the UK comes from and what impacts it has there. I observed paper being made in Scotland, traced my local recycling bin's contents to China, where I discovered the history of paper, watched trees being felled for a modern mill in Finland, witnessed pollution from older mills in Russia, and became enraged by human rights abuses in Indonesia and destructive forestry in Canada. I was also inspired by scientists, environmentalists, community leaders, corporate paper buyers and industry employees who explained to me the many ways in which they are working to safeguard forests for future generations.

The people I met showed me that paper use is the source of problems cutting across most of the issues that concern environmentally and ethically minded citizens. Industrial paper producers have colossal impacts: as well as demolishing forest habitats, they threaten fresh water supplies, contribute to global warming, create pollution and waste, abuse human rights and prop up a global regime where multinational corporations prosper at the expense of indebted southern countries. We are used to thinking about single issues at a time: fossil fuel use is bad for the climate; the multinational garments industry is bad for human rights; toxic chemicals are bad for health. Paper is bad for all of these and more. Moreover, the problems caused by paper are exacerbated as consumption grows.

Fortunately, unlike climate change, most of the problems posed by our paper use are tractable and there are many people around the world promoting solutions that we can all adopt to reduce our paper footprints. The most direct is simply to use less. If we cancel our orders for newspapers or magazines that we hardly read, and unplug the printer for a day, we may all discover that this can be much easier than we think.

CHAPTER 1: ADDICTED TO PULP

Paper, paper everywhere

From bills to books, cartons to catalogues, loo roll to lottery tickets, paper is ubiquitous. Each of our life stories is a medley of sheets beginning with a medical chart in a maternity ward, leafed and shuffled through until we finish with a death certificate and coroner's report. A modern European life's worth of paper would be a major art installation: twenty tonnes of packaging, newspapers, magazines, books and toilet rolls plus treasures like calligraphic scrolls or origami, mementoes like football match tickets and concert programmes, not forgetting all those credit card receipts, telephone directories, Post-its and pointless photocopying. All this paper would easily fill a double-decker bus.

Paper has huge aesthetic appeal. It is fundamental to the work of artists, from painters to calligraphers, from musicians to architects. It comes in a rainbow of colours and has its range of distinctive sounds: the rustling of the pages of a book, the whirr of a card-sharp shuffle, the crumple of newspaper to light a winter fire. It can be as tough as a board or thin enough to trace through, corrugated or shiny smooth. Long-awaited letters carry the scent of loved ones just as brand-new money has the perfume of opportunity and examination papers smell of fear. There are even papers made especially to eat – from the traditional rice paper for summer rolls to edible starch papers made for printing with edible inks, for those who want literally to eat their words.

Paper's diversity and penetration into our lives is extraordinary. Our mornings begin with tissues and teabags, coffee filters and cereal packets; our days are scattered with postcards, flyers, train tickets, diaries, documents, notebooks, receipts and stickers; our evenings bring cinema tickets, popcorn boxes, CD inserts and magazines. Shops are stacked with cardboard packets, labels, tags and more receipts. Our homes are awash with kitchen roll, junk mail, bills and last weekend's newspapers. Despite a wealth of new entertainments and technologies, paper's adaptability is hard to beat.

Paper has been an extraordinarily good tool for transferring ideas in space and time. What began as an intimate one-to-one or at best one-to-few communication, through letters and hand-written folios and books, evolved with the advent of printing presses and increasing literacy into broadcast news and views, enabling ideas to spread widely and more quickly than ever before. Yet as new devices have come along to serve the same function, such as radio, TV and the internet, paper has not only held its own, it has actually increased in usage. Junk mail and advertising proliferate as corporations use ever more sophisticated tricks to influence our behaviour as consumers, with paper often as the medium. Nothing in the world will make me deny the pleasure of curling up with a good book, the fun of a comic, the inspiration that can be gained from flicking through a well-designed glossy magazine, the democratic values served by a free press or the awe engendered by our great libraries. But the sheer volume of paper circulating in modern society is getting completely out of hand.

I have to confess to being an enthusiastic user of paper myself – it's an occupational hazard for anyone with a zeal for writing. I have something of a stationery fetish, a serious weakness for arty hand-made paper no matter how impractical and find it hard to resist smooth, creamy sheets that just beg to be scribbled on. I am a self-confessed notebook addict needing a regular supply and, like many writers,

I am fussy about these things, preferring narrow lines to wide and having a certain predilection for margins and ring binding. Feeding my habit with adequate jotters made of recycled or environmentally benign paper is something of a struggle, but it *is* possible, and the discovery of beautiful and sensitively made paper is one of life's little pleasures.

The earliest paper

Paper has been with us since early in human civilisation, though the first writing was paper-free, and is usually credited to the Sumerians, the residents of southern Babylonia, now war-torn Iraq, over five thousand years ago. They wrote their mysterious, long-extinct language by pressing wedge-shaped, or cuneiform, symbols into damp clay tablets, then baking them hard. Though the Sumerian culture was overthrown, its cuneiform script, the precursor of modern alphabets, survived and spread to other civilisations in south-west Asia.

In Ancient Egypt, the first paper-like material was made from a big wetland grass plant, *Cyperus papyrus*. I first saw this plant in the Okavango Delta in Botswana, travelling by dug-out boat in hippopotamus-infested waters. Between lily ponds with swoon-inducing perfume the boat pushed past papyrus stands so tall that moving among them was like paddling through a surreal forest, with trees replaced by long-handled green umbrellas. The Egyptians learned to make a writing material from this plant, by extracting the pith from the middle of the stems and flattening it into long, thin strips. These were laid vertically side-by-side and slightly overlapping, overlaid by a similar arrangement of horizontal strips and then pressed. The pith contains a natural gum that glues the strips together as it dries, resulting in a strong, smooth, paper-like sheet of papyrus, upon which scribes wrote sacred messages in hieroglyphic script.

The invention of papyrus encouraged the development of all the paraphernalia of writing: brushes and pens made from reeds, wood, feathers and bones, and inks from everything you can imagine. In this childhood of human writing, I imagine endless happy fiddling with mud, soil and ashes, and experiments with gums and dyes extracted from all kinds of animals and plants. But the writing of the Egyptian scribes, though wonderfully inventive, differed fundamentally in two ways from a modern-day book: it used neither an alphabet, nor real paper.

The next paper-like invention we know of was made in Pergamum, a city in what was then Mysia, a kingdom in north-west Asia Minor, and is now in the Asian part of Turkey. For greater portability than stone and more durability than wax or papyrus, the Mysians developed ways of treating animal skins to produce smooth, pale writing surfaces, making vellum from calf or goat hide and parchment from the skin of sheep. These had the advantage that they could be bound into books, whereas papyrus was generally rolled into scrolls. Right up until the Middle Ages, most European books were made from animal products.

Real paper, the material formed from a liquid pulp of cellulose fibres, spread into a sheet and dried, was not invented until two thousand years ago, when a revolution took place in China that went unnoticed in the West for more than a millennium. Writing had been long established, using the complex script of thousands of syllable characters that is still used today, and Chinese scribes engraved onto stone, wood and animal skins, much as did their contemporaries in ancient Rome. Calligraphic art was a vibrant part of the culture and calligraphic artists were always seeking a more perfect surface upon which to display their skills. Then, some time around AD 105, during the Eastern Han dynasty, an enterprising secretary to Emperor He, called Cai Lun, introduced a new technology to the court. This involved mashing the bark of the Qing Tan tree, diluting it into a pulp and then re-forming it into the thin, strong mesh of fibres that we have come to know as paper. He also showed how to make paper from other plant fibres, including flax, from which linen is made, and hemp. Ever since, Cai Lun has been credited as the inventor of paper and it has been made by hand his way, one sheet at a time, by dipping a gauze-covered frame, called a deckle, into a vessel of pulp, allowing the water to drain out, peeling the resulting mat of fibres off the gauze and drying it.

It is unlikely that Cai Lun came up with the whole paper-making process on his own. Like all such innovations, it was probably developed piece by piece, over a period of time, and in all likelihood he got the idea from someone else. This is backed up by a discovery made in August 2006 at Dunhuang, in the Gansu province of China, of flax paper up to 170 years older than Cai Lun, leading to speculation that he was merely the first court official to lay claim to it, or perhaps at best that he made technical improvements to an existing paper-making process, such as using bark rather than flax. The paper found at Dunhuang has been dated to 65 B and was found in an ancient garrison from the Western Han Dynasty, the dynasty prior to Cai Lun's. Another piece of paper found in the garrison, dating from 8 BC, carries Chinese characters still legible today, and seems to be part of a letter. As Fu Licheng, curator of the Dunhuang Museum, was reported by the Xinhua News Agency as saying, this shows that Chinese people 'have been writing on paper for much longer than we thought'.

There are those who claim that paper was not even a Chinese invention, and that the Khanzadas people, from Tizara in the Alwar district of Rajasthan in India, first made paper from cellulose fibres in the third century BC. Paper making is certainly an ancient tradition in India, although it was almost wiped out during British control of the subcontinent. Mahatma Gandhi helped to breathe new life into the art by demonstrating paper making at the 1938 Haripura Congress, a watershed event for Indian independence. The tradition is maintained these days in the village of Sanganer, near Jaipur, said to be the world's biggest centre of hand-made paper making. Perhaps before that the tradition of paper making came down from the highest land on earth, the Himalayas of Nepal, where exquisite hand-made Lotka paper is still made from the bark of daphne trees.

What is uncontroversial, however, is that it took Europeans ages to catch on to the idea. For centuries, paper making was an exclusively oriental pursuit, and even when it finally reached the West, it was made by hand and almost always from rags. It was only relatively recently (about 150 years ago) that paper began to be made from the trunks of trees, and that changed everything.

How paper is made now

Most modern industrial paper production uses trees as its raw material. It involves three steps. First, timber and extracted from a forest, is delivered to a wood yard, by truck, train or boat, unloaded, stripped of its bark and chopped either into chunks or chips. At this stage it is often combined with chips sourced from sawmills and other timber processors.

Second, the wood is pulped, which means that the individual cellulose fibres are separated out, either mechanically or chemically, and then diluted into a watery slurry. Mechanical pulping involves grinding the chips, just as flour is milled between grindstones, or shredding it down to individual fibres with huge rotating steel-toothed disks. Chemical pulp is made by stewing the woodchips in

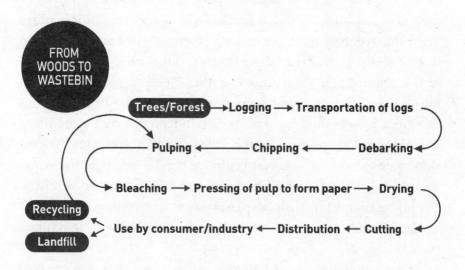

strong alkali solutions at high temperatures to separate the cellulose fibres from the lignin, the material in tree cells that makes them rigid. The pulp is also often bleached, involving more chemicals, which carry the risk of pollution. Pulp recipes, known as the furnish, vary the amount and type of fibre, filler and chemicals for each kind of paper, to produce different characteristics such as how much it will absorb ink or dyes, its smoothness, strength, how it will crumple and fold, and even what noise it will make when a page is turned. There are few industrial secrets more tightly guarded than the precise furnish for a successful paper.

The third stage of paper making involves spreading the pulp onto a web to form a sheet and extracting the water. Instead of making individual sheets using a frame and deckle, industrial paper machines make a continuous roll of paper using a long rotating gauze onto which pulp is sprayed. The resulting mesh of paper fibres is run through a press to squeeze out the excess water, then dried by pulling it between heated rollers and finally wound onto an enormous reel, for cutting into the shapes and sizes that customers require.

The paper-making process is nothing short of miraculous to witness. The first time I watched a paper machine in action was at Scotland's leading producer of cheques and bank drafts, Tullis Russell, an employee-owned firm based near Merkinch, in Fife, in a huddle of low-slung buildings and sky-scraper chimneys nestled in a wooded valley. I was shown around by Gregor Milne, a big, amiable man in an uncomfortable-looking dark suit. He seemed amused to be able to introduce me to my first ever paper machine, kitted me up in safety gear and led me into a long, narrow building. As he had predicted, my spectacles steamed up immediately in the humid atmosphere of hot pulp. As the blur subsided Gregor walked me down the 100-metre-long (330 feet) contraption, humouring me as I gawped in wonder. At the 'wet end' of the machine, jets squirted pulp onto a vast conveyor belt that blistered its way through a maze of casements and cylinders, and somehow a giant roll of paper emerged after a journey of baffling complexity at the 'dry end' of the building.

What most amazed me about the paper machine was its sheer speed: high-security bank paper was spinning off the web at an incredible 112 km (70 miles) per hour. It took a mere twelve seconds for the pulp, consisting of more than 99 per cent water, to form and dry into a printable sheet.

The result of this speed is that the productivity of modern paper mills is prodigious, and so, consequently, is their consumption of wood fibre. Forty-two per cent of all industrially felled wood is pulped for paper, and the pulp and paper industry is a core driver of forestry, too much of which is destructive. Contrary to some industry claims that they source their wood sustainably, the majority of the wood used for paper making comes from natural forests, including some that are endangered and irreplaceable. The alternatives to sourcing from natural forests are not always preferable: to satisfy the paper industry's desire for particular species, such as spruce, pine, acacia and eucalyptus, across the planet ancient forest ecosystems are being razed, wiping out not only the trees but also the birds, butterflies and bears (and, as you will gather, I am particularly bothered about the bears), to be replaced by monoculture plantations of exotic species with little ecological value.

It is these forest impacts that first got me interested in paper. It all stems from a passion for forests, born in the woods of Northumberland and nurtured on journeys from tropical jungles to ice-swept *taiga*. For ten years as a forest researcher and activist I have had the good fortune to travel to most of the forested regions of the world, from Siberia to the Amazon, gradually becoming aware that the paper industry was behind many of the most worrying trends in the forestry world.

Runaway consumption

While I was travelling to research this book I wrote a column for my local news magazine, *Am Bratach*, and when I returned home, I was asked to do a public talk about the journey in my local village hall in Lochinver. I wanted people in my community to be able to relate my stories about the global paper industry to their own day-to-day encounters with paper, so I decided to build a display. It took six back-wrenching wheelbarrow loads to get it into position and it made my neighbours gasp when they realised it represented an average British person's annual paper consumption of over 200 kg (440 lb). It consisted of 120 toilet rolls, obtained on a 'sale or return' basis from the local grocer, representing the 20 kg (44 lb) of tissue products we each use in a year. From the same shop, I borrowed two large bales of flattened cardboard boxes, weighing 60 kg (132 lb), to represent paper packaging. Several hundred greetings cards, a case of wrapping paper and a big bunch of brown paper bags represented the 10 kg (22 lb) or so of paper categorised as 'other' by the UK's Federation of Paper Industries. But by far the biggest category was printing papers. Each year we each get through on average 80 kg (176 lb) of graphic paper, which breaks down as roughly 100 paperbacks, 400 magazines and catalogues, plus 5,000 sheets of reports, letters and whatever else churns out of the printers in our far-from-paper-free offices. The village newsagent donated around 500 unsold newspapers, representing the additional 40 kg (88 lb) of newsprint the average Brit ploughs through in a year.

Contemplating this paper mountain, it became easier to visualise the sheer scale of our consumption, which, throughout the world, is already excessive yet still growing fast. World paper use is currently running at 335 million tonnes per year, and its growth rate is dramatic, having increased fourfold in the past forty years and fast approaching a million tonnes per day. A million tonnes of copy paper is sufficient to wrap around the equator of the earth 1,500 times. The same weight of toilet roll would stretch to the moon and back two hundred times. And that's just the paper we use in one day.

Understanding why our paper use has ballooned over the course of a generation is not hard. It has been facilitated by technological developments such as desktop printers, and economic growth that has put such technologies within the reach of most households, but it is driven by deeper, underlying changes in our society.

A Glaswegian community worker commented to me recently that he interprets the paperwork swamping his office as a symbol of a growing social distrust, whether it's the bureaucracy involved in working with children or the paper trails required by regulations and insurance. The substitution of tissues and kitchen roll for handkerchiefs and dishcloths, shops full of multi-layers of tamper-proof packaging and the compulsive wrapping of handled objects can likewise be seen as signs of diminishing trust in the safety of our food, our environment and the people we interact with.

To avoid being overwhelmed by the sheer scale and breadth of our paper use I wanted to understand what is behind it. To do that I have travelled all over the world, looking at the whole human system that supports paper's role in our lives: the paper-producing companies; the forestry operations that supply them with raw material; the industrial providers of their other needs such as water, energy and chemicals; the financial institutions that grease their wheels; the converters, such as publishers and packaging firms, that transform paper into merchandise; their distributors and retailers; the end-consumers; and the waste managers that recover paper and either recycle, landfill or incinerate it. Governments create the legal frameworks that allow the whole system to operate. But it is we consumers who demand the goods and services and provide the money that feeds the industry, allowing it and its impacts to grow. The greedier we become, the faster and more rampantly the industry responds. The more we accept without question the vast quantities of paper thrust upon us, even when we're spending money on something else entirely, the worse the situation becomes.

Considering paper production and consumption as all one system enables us to identify the places where pressure can be brought to bear to make it change. This is crucial, because the quest to understand our society's obsessive paper use and its impacts must also be a quest for options for change and solutions to the problems. The simplest solution, of course, is to use less paper, but reduced consumption is not what the paper industry has in mind for us at all.

At a global scale, the paper industry is gearing up for ever higher levels of paper use. Collectively, Americans make and use more paper, by far, than anyone else. The USA's 92 million tonnes per year total paper usage is more than twice the second-biggest user, China, at 43 million tonnes, almost three times Japan's 31 million tonnes, five times Germany's 19 million tonnes and more than seven times the UK's 12.5 million tonnes. Most of these consumption levels are at least twice what they were in the 1980s and although sales of some products, such as newspapers, seem to have reached a plateau or are even starting to reduce in Europe and America, these trends are more than compensated for by growth in countries like China and India. Overall, global paper consumption is predicted to keep on rising and is expected to double 2005 levels by 2020, as more and more people around the world get caught up in the trappings of modern society and acquire the obsessions with hygiene, convenience and communication that underpin the exponential increase in the use of tissues, packaging and printing papers. Perhaps the digital revolution offers us alternatives to paper, but only time will tell if their uptake will reduce overall consumption.

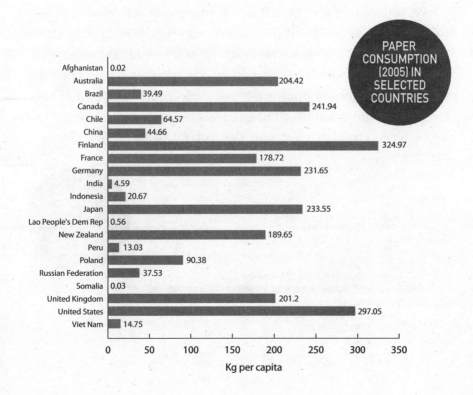

PAPER CONSUMPTION (2005) IN SELECTED COUNTRIES

Country	Kg per capita
Afghanistan	0.02
Australia	204.42
Brazil	39.49
Canada	241.94
Chile	64.57
China	44.66
Finland	324.97
France	178.72
Germany	231.65
India	4.59
Indonesia	20.67
Japan	233.55
Lao People's Dem Rep	0.56
New Zealand	189.65
Peru	13.03
Poland	90.38
Russian Federation	37.53
Somalia	0.03
United Kingdom	201.2
United States	297.05
Viet Nam	14.75

As a writer, I have to be vigilant to prevent the printer in the corner of my studio from doing its bit to increase the world average. I obsessively reduce documents to single-spaced, 9-point font size with 1 cm margins, usually reducing the amount of paper required by a factor of three. I print on the back of any single-sided piece of A4 I can lay my hands on. Yet I still cringe at the thought of how much of the stuff I go through. As a friend and writer Linda Gillard puts it, 'It's bad enough struggling with a lousy draft on a bad day, without thinking "Trees died for *this*?"'

But, in fact, trees are only part of the story. A key concept in understanding the impacts of a product is to analyse its 'life-cycle'. This is the totality of resources that are required to gather and process the raw materials from which it is made, convert it into saleable commodities, transport it to consumers, use it and then dispose of it. A life-cycle study of the paper industry has calculated that production of 1 tonne of paper requires 98 tonnes of other resources, including water, metals to make machines, fuel to power them and so on.

We can assess the land area that is required to supply each person with the raw materials and natural resources that go into the products and services they consume. This area is often referred to as the 'environmental footprint' and it has become an important tool for identifying unsustainable consumption patterns. Collectively Euro-peans have footprints twice the area of Europe, meaning that we have a massive dependence on other countries, particularly in the global south (a

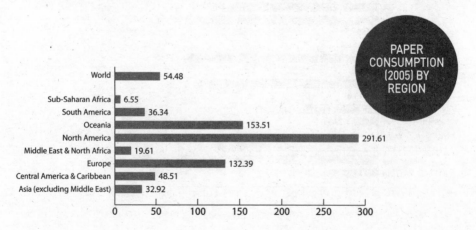

term I use in preference to 'third world' or 'developing countries'). If everyone on earth lived like the average European we would need two planets. Some Europeans have bigger 'feet' than others; the average British person has a 'three planet' lifestyle. The USA exceeds all other countries, with a 'five planet' footprint. Because of its intensive use of natural resources, paper adds significantly to our footprint. One of the hallmarks of northern countries (the term I use for the so-called 'developed', high-consuming nations of North America, Europe and Australasia) is per capita paper use several times the world average.

Global paper consumption is deeply unfair, with huge disparities between the consumption rates of rich and poor countries. Leading the world in excess per capita paper consumption is, surprisingly, not the USA, at 297 kg (655 lb) per year each, but Finland, whose average citizen gets through a staggering 323 kg (712 lb). This is more than six times the world mean, and more than 15,000 times as much as Somalia's annual average of 30 g (1 oz), a mere four sheets of A4. The average person in Laos consumes far less paper in a year (560 g/20 oz) than the average British citizen in a day. It is only reasonable for southern countries to want to increase their use of paper to gain its many benefits. Cutting our consumption would enable such nations' needs to be met without expanding global production.

Waste

Paper is not only all-pervasive and its consumption vast; it is also often wasted. There is a famous and much-copied Canadian cartoon of a stand of temperate rainforest trees, in which a sapling, looking up to its parent towering over it, says 'When I grow up, I want to be part of something great, like a Pulitzer Prize-winning novel.' Over the next few frames the young tree does indeed grow up tall and fine and is eventually felled. To the end it is still optimistic about its life after death, dreaming of nestling on bookshelves, appreciated by readers. But in the final frame the tree's destiny is revealed: an office worker struggles over a photocopier, cursing as it churns out stacks of incorrectly copied sheets and dumping them

13

unceremoniously in the bin. Every day, millions of trees meet this ignominious fate.

A great many of the sheets we encounter in our daily lives have only a fleeting role: either flushed down a toilet or, like the free news sheets handed out at train stations or printouts of emails and web-pages, binned after a quick skim. Forty-five per cent of office printouts and photocopies are tossed in the rubbish the same day they are printed, defying the opportunities provided by computers and the internet to keep information in electronic, lasting, paper-free form. We're hooked on information and infatuated with newness and we want it in physical, preferably glossy, form.

In our addiction to our daily dose of disposable bumf, we have grown complacent about its origins and impacts, and with the advent of office recycling bins and local council 'green bin' pickups, we have even managed to recast our excessive throughput of unread photocopying and newspapers as virtuous. 'We recycle all our paper,' we trill each week as we scoop up armfuls of unopened mailings from the doorstep and send hundreds of pages of barely ruffled Sunday papers off to 'be recycled'. How many of us stop to consider where it all goes or at what cost it came to us in the first place?

It is a tragic irony that this most ephemeral material is made from the longest-lived organisms on the planet. The reality is that wood growing in the trunks of ancient trees in a forest is cut, pulped, made into paper, photocopied on one side and binned, to be found in a matter of a few weeks rotting in a landfill site. In Britain and America, about 40 per cent of domestic garbage is paper, and all over the world, paper and cardboard products are the single biggest contributor to waste streams, though 'stream' seems an inappropriate trickle of a word for the Amazonian scale of this flow. Every year hundreds of millions of tonnes of paper floods out of the forests and into landfill, with barely a rustle of leaves in between.

Unlike cloth, which we treasure and launder and pamper and repair, we treat paper with utter contempt. We unthinkingly pick up countless paper napkins from free dispensers only to pitch them in a bin a few minutes later, barely crumpled, let alone soiled. We gather glossy leaflets and flyers like magpies, just to take them home, strew them around our nests and then throw them away mostly unread. As much as 75 per cent of the paper involved in the production of magazines is never so much as glimpsed by a human being, only making it as far as a warehouse or newsagent's shelf before being dumped. Our bins are full of cardboard packaging designed merely to catch our eye long enough for us to lift its branded contents from supermarket shelf to trolley.

Such wasteful paper habits present global society with a massive trash management challenge. In Britain alone, 5 million tonnes of paper are dumped into landfill every year. For each tonne of paper, 3 square metres (32 square feet) of landfill is required. Landfilling all of the world's waste paper would require a dump measuring nearly a billion square metres, the size of a large city like London.

But used paper is NOT a waste material: it consists of strong plant fibres that can be easily washed and used again. Paper is easily recyclable, and indeed recycling it is much cleaner, safer and more efficient than making it from scratch, using what is termed 'virgin fibre', yet less than half the paper used in the world is recycled. It should never be sent to landfill, where it will rot, releasing methane, a greenhouse gas twenty-three times more potent than CO_2.

The UK is not alone in squandering this resource: less than half of the paper consumed in the world is recycled after disposal. Except in a few places, such as some German cities, effective systems for recovering, collecting, sorting and recycling it have yet to be designed and delivered. In New York City fines of $2,000 are imposed for the theft of waste paper from garbage left out on the street for collection, indicating that it is valued at least by 'rustlers', but nationally, paper recycling was still at only 53.4 per cent in 2006 with the national target set at an unambitious 55 per cent by 2012. Throughout Europe and North America society fails to provide every household with the opportunity to pass their paper and cardboard over for recycling instead of sending it to the dump, and there are virtually no systems for sorting paper so that high-quality office paper, for example, is separated from newspapers and packaging.

In the UK local authorities have recently gone into recycling over-drive because of a European directive making it illegal for them to landfill more than 50 per cent of the waste produced in their region. Even my home village of Lochinver, in north Scotland, for years deemed far too remote to merit paper collection, has been granted a recycling bin. I asked my local authority, Highland Council, where the paper goes when it leaves here. The answer was that, along with all the other waste paper from the Highlands, it was driven to Stirling Fibre, in Croy, Lanarkshire, where I was assured 'it is reprocessed and within weeks it is back on the shelves as a recycled product'.

But was it? Stirling Fibre's website proudly proclaimed the company to be a 'worldwide wonder', with a thriving international trade. It stated, 'As one of the UK's largest purchasers of waste paper we then supply this material throughout the world. We export into Scandinavia, the rest of Europe, North America and as far afield as China.'

Stirling Fibre is not exceptional. In the UK we have nowhere near enough capacity to recycle all the waste paper we collect. To meet its targets from the EU directive, the UK government has made drastic increases in paper collection, but with no corresponding encouragement of waste processing. As a result, the volumes of paper recycled into a new product in the UK actually fell between 2000 and 2004, whilst in the same period, waste paper exports increased fivefold. In 2005, 68 per cent of these exports went to Asia, with China the biggest single recipient. What, I wondered, would happen to it there?

CHAPTER 2: FROM ARTISANS TO INDUSTRIALISTS

Recycling

In February 2006, I fulfilled a long-standing desire to investigate the fate of all the newspapers, junk mail and printouts that end up in China after I have deposited them into my local paper recycling bin. Unlike the 3 million tonnes of waste paper that is shipped from the UK to China every year, I made my way there overland, a six-week journey by train through Russia, stopping off at various pulp mills, forests and other paper-related hotspots along the way. I eventually reached Ningpo, one of the major ports on the east coast of China, just south of Shanghai, where imports of waste paper arrive. Here I hoped to catch sight of some waste paper from home, and find out what happens to it once it reaches China.

Chinese imports of recovered paper (from the UK, USA and Canada, along with other northern countries) amount to more than 10 million tonnes, which represents almost half of the global trade in this commodity and supplies more than two-fifths of China's paper production, far more than anywhere else in the world. I had a list of companies known to deal in this waste, but unfortunately, because my main local contact, a Chinese environmental activist working for Greenpeace, had gone to Papua New Guinea, I had no one to make formal introductions on my behalf. This is important in China: there is an etiquette to follow for establishing contacts and setting up meetings that really needs to be handled by a Chinese person with social capital and skills.

Ningpo dock was lined by red cranes like supermarket check-outs with container ships shuttling in and out transferring their loads. I took a ferry out to a nearby island and back, partly to enjoy a taste of the salt air after weeks of continental interior, but also to get a water-level view of the traffic. It was foggy, so the views were limited to nearby vessels, tooting and honking their way towards the harbour. As the ferry I was on wove among the container ships, I kept my eyes peeled for names on boats or containers that corresponded to my list of waste paper importers, but most were anonymous or at best displayed the name of the international shipping company. Tracking individual shipments, let alone setting eyes on copies of the *Daily Telegraph* or *Sun*, was not going to happen at the port.

I took a bus a few hours inland from Ningpo to a small town called Fuyang. I knew that somewhere nearby was a waste paper depot where the contents of European and North American recy-cling bins were stockpiled before being sold on to reprocessors. I did not know exactly where it was, but I was armed with what I believed to be its address in Chinese characters so, on arrival in the town, I showed the address to a bus driver, a couple of cabbies at the bus station and anyone else who cared to look. They all shook their heads as if they had never heard of the place.

My only option was to try to spot trucks carrying waste paper. When a blue pickup loaded with what looked like shredded office waste finally passed through the centre of town, I was ecstatic. I searched manically for a taxi to jump into with a triumphant 'Follow that truck!' but by the time I tracked one down the truck had gone. I consoled myself by buying strawberries from a woman with two shallow baskets on a yoke. Mid-transaction, a motor trike stuffed with cardboard wobbled round the roundabout and disappeared up a side street. I chased after it, but the trike driver threw me off his trail in no time. Two paper transporters in such quick succession had got my hopes up, but over the course of the afternoon I scrutinised lorry after lorry carrying everything from plastic piping to pigs. Everything, that is, except for paper.

My patience was wearing thin when I spotted a tall, slim man in a leather jacket bundling cardboard in the market, next to the beautifully laid out vegetable stalls, whose sellers brought him their empty boxes. I leaned nonchalantly against a white van, pretending to take pictures of the market stalls, while he flattened boxes, ripping off all the tape and staples and stacking the paperboard into neat heaps. I was itching with anticipation and he was taking all afternoon. He chatted with passers-by. He smoked a cigarette. I was starving but daren't go off to buy anything to eat in case I missed his departure. He weighed his bundles in a leisurely manner and strapped them onto the back of his tricycle. A lengthy cash transaction ensued with the stallholders and it was hard to restrain myself from asking him to get a move on. Then all of a sudden he pedalled off across town as if he was racing for the nation. I followed on foot, grunting and sweating, but he lost me, presumably relieved to have escaped the foreign spy. Disappointed, I gave up on the Fuyang depot.

Instead I started contacting the recycling mill I identified as my next best bet, making repeated phone calls to someone called Lucy. The mill belonged to the Jinjiang Paper Company and was based in a town called Lin'an and I had strong evidence that it used paper from the UK. Lucy told me her 'leader' was not available and she did not have the authority to let me visit. I wondered what might induce Lucy's leader to be willing to meet me.

I phoned and faxed the company again and Lucy promised to call me back later. When she did it was to ask how long I would be in the region. She regretted that her boss intended to be 'back in the office' the day after I intended leaving. It dawned that I was failing to get permission to visit, only in a polite, Chinese kind of way that avoided outright refusal. I asked for directions to the mill. She was cagey, but eventually revealed that it was only five minutes by taxi from the centre of Lin'an. I decided to be a rude Westerner and pay her a visit, but I needed an interpreter.

My method for securing affordable translation help was a by now well-practised routine of chatting up English-speaking Chinese people hanging out at the international hostel. One of them put me in touch with Christina, real name Xiao Na, a 26-year-old optical engineering masters student who agreed to come with me to Lin'an. Next morning she arrived, dressed for a catwalk in a white bomber jacket, brown jeans and elaborately buckled knee-high leather boots. She spoke excellent English and, when I made a comment about Chinese being hard for me to pronounce, she chided me for having a language that includes the words trough, bough, through, though, borough, rough and thought. *Touché*.

We took the bus through a landscape ravaged by development, filling with houses faster than a Monopoly board. I explained to Christina that I was writing a book about paper, and wanted to discover what happened to waste paper from the UK once it reached China. While we travelled, Christina did some diplomacy with Jinjiang Paper by mobile phone, and by the time we got to Lin'an, Lucy had relented and agreed to our visit.

The Jinjiang paper mill was a meek little grey factory with a single steaming chimney, barely bigger than a drainpipe, sticking out from halfway up one wall, but it had a massive forecourt, the size of a major intercity bus station. This was filled from one end to the other with mounds covered with huge green tarpaulins, each easily the size of a double-decker bus. There must have been several hundred of these piles.

We were met by Lucy who was tall, slim and wore a hairy pink coat. She invited us into the line of prefab huts that passed for offices and introduced us to her leader, a very suspicious Mr Chung, who (surprise, surprise) turned out not to be absent after all. Mr Chung, who looked to be in his forties, was round-faced and slack-suited. He spoke English sometimes, appearing to understand my questions and not always waiting for Christina's translations, then answering with boxed-in monosyllables. I stuck to straightforward questions like what the factory made and where they sourced their waste paper. I received terse responses. The Jinjiang factory made newsprint for various Chinese papers, and Mr Chung confirmed that they used recycled paper, exclusively imported waste from North America and Europe, including the UK. 'China's waste recovery and sorting system is inadequate,' he explained, 'and the consistency of the recovered paper grade we need – newsprint and magazine paper – is better from imports.'

Overall, China is heavily dependent on imports of waste paper, which constitute 40 per cent of the paper reprocessed. This demand for waste paper lifts its international price, so from a market perspective this can be perceived as a good thing, but the environmental cost of shipping waste around the world has to be considered. The Chinese recycling industry is growing rapidly, with consumption of waste paper forecast to grow by up to 60 per cent in the next five years. To help to ensure that the country continues to meet its own needs for paper from Chinese production, China levies no import tariffs on waste paper or raw logs, but provides huge disincentives for the import of finished paper products, for example it imposes a tariff of more than 50 per cent of the cost of imported newsprint.

Mr Chung agreed to let me look more closely at the paper stockpile. Out on the factory forecourt, he uncovered a shipment of paper recovered from the USA: bales of *San Francisco Chronicle*, *New York Times* and the *Daily Record* mixed in with telephone directories and magazines from *Newsweek* to *Computer Weekly*. I asked if they had any paper from the UK and Mr Chung nodded, but was not willing to seek out a British stack. Somewhere under those tarpaulins there would have been the *Beano*, *Guardian* and *Economist*, I was sure. I would have loved to rummage there all day to try to find some papers from close to my home, but his folded arms and unsmiling face made it clear that our welcome was running out fast. Lucy was more friendly, chatty and enthusiastic about my project, clearly quite impressed by my persistence and determination to get to see their factory. She laughed at my delight at finding English-language newspapers under the green naps. Encouraged, I asked if we could go inside the plant, trying to flatter them by mentioning that I understood the mill had a very modern de-inking process funded by Finnish investment and that I would be keen to see this in action. Mr Chung refused and led us to the gate. We were given, as you might put it, 'the bum's rush'.

Twenty-seven generations of tree-free paper

Sometimes research failures can be more interesting than successes. My efforts to discover what happened to the contents of my local recycling bin barely scraped in as successful, but while I hung around in China I began to realise that there were much more profound lessons about paper to learn there than any recycling plant would teach me.

The most significant of these is that paper does not need to grow on trees. Any strong fibrous material can form its basis. This is well demonstrated, if somewhat bizarrely, by the novelty papers made from animal dung. A Tasmanian paper artisan called Joanna Gair attracted global interest when she started marketing 'Roo Poo' paper made from kangaroo dung. Scandinavians make it from elk droppings, Africans make it from buffalo turds and fibre from elephant dung is used for 'Ellie Poo Paper', sold in aid of elephant conservation.

These are gimmicks, but they take us towards the fascinating heritage of paper, which began in China two millennia ago. For most of the past two thousand years, pieces of paper were tree-free works of hand-made art. Even now, in quiet backwaters of this vast country, the art of paper making is still being practised, though its industrial counterpart is racing to obliterate it. Still, at present half of China's paper production is from rice straw, sugarcane waste and bamboo, and together with its huge recycling effort, this means that as little as 15 per cent of the paper made in China is pulped from trees, by far the lowest proportion of any country in the world.

I wondered what the present-day calligraphers use for their work. With the help of a reference book and an American woman studying at the Hangzhou Art College, I discovered that Xuan paper, made from the bark of the Qing Tan tree, is still the paper of preference and that the most perfect paper is still hand-made by a small company in a town called Jingxian, in Annhui province. I even found an email address and, after a bizarre series of exchanges in which I sent messages in English and received responses in Chinese, I reached the conclusion that I was actually welcome to visit the factory to see calligraphy paper being made the traditional way.

Tradition is important in China, particularly with regard to calligraphy, this most ancient of arts, the four tools of which, paper, brush, ink block and grinding stone, are treated with great respect. The brush was traditionally made using rabbit fur, the tail hairs of a weasel or even a newborn baby's hair. The ink, made from soot and gelatine and often perfumed, comes in a stick or block, which is rubbed on the grinding stone or ink slab with a little water. Ink slabs may be made of a whole range of hard materials such as stone, bronze or even jade, and they are often elaborately shaped. Ancient inks, slabs and brushes are all high-value collector's items. To achieve perfection, these tools must be wielded on a surface that is pale, delicate and absorbent yet strong and long-lasting.

Paper has great cultural significance in China. Several paper crafts are imbued with spiritual meaning: flying of paper kites is a form of meditation or contact with spirits of the air; masks made from paper are central to theatrical traditions for telling stories of gods, demons and mystics; paper-cuts are used to decorate shrines; prayers are written out on paper then burned; and, perhaps strangest of all, 'ghost money' is made and given as gifts to the spirits of ancestors. The act of giving cash to ancestors is a good indication of how much respect is paid by many Chinese people to their ancestors, whose presences are everywhere. There is even a national holiday for remembering them.

My translator for the trip to Jingxian was a helpful twenty-year-old who like many English-speaking Chinese students had adopted an English name, Chris. During the five-hour bus journey, I was struck by the red paper strips painted with calligraphies in golden writing hanging on either side of every house doorway. Chris explained they were good-luck messages for spring. They illustrated how calligraphic paper is not used only for esoteric art, but is as much a household feature as are greetings cards to Americans and Europeans.

The factory on the edge of Jingxian was rather like an old farmstead, with small stone barns around a central paved yard. The buildings were about the size of the milking parlour on the farm near where I grew up and emitted a similarly strong smell of straw. I was greeted by Cai Zhang, a young man exuding chubby well-being. He invited me up stone steps to a dusty room full of unrecognisable wooden artefacts, where he offered tea, then engaged Chris in a long discussion, presumably about me. Eventually he seemed satisfied, and he and I were formally introduced.

Cai Zhang ran the Xuan paper company with his brother, who managed sales and marketing from Beijing, about 1,600 km (1,000 miles) north. Cai Zhang oversaw production, which was done the traditional way. The factory employed one hundred people, of whom thirty were professional paper makers. He didn't get many visitors, he said. Foreigners had never been to see the factory before. Would I like a tour? I nodded enthusiastically and he gave me a shy, if somewhat perplexed, grin.

One of the stone barns turned out to house the raw materials: bundles of rice stalks and other straws, leaves of plants that were not in the dictionary, barks of trees including mulberry and, of course, the bark of the Qing Tan tree, which was sourced locally, including from a patch of trees right next to the factory. Rather than cutting down the whole tree to strip its bark, Qing Tan trees are decapitated at a height too high for grazing animals to nibble them and allowed to resprout, a process called pollarding, which can be repeated every few years without harm to the tree. In an open-sided barn, Qing Tan bark was bubbling with caustic soda in a stone vat about the size of a small jacuzzi, heated by a wood-burning stove.

Inside the main building of the factory, there were several paper makers in action, teasing delicate tissues from stone tubs of milky-looking pulp. Their skill was staggering. I watched one man working with a rectangular wooden 'frame and deckle', about the size and shape of a window-frame with a removable gauze instead of glass. He dipped it, scooped up a sheet's worth of pulp from the vessel and shook it even, rocking it back and forth to let out the water. There is a wonderful Scots word, 'shoogle', for precisely this rocking motion. After shoogling the frame, he let it drip for a few seconds, then, as if opening the window, he raised the deckle and lifted out the gauze. Then he performed a miracle by peeling the fine sheet of wet fibre, without ripping it, off the net fabric and onto a stack to be pressed and dried. The wet sheet was amazingly strong, the fibres hanging together like woven cloth. He put the gauze back into the frame, replaced the deckle and repeated the process. I went into a trance-like state watching the paper-making meditation: dip, shoogle, drip, peel; dip, shoogle, drip, peel; dip, shoogle, drip, peel.

Nearby, two men were working together to make huge sheets of paper on a web too big for a single person to handle. They swooped the frame into the pulp tub, rocked it to spread the fibre evenly, tilted it to drain, lifted the deckle and then one of them peeled the sheet onto the growing stack while the other readied the frame for the next dip. They operated with the even rhythm of experienced dancers, waltzing in perfect step, their movements so synchronised and graceful I was mesmerised. These two were making the factory's highest-value Xuan paper, prized by top calligraphic artists as the best in China. Walking around the factory there was a tangible sense of prestige in the work and pride in the beauty of their hand-made products.

The factory showroom was a paradise for a stationery fetishist like me and I was almost weeping as Cai Zhang showered me with gifts of the most beautiful paper I have ever seen. With over two hundred varieties of different textures and weights, the makers of these sheets have perfected paper production as an art, not merely an industrial process.

When I asked Cai Zhang what his ambition was for the future of the factory he said, 'The same as now. I want to carry on this tradition. This is the right way to make the best paper.' He said his attitude was Taoist: to reject labour-saving devices and treat labour as inherently noble. Despite the outward appearance of a modern businessman, his ethos was firmly rooted in tradition. 'The only break here since the Qing Dynasty was during the Cultural Revolution when the factory was forced to close,' he said. 'Then all the paper makers were made to work at the state-owned mill.' The state factory he referred to makes the politically correct 'Red Star' brand of paper. 'We were allowed to re-open in 1986 and many of our paper makers came back. Here they are treated as professionals, not workers.' His round face puffed up proudly as he smiled.

I probed, hoping I was not being rude. I was desperate to know if it was a coincidence that his family name, Cai, was the same as the man credited with inventing paper, Cai Lun. He could not be a direct descendent, because Cai Lun was, according to the history books, a eunuch, and anyway, that was almost two thousand years ago. But I was astonished to learn that Cai Zhang could trace his lineage back twenty-seven generations and that the family-owned factory had made paper continuously throughout that period, perhaps for as much as a thousand years. He was one of an ancient clan of master paper makers. I had no idea anyone in the world had a family tree so tall, let alone a family business that could endure so long.

After seeing around the factory, Cai Zhang took me for lunch at the Paper Room in a local restaurant, an intimate banqueting room on the walls of which hung traditional tools and ancient paintings of the paper-making process. He was peacock-proud of the painting of his ancestral factory founder. If I had any remaining doubts about his authenticity, as I looked at this, they evaporated. I swear I could even see the family resemblance. I felt I was reaching across history, looking down the generations, and when I shook Cai Zhang's hand to say goodbye I was sure I had made as direct a contact as it is possible to make with China's ancient paper-making heritage.

Transition to a modern industry

Paper making took more than a thousand years to make its way from China to Europe and several hundred more to really catch on in the West. By the seventh century AD, paper making had spread to Korea and Japan, but the idea did not move west until the Tang Dynasty, in AD 751, when some Chinese paper makers were captured during the Battle of Talas, in Kyrgyzstan, by the Arab Abassid Caliphate, and taken as prisoners of war to Samarkand, in present-day Uzbekistan. The oldest paper document known to exist in Europe is the Missel of Silos, found in Burgos, in north-west Spain, dating from the eleventh century. The first recorded paper making in Europe was in Italy in the thirteenth century. It took until the late 1400s for the first paper mill to be built in the UK, on the River Beane near Hertford.

The Industrial Revolution transformed the paper industry as machines were invented to speed up and increase in volume all aspects of the paper-making process. Beating of fibres to pulp by hand was superseded by a steam-driven invention from Holland, and modern versions of this machine are still known as hollander-beaters. But revolution really hit the industry with the invention in 1803 of a mechanical paper-making process named the Fourdrinier machine after the family of stationers who owned the Frogmore paper mill in Hertfordshire where it was installed, ignoring the claims of Nicholas Robert, its inventor, and Bryan Donkin, the engineer who made it work.

Up until the late nineteenth century almost all paper in Europe was made from rags, and in fact a Scottish regulation made it illegal to make paper out of anything other than waste materials, in an effort to protect the textile industry's supplies of flax, cotton and other fibres. During the Second World War a great deal of paper was made from straw. Even into the 1950s some Scottish paper mills used esparto grass or rags as their exclusive source of fibre. A kind of glue called size is used to strengthen and coat paper for printing, and this was mostly made from the gelatine from animal bones. The British tradition of door-to-door collection of old clothes and fabrics by the 'rag and bone man' stemmed from the demand by the paper industry for rags for fibre and bones for size.

Throughout the nineteenth century, the development of better machines meant that paper could be made in ever greater volumes, and the pressure on the rag trade led to a search for alternative fibre sources. In 1857, a method was invented in Germany of grinding wood down into fibres mechanically and in 1864 the British inventors Charles Watt and Hugh Burgess showed how wood could be pulped by 'cooking' it in chemicals. The paper industry was changed for ever.

The British paper industry flourished in the late nineteenth and early twentieth centuries, but during the past few decades, as the industry has globalised, hundreds of paper mills have closed in the UK and the paper industry has been almost completely rubbed out of the industrial landscape, with the near total loss of a skilled profession. On the Water of Leith, for example, the river that flows through Edinburgh in Scotland, there used to be seventy-two paper mills, all of which were successively closed between the 1950s and 1980s. A similar story can be told about the Kelvin River leading into Glasgow, and the riverbanks of many other UK cities. Although one effect has been a sharp improvement in water quality in these rivers, the negative impacts of paper production have not disappeared; they have simply been exported to more forested countries.

These days paper making is a far cry from its humble hand-made beginnings. It has become a capital-intensive industrial process, run by multinational corporations that shift their operations around the world according to the whims of investors, seeking cheap labour and raw materials and unrestrictive regulatory regimes. After centuries of being dominated by northern countries, the paper industry is making its way back east.

China's industrial revolution

The paper industry has changed beyond recognition since its earliest beginnings as the provider of surfaces for calligraphic art in China two millennia ago. It has diversified, globalised and industrialised at an astonishing rate over the past century and it continues to transform.

In terms of the global paper industry, China is crucial. It currently stands second behind the USA in both consumption and production of paper. However, its consumption and production growth rates in recent years far outstrip the USA and it is predicted to overtake and move into first place within the next few decades. In the four years between 1998 and 2002, Chinese paper consumption increased by 30 per cent and the growth curve shows no sign of flattening off. By 2000, it was growing at 15 per cent per year. Newsprint consumption has been increasing particularly fast. In 2005 China used more than 60 million tonnes of paper, five times the total UK consumption, though less than a tenth per capita, and as aspirations for consumerist lifestyles grow its demand for paper and packaging are on an inexorable upward trend. It will be interesting to see whether the availability of online news will dent this growth, as it has particularly in North America.

In most northern countries, heavy industry is dominated by small numbers of enormous companies, but China is different. It has a very diverse industrial system, with many small localised companies governed by district authorities with significant devolved power. The Chinese paper industry is typically diverse. In North America, for example, ten companies represent more than 50 per cent of the paper industry, but in China there are only a tiny handful of companies with more than a 1 per cent share in the industry. Finland, Europe's leading source of pulp, has only nineteen pulp mills, yet China uses five thousand mills to produce less than three times as much volume. Foreign paper companies, such as the Europe-based UPM-Kymmene and StoraEnso, are moving in aggressively to 'consolidate' China's paper industry and analysts predict a similar collapse in the number of paper firms in China, as happened in Britain in the 1960s and 1970s when the Scandinavian paper corporations achieved a dominant position in European markets.

It is already clear that China is the country receiving most investment in new developments by the paper industry, which, if it continues, will cause a momentous transformation of China's paper-making sector. According to the American Forest and Paper Association, there are plans for up to forty-two new large-scale pulp and paper mills, involving investment of around $25 billion by 2010. It is seriously doubtful whether, at the global scale, such expansion is sustainable.

Many of China's thousands of small-scale paper mills are quite a bit larger and more mechanised than Cai Zhang's, but most are still small or medium-scale enterprises that form an important part of the rural economy. Unfortunately many of them have little in the way of effluent treatment facilities and so they are collectively responsible for water pollution on a national scale. Local governments taking action to try to improve water quality have caused widespread mill closures.

A common first reaction on learning about these closures is that, because this will mean less pollution, it must be a good thing. However, the grand plans afoot to replace the many small mills with modern, Scandinavian-style mega-mills may be a double-edged sword. Although these would incorporate the most effective effluent clean-up technology, and thus may have a positive impact on water quality, the wider impacts of this modernisation may not be so benign.

Firstly, shifting Chinese paper making from straw to wood pulp would be bad news for both farmers and forests. The Chinese paper industry is remarkable in that 85 per cent of its production does not involve wood pulp, with about 40 per cent of the paper made from recycled fibre and almost half from agricultural residues such as straw, sugarcane waste (bagass) and bamboo. But Scandinavian-style mills pulp wood, not rice straw or bagass, and certainly not the bark of sustainably pollarded Qing Tan trees. The shift from small agricultural-residue paper mills to wood pulping mills would cause an enormous systemic change in the fibre supply to China. The only forest big enough to provide China with sufficient volumes of timber in the short term is Russia's *taiga*.

China is short of wood since a logging ban was imposed across much of the country following disastrous flooding in the Yangtse and other valleys in the late 1990s, which was deemed to be caused by the loss of the water-holding properties of river watersheds as a result of deforestation. The ban has been widely upheld, which is good news for China's remaining natural forests, but the sudden brake on the domestic wood supply has meant that China now only supplies 40 per cent of its own timber. Its wood shortfall is forecast to increase from its current level of 65 million cubic metres (m^3) to 140–150 million m^3 by 2015. (One cubic metre is five telegraph poles, enough, almost, to supply an average UK person's annual paper and wood requirement, or to make about 1,500 toilet rolls.)

Russia is expected to play the major role in filling China's wood gap. There are already eight hundred Chinese-owned sawmills in the Russian Far East and the Chinese government is investing hard in transport links with Russia. Every day 180 railway wagons full of logs chug over the border from Russia into Manzhouli in China on the Trans-Manchurian railway line. The other major Chinese rail port, Suifenghe, processes even more: up to four hundred wagons of Russian wood per day. Both towns are experiencing what is being described as a Gold Rush, as China's imports of Russian logs have risen exponentially in recent years, from 1 million m^3 in the mid-1990s to 14 million m^3 in 2003. Russia now supplies 90 per cent of China's log imports.

China is also proposing to develop more than 12 million hectares (30 million acres) of fibre tree plantations, leading to the displacement of other ecosystems and agriculture. Add to this the loss of income to China's farmers who will lose their market for straw and other agricultural residues as pulp mills shift to wood. In a rural economy already struggling to keep people on the land, this could be disastrous.

A second loss of replacing China's many small mills by a few giants would be the loss of jobs. Modern Scandinavian-style pulp and paper mills produce many thousands of times the volume of paper produced by Cai Zhang, yet employ as few as five hundred staff. Mechanisation in the paper industry causes some of the most dramatic job-shedding in any sector and it leads to what has been dubbed in America the 'job-free economy' where a handful of giant machine operators clear-fell monoculture tree plantations and feed them to automated cellulose factories churning out colossal volumes of magazines, junk mail and catalogues, up to 75 per cent of which are landfilled or recycled without ever having been opened. In China, the closure of up to five thousand mills, each employing a couple of thousand people, could lead to the loss of up to a million jobs.

The third loss caused by the closure of China's many small straw paper mills would be the loss of technical knowledge and development opportunities for the agricultural fibre sector, a sector that is just starting to excite interest in North America and Europe as a potential source of sustainably produced paper using wastes that are currently often burned on the field. China is well placed to lead the world in making paper from straw, but if it closes all its small mills this knowledge and opportunity will be lost.

There is an alternative: China could retrofit its existing mills with effluent treatment facilities to clean up the pollution. Unfortunately, multinational financial institutions such as the World Bank call the shots on this issue, and they have a tendency to prefer to fund small numbers of giant investments rather than the many thousands of small-scale investments that would be needed to clean up China's existing paper mill infrastructure. There is also pressure from the consultancy and engineering companies with wood-based expertise that will benefit from

China converting to wood pulp, and a strong lobby, particularly in North America, claiming that agricultural fibres are less recyclable than wood fibres and dilute the quality of recovered paper. Political will by the Chinese government to support its rural economies could, of course, play an important role in the decision of what long-term strategy will be adopted, but many Chinese officials are addicted to modernisation and are happy to close what they perceive as 'antiquated' mills.

Chinese officialdom's love affair with mega-industry is exemplified by the massive Yangtse Dam, the biggest water engineering project in the world. It takes three days chugging by boat from the Yangtse Dam up the three drowned gorges to reach Chongqing, a city state of four thousand bridges and more people (thirty-two million) than any other city in the world. Chongqing's monthly magazine, the *Chongqing Current*, describes the dam, and the 640-km long (400-mile) reservoir behind it, apparently without irony, as 'the greatest success of planning in China, successfully submerging 129 towns and relocating 1.3 million people'. Up to four million people will have been resettled by the time the project is complete in 2020, the equivalent of displacing the entire population of Ireland. With successes like these, who needs natural disasters?

CHAPTER 3: CHECKS AND BALANCES

Money does not grow on trees

Although the history and the future of the paper industry may belong to China, at present it is very much still dominated by the USA. Many new pulp mills being built around the world are projects of multinational corporations based in the USA, designed by consultants based in the USA, funded by money raised in the USA or aiming to make products destined for the American market. Collectively, Americans make and use more paper, by far, than anyone else and, per capita, Americans consume six times as much paper as the world average.

The USA is also the source of the most widely recognised piece of paper in the world, that emblem of globalisation, the dollar bill, or 'greenback'. There is no sign that American cash is being usurped by electronic banking: since the 1970s the annual print run of 'greenbacks' has trebled. By 2005 it was 8.6 billion bills, enough to go right around the equator twenty-four times.

Although the vast bulk of the paper made and used in the USA is the result of pulping wood in heavy industrial processes, cash dollars actually have more in common with a lot of Chinese paper than with the typical North American sheet: like most money worldwide the paper used to make dollar bills is not made from wood fibres, being a blend of 75 per cent cotton and 25 per cent flax-fibre (linen).

Banknotes have some remarkable properties. It is easy to take for granted the fact that they are far more robust than normal pieces of paper. Most people expect to be able to crumple and fold them with impunity and even get them wet without any ink run or disintegration. The manufacturers of the paper used for American money claim to make the most durable banknote paper in the world, which it is possible to fold four thousand times before it will tear. They have also incorporated elaborate security features like red and blue fibres, watermarks and threads running the width of the note, in different positions for different denominations, which glow red under ultra-violet light.

There are dense regulations surrounding the production of paper money. In America it is illegal for anyone other than the USA's Bureau of Engraving and Printing to use the same blend of fibres, or indeed to handle or possess a similar paper. Apparently it is even strictly speaking a federal crime to ship the currency paper from its manufacturer, Crane & Co., in Massachusetts, to the Bureau of Engraving and Printing in Washington, DC.

In the UK, since 2003, Bank of England banknotes are 100 per cent cotton and produced by De La Rue plc, the world's largest security paper and printing company, which also produces the banknotes for 150 other currencies and, with its subsidiary company Portals, controls about 60 per cent of the world's banknote market, including making some euro banknote paper. De La Rue also has a 26 per cent share in Camelot, which runs the UK National Lottery, and it makes other security documents such as passports and stamps, priding itself on 'pioneering new technologies in government identity solutions for national identification'. When I set off on a journey, I have a ritual check that I am carrying the fundamentals of 'tickets, passport, money', so I was surprised to discover that one corporation may be responsible for the paper used in all three.

It is worth dwelling a little on the fibres used to make money and considering whether some of their attributes could be more widely exploited. What would it be like if more of the paper used in America came not out of the forests, but off the fields? Some trials are already under way to make paper with some of the prairie straws currently burned as waste by agribusinesses, thus supporting rural economies as well as cutting waste and reducing pressure on forests for fibre. A non-profit organisation called Fiber Futures is spearheading this work through their Second Harvest Paper Project, working to interest American farmers and the paper industry in the potential of farms as a source of paper fibre. As well as straw, they are running trials of specially grown crops, such as kenaf, flax and hemp, which are known to produce excellent fibres for paper, in much shorter rotation periods than trees.

Unfortunately, however, for now the vast bulk of American paper is nowhere near that sustainable. It is made from wood from forests all around the world and manufactured in heavy industrial processes that bear little resemblance to the hand-made paper produced in China's rural factories.

The USA boasts the biggest paper company in the world, International Paper. It also hosts three others of the top five: Georgia Pacific, Weyerhaeuser and Kimberley Clark, which along with other American companies Smurfit-Stone, Procter & Gamble, Meadwestvaco and Boise Cascade dominate the league table of giant paper companies most years. In the 2007 PriceWaterhouseCooper annual industry survey report, they were all up there in the top fifteen. (Their closest rivals are Finnish StoraEnso and UPM Kymmene, Japanese Nippon Unipack and Oji Paper and the Swedish Svenska Cellulosa Aktiebolaget (SCA).)

The collective impact of the big multinational companies on the world's forests has been catastrophic, and American forests have not been spared. In the USA a host of environmental organisations, such as ForestEthics, Dogwood Alliance and the Natural Resources

Defense Council (NRDC), are campaigning hard to try to reduce their impacts on the remaining woodlands, particularly in the south-east of the country, the biggest source of wood for paper.

Scot Quaranda is a bouncy, fast-talking American with wide eyes and big ambitions for the campaigns at Dogwood Alliance. The focus of those successful campaigns has been to persuade giant paper traders, such as Office Max and Staples, to source their paper from responsibily managed sources. Scot said Dogwood Alliance has adopted the strategy of trying to weaken demand for papers from endangered swamp and hardwood forests rather than seeking legal protection for them because trying to get such laws enacted was 'like beating our heads against the wall'.

The industry's appetite for wood does not only affect trees. Academic researchers in the south-eastern states of the USA have established that the paper industry also threatens local economies. Their research shows a downturn in the well-being of rural communities where the paper industry is concentrated. The catchments of pulp mills are economically worse off than other rural communities, experiencing higher levels of poverty and unemployment and lower expenditures on public education. This is because although the industry brings some economic benefits to landowners, small landowners tend to be paid less for their wood. The result is a marked consolidation of forest land holdings, concentrating the economic gains among fewer and fewer people. This is compounded by mechanisation in forestry and mills that has led to job shedding. The same pattern is repeated in other major paper-producing regions of the world.

Global impacts

Most of the giant paper corporations with USA headquarters are really running businesses on a global scale and their impacts are felt all over the planet. As local supplies of fibre become scarce in the USA and, more significantly, as supplies of fibre in other parts of the world can be sourced more cheaply, the big paper companies are shifting operations to other countries. American corporations and investment institutions hold the key to the global industry's future, with USA-based companies stoking the engines of supply and demand in the paper industry.

On the supply side, this means encouraging new ventures to create more paper pulp. New pulp mill projects are gargantuan investments, costing no less than a billion dollars. To keep the costs down at that level, most new pulp mills are built in countries in the global south; in wealthy countries they can cost twice as much. For example, a proposal for a pulp mill has been explored in Scotland by a team of entrepreneurs called Forscot, and their cost estimate is for £1 billion, roughly $2 billion. A similar mill can be built in Latin America for half this amount, but still, raising the finance to build projects of this scale requires the backing of the biggest global investment structures.

The funding tends to come from a mixture of sources. Most of the projects seek the backing of the large multilateral financial institutions, such as the World Bank, the International Finance Corporation, the European Investment Bank and the Asian Development Bank. Partial funding by one of these institutions is often seen as a kind of guarantee by a range of commercial banks, which will then step forward to provide additional finance. The export credit agencies of North American and European countries also play an important role, particularly in funding the purchase of equipment from these countries to be used in construction of pulp mills and in encouraging the production of pulp to be exported from the producer country to be consumed in the north.

Sometimes all of these financial sources fail, as has happened for a major pulp mill planned by United Fibre Systems (UFS) for South Kalimantan, in Indonesia, which has been widely criticised as it would involve the destruction of huge areas of fragile tropical forest, devastating the lands and water courses of tribal people, wiping out the habitat of animals such as orangutans and tigers, and profiting a group of people notorious for corruption during the Suharto regime.

Tracking the efforts by UFS to fund their Kalimantan plans requires an expert in corporate financing like Stephanie Fried, of Environmental Defense, a non-profit outfit based in the USA. She first became aware of the UFS proposal when it tried to get backing from the World Bank's Multilateral Investment Guarantee Agency (MIGA). Despite having substantial investment from the Chinese state, UFS needed international backing to prove its viability. 'We made the MIGA aware of the dubious environmental and social impacts of the proposal, and insisted that they apply their full due-diligence procedures to assess the impacts of their investment,' Stephanie said. 'We pointed out that supporting these projects could damage the bank's reputation. Highlighting the role of "politically exposed persons" is particularly effective because their involvement triggers legally required scrutiny of the risk of money launder-ing.' Subsequent bids for money from the credit agencies of several European countries were seen off in the same way, and then several commercial banks, including Deutsche Bank and JPMorgan, were persuaded not to invest in the project.

Paper companies involved in pulp mill proposals that do not get mainstream funding are now turning to more fluid and high-risk finance, such as hedge funds. These are private investment funds that seek to earn high returns for a select group of clients through hedging, namely managing a portfolio of linked short- and long-term investments to offset their risks.

UFS turned from banks to seeking the support of a hedge fund and in September 2007 the Hong Kong-based Abax Global Capital offered to pay out $225 million towards the new mill. North Amer-ican and European institutional investors are involved in Abax: notably Morgan Stanley is reported to own a significant minority share; Goldman Sachs and Merrill Lynch serve as brokers. These have become the targets of campaigners like Stephanie who have begun to supply them with information about the impacts of the proposed mill, in the hope of persuading them to withdraw their investments.

Increasingly, hedge funds are moving in where banks fear to

tread, according to Stephanie. 'There are concerns that capital flows associated with hedge funds and private equity may be playing an increasingly important role in bankrolling environmentally and socially destructive mega-projects,' she said.

Pulp mill technologists are also key to the progress of new pulp mills. Finland-based Pöyry is the largest firm of forestry and paper industry consultants in the world and they have a disproportionate impact on the planning of new pulp mill projects. Environmental commentator Larry Lohmann has pointed out (in an insightful analysis called *Pulp, Paper and Power*), 'The evolution of pulp and paper technology has always been intertwined not merely with profit but with the attempt of small elites to rearrange structures of power in their favour.' A key part of their role is to persuade funders to back new mills.

A recent study of the financing of pulp mill projects by a German non-governmental organisation (NGO), Urgewald, has identified up to fifty new mill proposals (in Australia, Brazil, China, India, Indonesia, Laos, Malaysia, Russia, South Africa, Uruguay and Vietnam) that are currently seeking the backing of financial institutions, a development that the study's author, Chris Lang, dubbed a 'pulp invasion'. Along with other NGOs Urgewald is urging banks to question the ethics of investing in pulp mills, whose lifelong impacts could be socially and environmentally catastrophic.

Margareta Renstrom, from the World Wide Fund for Nature (WWF) International Paper Team, said, 'We cannot wait until pulp mills are actually causing forest destruction to complain about them – we have to try to stop the destructive projects when they are in the planning stage, and that means the financial institutions are crucial.'

Greater restraint in pulp mill investments may not just be good for the environment; it may also be economically prudent. After one of Asia's biggest paper companies, Asia Pulp and Paper (APP), spectacularly defaulted on $14 billion of loans, deep questions have begun to be asked about the industry's financial pattern of boom and bust. The Center for International Forestry Research (CIFOR) set a financial analyst, Machteld Spek, the task of assessing the financing of pulp mills. Her research results are described in CIFOR's 2006 annual report as 'a disturbing portrait of how little the financial industry seems to have learnt from APP's debt debacle'. She catalogues incompetence and inexperience in the financial sector, and repeated failures to understand the impacts of the paper industry, identifying a lack of due diligence that 'could lead to a new wave of projects which are risky for investors and potentially disastrous for the environment and forest-dependent communities'.

In Australia, a huge controversy has emerged over proposals by Australian forestry company, Gunns, to build a pulp mill at Bell Bay in the Tamar Valley in Tasmania. Opponents point out that 80 per cent of the wood used by the pulp mill would initially come from native forests and that the mill's water consumption would almost equal current total water use in northern Tasmania. They cite scientific concerns that the logging will cause local extinctions of wildlife including the Tasmanian wedge-tailed eagle, spotted-tail quoll and giant freshwater crayfish. Despite many objections, the Tasmanian government approved the planned mill in August 2007 and the Australian federal government followed suit in October 2007. Australian bank ANZ has since been the target of intense lobbying as it indicated it was a potential financier of Gunns' plan, in response to which it has committed to an independent review of the mill proposal.

It may come as a surprise to many bankers to discover environmentalists who want to treat them as allies, but there are tools in the financial world that can be used to make sure that money is diverted away from damaging projects and into more ethical investments. In 2003, the World Bank and the International Finance Corporation instituted a set of principles for socially responsible and environmentally sound investments, known as the Equator Principles, and invited national banks and financial institutions to sign up to them. So far around fifty banks have done so, representing most of the major global financial institutions, including American giants Citigroup, Bank of America, HSBC and JPMorgan Chase.

If we invest the current generation's money according to these principles, we should bequeath a better world to the generations to come. In terms of the fifty pulp mills that are still just twinkles in the eyes of their proposers, the Equator Principles must be used to ensure that they will only reach production if they will not harm people or the planet.

American reams

The influence of American financial institutions on the paper industry is not restricted to their investments: they are themselves huge paper consumers. Yet these institutions stand to gain financially by not generating paper that has no real value (like junk mail), and avoiding waste.

Bank of America, one of the twenty biggest corporations in the world, is a global leader in finding ways to reduce paper use. It has committed top executives who have made it company policy to reduce its forest footprint, and this policy has fanned out across the organisation, with all staff being encouraged to cut their own paper use and come up with innovations that can help the company to use less resources. Bank of America does not do this because it is run by tree-huggers, but because increasing efficiency by using fewer natural resources, including paper, saves money. A cost cut of $20,000 was made on a single report, by sending out postcards notifying clients that it was available on the internet, instead of printing and posting the document. When it made the receipts from its hole-in-the-wall cash machines (ATMs) smaller, lighter and optional, it saved $500,000. A year after instituting a campaign to get staff to print and copy double-sided (duplex), copy paper use was down 18 per cent, computer paper was down 32 per cent and the company had saved a cool million dollars. Putting forms online was worth an estimated $10 million, not including the savings in postage and storage.

Other American companies have had similarly dramatic results. AT&T instituted greater use of email and the internet, avoiding the use of ten million sheets of paper and saving a conservative estimate of three thousand trees. Online billing to their customers produced even more dramatic cuts, cutting average bill costs from $6.75 per bill to $0.03, a 99 per cent saving.

Sometimes these changes do not need to happen across the whole company; individuals can make a real difference. One woman in a Californian government tax department reformatted a property tax form and saved the county $27,000 and more than 2 tonnes of paper.

When I met Heather Serantis back in 2002, I thought she was far too smartly dressed to be an environmentalist, so I was taken aback to discover she was working on paper issues at ForestEthics, a campaign group known for their hard-hitting consumer-oriented environmental campaigns. All became clear when she revealed that her work focused on research into big corporate paper users, for whom power dressing was *de rigueur*. One of her findings was that the cumulative cost of forms in the USA is staggering. 'Businesses,' she had found, 'spend $1 billion a year designing and printing forms, $25–35 billion a year filing, storing and retrieving those paper forms, and $65–85 billion over the entire life-cycle of those documents maintaining, updating and distributing them.' What is worse, a third of all forms are outdated before they are used, and thus end up as waste.

The use of electronic systems is no panacea unless it is combined with staff education or reward systems. In fact when email is introduced to an organisation it results, on average, in a 40 per cent increase in paper use, because people who are used to a system of paper memos tend to print messages out. The convention of keeping the text of the original message in a reply to an email can mean that printing a two-line message can produce pages of printout, if it is the result of a dialogue involving several exchanges. A recent study by Xerox showed that 45 per cent of office paper is binned on the day it is printed, and with the average American office worker using five sheets of paper per hour, the result is an estimated trillion sheets of waste paper per year.

It is not the computers that are the problem, of course, it is the printers attached to them. There are now an estimated 281 million printers on the planet, being used unnecessarily to convert electronic information into paper rubbish. Printing paper use has trebled in the past two decades and office paper sales are increasing at 6 per cent per year. Depressingly, only 5 per cent of office paper has any recycled content at all, and less than 15 per cent of office paper is recycled after use. This is an area where huge improvements are easily possible. Learning how to make better use of digital archives and resources is an excellent opportunity to save both money and trees.

The cost of the paper itself is only a tiny fraction of the cost of office paper use, and is dwarfed by the cost of storage, time spent searching files, postage and obsolescence. Heather Serantis quotes a study of the government offices of Alameda County, California, which found that only 11 per cent of the costs of paper use was down to purchase, with 33 per cent spent on copying and 56 per cent on distribution. Storing a million sheets of paper costs upwards of $20,000 in filing cabinets, and many bureaucracies keep files in warehouses the size of football fields that would fit on a single bookshelf if stored electronically on a few hundred CD-ROMs. Lost and misfiled paper also costs money and time: a time-and-motion survey found American managers spending three hours a week hunting for bits of paper. Electronic filing is faster and easier to search, but again, unless it is combined with strong paper use policies, this can mean that office workers print a copy of information and bin it, only to print it again the next time they need it, rather than keep, file and search for the original paper copy.

At Bank of America, the strong trend to reduced paper use has been achieved at least partly by having a full-time employee dedicated to tracking how much paper is used in the corporation, by whom and for what. Heather Serantis says that this means the bank can 'explain to its employees how cost savings from paper reduction helps contribute to overall efficiency. Employees can then begin to see the economic benefits for each action they take.'

The secret of the bank's success, Serantis believes, is because it has not set out to achieve a 'paperless office', which would be setting itself up for failure. Instead, it has committed to 'steady dedication', bringing about shifts and changes over a decade that amount to substantial savings, many of which they have used to invest in new systems to bring about further reductions down the line, or to pay for other environmental improvements that cost more.

Wiping away ancient forests

There are some kinds of paper deemed to be essential, which even the most ardent environmentalist may balk at cutting down on. Cash comes to mind, as does that most iconic of papers, the soft, strong and very, very long toilet roll. Touched once, then flushed away, it serves an important purpose yet perfectly demonstrates the transience of this material. There is no better symbol of a world that has lost sight of the ecological value of forests.

The norm for loo roll now seems to be that it should be quilted, textured and softened, a spa-worthy treat that 'keeps skin happy' or perhaps even promises 'a protective balm containing calendula'. Even dry roll is no longer good enough, and moistened tissues are now available to 'put a smile on your cheeks' as the Andrex wet wipes label puts it, and that's not instead of dry paper, but as well: 'Use together with Andrex toilet tissue to feel cleaner and fresher. That's progress for everyone!' The same bizarre concept of progress has led to tissues 'enriched with aloe vera and vitamin E' and 'with added balsam'. The mind boggles.

Not so long ago, most people washed with a face cloth, blew their noses on a handkerchief and wiped the table with a dish cloth, all of which were laundered weekly. Now we are encouraged to wipe with tissues or mop up with a handful of napkins. The use of disposable kitchen roll rather than reusable cloths is widespread, no doubt partly because so many people believe that it is more hygienic, but also because it is simply easier to throw away the mess than to rinse out a cloth and keep it clean by regular laundering. Indeed, the success of the tissue marketers in persuading the people of Europe that disposable wipes are better than reusable ones means that tissue is the fastest growing paper consumption sector. The burgeoning use of paper table napkins for pointless things like wrapping cutlery means that the growth trend for tissue is forecast to continue through the next decade.

The language and imagery of tissue marketing is bizarre, mostly seeking to avoid any reference to either what the product is made of or what it is made for. The leading UK toilet roll brand, Andrex, is made by Kimberly-Clark, probably the only paper corporation to be a household name and the world's biggest tissue producer. It is promoted by means of a blond Labrador puppy, and for years its advertisements have been filled with images of the toddler dog cavorting in the garden with the roll, demonstrating how 'soft, strong and very, very long' it is. The company's ageless puppies have since reached undreamed-of levels of cuteness and these days its slogan is the crooning 'tuggable, huggable softness'.

The reality is completely different from the image. Kimberly-Clark makes toilet roll out of ancient and endangered forests, as Greenpeace has revealed through its hard-hitting campaign Kleercut, a play on Kleenex, the company's global tissue brand. In contradiction of Kimberly-Clark's assurances that 'We adhere to a corporate policy that prohibits the use of fiber from virgin rainforests or ecologically significant old growth areas, including designated areas in Canada's Boreal Forest', Greenpeace has tracked wood used by Kimberly-Clark from Canadian forestry operations that raze irreplaceable wild forests, logging trees that are hundreds of years old and leaving empty clear-cut scars in the land. While these logging operations are not illegal, it could be argued that they do indeed take trees from 'ecologically significant old growth areas'. More recently, Kimberly-Clark has acknowledged in the press that it has indeed used wood from British Columbia costal areas. A more appropriate symbol for Andrex than the puppy might be a homeless young black bear cub, one of the victims of the habitat destruction that is caused by the toilet roll's production.

Greenpeace complain that most of the consumer products sold by Kimberly-Clark contain no recycled content whatsoever, and that in making the 3.7 million tonnes of tissue it sells each year (enough to stretch to the moon and back 750 times), the company uses 3 million tonnes of wood, too much of which comes from unsustainable and destructive forestry.

Greenpeace's claims are backed up by the World Wide Fund for Nature (WWF), whose analysis of the environmental performance of the five biggest European tissue producers, SCA, Kimberly-Clark, Metsa, Georgia Pacific and Procter & Gamble, scored Kimberly-Clark worst overall and gave them a miserable 18 marks out of a possible 100 for their 'responsibility in sourcing wood fibres'.

Kimberly-Clark seems complacent about its use of forest fibre, claiming that only the fibre from freshly cut trees (known in the trade as 'virgin fibre') is good enough to deliver the 'dream cushiony softness' of its products. Greenpeace point out that Kimberly-Clark's website proudly states that 'Kleenex Facial Tissue is made from 100 per cent virgin fibre and contains no recycled fibre. Virgin fibre is used in our tissue because it provides the superior softness consumers expect from a premium facial tissue product.'

Greenpeace paper campaigner Judy Rodrigues argues that 'there are many tissue products on the market that contain a very high percentage of recycled fibres and are just as soft and strong as 100 per cent virgin fibre tissue products. Kimberly-Clark is choosing to ignore consumers' preference for forest friendly tissue products and their demands for tissue products that have a high post-consumer recycled content instead.'

There can be no justification for cutting down trees to flush them down a toilet when there is plenty of recycled fibre that can do just as good a job. These days it really is hard to tell the difference between a good recycled paper and the big-name brands. The days of grey, scratchy, unabsorbent recycled tissue are long gone. One day legislation will outlaw the use of virgin fibre in toilet paper, but until then it is up to each of us to make sure we only buy recycled.

Cardboard cartons

Packaging accounts for more than a quarter of global paper use and is another rapidly growing sector of the paper economy, as goods travel further and further and manufacturers and retailers seek ever more eye-catching exteriors for their products. The packaging industry is worth a staggering $600 billion per year, roughly equivalent to the GDP of Russia. Around 60 per cent of all packaging is paper-based and some of the volumes of food packaging in particular are breath-taking. Every day in the USA, 320 million takeaway drinks cups are supped from and discarded.

Although the levels of packaging that we encounter, for example, in supermarkets, can be exasperating, in fact the packaging sector makes more use of recycled fibre than any other, particularly in heavy products such as corrugated cardboard. In addition, these products are rarely bleached, so they are less implicated in problems like chlorine pollution. For these reasons, few environmental paper activists target the packaging industry in their campaigns. However concern is growing about the impact of other parts of the packaging sector, particularly the white carton board used for things like cosmetics packets, which is known as 'solid bleached sulphite' or SBS, and is made almost exclusively from wood fibre.

In south-eastern USA, where International Paper leads the field in paper production, there are more than ninety pulp and paper mills and half of their production ends up as packaging. The native forests of the region are clear-cut to make boxes and replaced by single-species tree plantations, which are no substitute for the rich diversity of the original forests. The environmental network Dogwood Alliance has begun to encourage packagers to shift to more environmentally friendly sources of fibre and to reduce their volumes, lobbying the fast-food industry to look at more efficient ways of making such things as pizza boxes and cola cups, and the cosmetics industry to avoid unnecessary layers of throwaway wrappers.

There are some good examples of paper saving in the packaging world. The paper used for packaging ranges from durable to delicate, from paperboard cartons for flat-pack furniture to grease-proof paper food wrappers. At the durable end of the spectrum, its role is to protect the goods inside from bumps and bruises during travel. In theory, this means the goods can be tossed into and out of the backs of lorries without being damaged. In reality, it may mean they are simply handled more roughly, as Hewlett-Packard discovered when it redesigned the packaging for its office printers, of which it ships five million per month. Kevin Howard, packaging designer for the company, had the innovative idea that 'by taking away the package you can lower the damage'. Instead of robust boxes filled with complex moulded buffering housing individual printers, the company shifted to distributing printers to big stores in a specially designed, reusable shelving unit wrapped only in see-through light plastic, like cling-film. The unit was made to be easily lifted by a fork-lift vehicle, and the fact that the fragile printers were fully visible meant that those moving them could see that they needed to handle them with care. The result was that the packaging volume reduced by more than 90 per cent and breakages in transit also reduced by about 5 per cent, a real win-win situation.

There is huge scope for similar improvements in materials efficiency throughout the packaging industry. The UK consumes more than 3 million tonnes of paper packaging each year, enough to make about ten billion cardboard boxes the size office paper comes in. During the 1990s, cardboard-box production in North America increased by 30 per cent and globalisation means that countries such as China now predict meteoric rates of increase in packaging production. Reversing the growth trend is going to be a challenge.

Branding and bills

A major role of packaging is to signal to, attract and inform potential customers. Many food product labels are made of paper: sashes on tins, sticky labels on fruit and the myriad cardboard packets that are used to conceal the cellophane-wrapped contents within, be they sausages or sweeties. Non-food products are also often wrapped in distinctive packaging, not so much to protect the contents physically, but for brand identification.

The producers of packaging are using increasingly sophisticated techniques to support branding and to protect brand identities. High-value perfume boxes incorporate holograms or even computer chips into the paper, to try to reduce piracy. Counterfeit goods account for up to 7 per cent of global trade, with losses estimated of €440 million per year. Proportions are even higher in some sectors, for example, 40 per cent of India's medicines are counterfeit, and pharmaceutical companies are understandably worried by threats of litigation for damage caused by fake versions of their products. They are thus using packaging as a way to make forging their products much more difficult. As well as chips and holograms, other security techniques include watermarking and the use of special fibres, such as those that are ultra-violet or infra-red sensitive. Chemical treatments of various kinds can sensitise paper to show distinct colour changes in the presence of acids, alkalis, solvents and bleaches, helping to prevent fraudulent use.

Such techniques are normally developed to help resist financial fraud. Security paper company Tullis Russell, which makes the vast bulk of all of the cheques and bank drafts used in the UK, has joined forces with computer chip company Xaxys, to produce a new paper system called Fibreloc. Gregor Milne, the company's product manager, explained that random distributions of sensitive fibres give each sheet of paper 'a unique fingerprint', so that it can be scanned and its identity verified by checking against a database of paper identities. Bank security paper is one area of the paper industry that is actually in decline, with the advent of credit cards and electronic banking meaning the use of cheques is shrinking by 6 per cent per year, though Gregor told me that he expects the decline to continue for some time and then bottom out. 'There will be a legacy value,' he said. 'People like to know "the cheque is in the post", and we believe most businesses will continue to use cheques. Plus there are new markets in Central and Eastern Europe, the Far East and South Africa. Where banking is growing, cheques have status and customers will pay for them, so they are good for banking businesses.' Meanwhile, by making higher value paper with more security features, Tullis Russell is increasing its profit margins. It is another good example of how the paper industry can increase profits while cutting production volumes, making more money from less paper.

Catalogues of disaster

Although some banks have taken a lead in cutting their office paper use, sometimes this is a matter of one hand giving while the other hand is taking away. The most flagrantly wasteful paper use is the unsolicited postal items known officially as 'direct mail' but more widely called junk mail, the vast bulk of which goes straight in the bin without being opened. The finance sector has been identified as the worst junk mail offender in the UK, with the single biggest source being MBNA, the world's largest credit card company (recently taken over by Bank of America), which sends out almost a hundred million unrequested items per year. The average rate of response to junk mail is apparently just 1 to 3 per cent in the UK, but with volumes like this, it is still considered a worthwhile marketing strategy.

In the USA, the situation is even worse, with an estimated ninety billion items of junk mail posted every year (and a 0.25 per cent US response rate still considered 'acceptable' by the industry). Even assuming each is only 2 millimetres thick this would make a stack 180,000 kilometres (112,000 miles) high, halfway to the moon, or twenty thousand times the height of Mount Everest. The mail order sector is responsible for most tonnage, sending out twenty billion catalogues, more than sixty for each man, woman and child in the country. Most catalogue paper is made from virgin fibre and thus the mail order companies alone are responsible for consigning more than eight million trees to the bin every year.

In 2005, American environmental organisation, ForestEthics began a high-profile market campaign against lingerie catalogue, Victoria's Secret, taking out full-page adverts in national newspapers of chainsaw-wielding women in their underwear. They accused Limited Brands, the company behind Victoria's Secret, of printing on paper sourced from endangered forests in Canada and in the southern USA. Victoria's Dirty Secret, the campaign slogan, was a viral success, and after a million people logged onto the website, in December 2006 Limited Brands caved in to pressure and adopted a new policy to shift onto environmentally friendly paper. There is still a lot to be done, but successful campaigns like this one give cause for optimism that it is possible to tackle even the most recalcitrant paper wasters.

ForestEthics has moved on to target Sears Holding Corporation. The Sears/Land's End company sends out 425 million catalogues each year, and ForestEthics has claimed they are made from wood from endangered forests. Moreover, because it is now the biggest catalogue company that does not have a positive environmental paper policy, it risks damaging its reputation. Sears did not respond to repeated requests for comment on their use of paper. Ginger Cassady, ForestEthics paper campaigner, said, 'In an era of increasing competition and growing concern about corporate responsibility, companies must demonstrate their values and protect their brand by implementing better environmental policies.' All the major catalogues are being graded by environmentalists as forest friends or fiends, so the pressure is on.

Individuals can also do their bit in direct paper campaigning, as encouraged by a Silicon Valley blogger, Pete Kazanjy. Concerned by seeing paper napkins being wasted at his local burger joint, In N Out, he came up with the idea of a sticker on the tissue dispenser that simply said: 'Remember, These Come From Trees'. After careful field testing and trials in friendly coffee shops, he perfected a striking, waterproof sticker design. He discovered that each sticker reduced napkin, paper towel or toilet roll use by about 15 per cent, with each sticker saving an average of 50 kg (100 lb) of paper, the equivalent of a whole tree, as well as saving money. In what he called 'the world's first guerrilla public service announcement', he made the stickers available from his blog site and encouraged people to ask their local café or restaurant if they could put them on their paper dispensers. The design began to spread around the world and it was soon available in several languages, from Arabic to Italian. Pete described sending out the 10,000th sticker as 'awesome' and, by early 2008, 50,000 had been distributed. As he put it, 'It saves the store owner money, saves the earth some trees, and helps educate each other in our day to day lives when it's easy to forget where things *really* come from.'

All in all, very little economic activity happens without the use of paper: goods are boxed for transit; catalogues spawn mail order sheets and retail receipts; banks shuffle cheques and statements; insurers and financial services stuff warehouses with documents; shareholders scrutinise newspaper business pages and investment magazines; we all like a wad of cash. And all except the cash comes at the expense of forests, a priceless inheritance that it is folly to squander.

CHAPTER 4: FOREST FOOTPRINTS

Old growth

It was a September dawn in the Far East of Russia and the night mist was still lacing the firs and birches. I stood at the edge of the clearing and watched the sunshine creep down from the highest branches. In forest, the sun does not rise. It strikes the tree tops first and only later in the morning is it ever high enough in the sky to penetrate down into the dense undergrowth of the forest floor. A brown bear cub strained on the end of a chain wound round an aspen trunk, eyes shining, making puppy-like squeaks and whines. I resisted the urge to stroke him, holding firm in my outrage that anyone could chain up a wild creature like this.

The chatter of breakfast burst out of a cabin as a man emerged, dressed head to toe in brown camouflage gear. This was Vadim, a hunter who knew every inch of this Krasnoarminsky forest. He was also the man responsible for the captive bear. 'Anton, little one,' he crooned, taking a pot of *kasha* (porridge) to the animal and stepping aside. The cub dashed in delight between the food and the man, not seeming able to choose which pleased him most, until Vadim simplified things by crouching beside the bowl and scratching the bear between his ears as he scoffed, grunting and slurping.

It was 2004 and I was here taking time out after a conference in Vladivostok with Andrei Laletin, director of Friends of the Siberian Forests and one of Russia's most effective policy activists. I wanted to see what we stand to lose as the paper industry expands into the Russian Far East. Before long, we were ready to set out into the forest. Vadim asked us to be quiet and follow him, then padded off, gun slung casually over a shoulder. Behind him, Andrei was wearing pin-striped trousers from a once-smart suit, teamed with a turquoise tracksuit top that had seen better days and sneakers, which looked much more like street shoes than trekking gear. Yet he scampered along behind the loping hunter with a noiseless speed and agility that made me feel as clumsy as a cow. My hiking boots crunched among leaves, twigs snapped underfoot and all my efforts to tread quietly backfired as I struggled to keep up with their pace.

From time to time we passed mossed-over stumps, the signs of past logging, but this was still magnificent forest. The oak trees were lofty and grand, the pines too, and the undergrowth was tangled and dense with flowers and ferns. They paused to let me catch up and pointed out a rowan tree with broken upper branches. 'Bear,' grinned Andrei. 'And here is where he sleeps in winter.' He pointed to a hollow snag, an ancient ruin of a huge tree now serving as a hibernation den for an Asiatic black bear. Brown bears, like Anton, live here too, and wolves, and the Amur (or Siberian) tigers, the biggest cats in the world, which survive the winters at minus 40 degrees by feeding on deer. There was no danger that day of a noisy hiker like me crossing paths with bear or tiger, certainly not catching them by surprise, but there were tracks, scat and other signs of life, like the muddy hollows where wild boar would roll and smear themselves against the biting flies in summer.

The broadleaf trees were in full autumn colours, vine leaves shouting red up aspen trunks crowned with fluttering gold coinage. The grapes were purple, with a white bloom, small as blueberries and sweet. The sticky green cones of pines were stuffed with succulent nuts and the forest under-storey was jewelled with rosehips, redcurrants and wild kiwi fruit. Here on the eastern fringe of the Russian empire, trees stretch unbroken from the northern tundra down into this more temperate zone and on into China, Korea and thence the subtropics. Having escaped the ravages of the last ice age it acts as a refuge of staggering biodiversity. It is the most southerly reach of the vast boreal forest, which forms a halo around the northern hemisphere and comprises more than half of the planet's woodland.

I don't suppose my footsteps got any quieter as the day went on, but my thoughts did. My anger about Anton the chained-up bear simmered lower and lower and began to be matched, and then overtaken, with curiosity about Vadim. His eyes sparkled as he pointed out each animal sign. With the patience of a teacher he helped me spot the fleeting movement of a tree-top bird. His big, powerful hands cupped a green beetle like a dear friend. His blunt finger rolled it over onto its back to reveal its gold belly before he gently let it down to trundle off to safety. With a curator's passion he showed me every treasure the forest housed. He made me laugh by impersonating a roaring stag and played the gallant knight when we came to a gorge, attentive as I shuffled along the single log that bridged the plunge.

After a *banya* (the Russian sauna) we drank, ate and laughed together long into the night. The vodka was strong, fortified by a root related to ginseng. Vadim sat at the head of the table, Andrei beside him translating as he related stories of hunting adventures. Early in his hunting career, he said, he sought a territory that was not used by other men and acquired a licence to use a remote hunting cabin deep in the forest, one that no one seemed to want. It took a full day's walk through the forest to reach it. The first time he went, he set traps along the way, arriving at the hut late at night. He slept badly. The next morning when he set off back to his traps he was terrified to see that his footprints were overlaid with the pug marks of a big Siberian tigress. He had been followed to the hut. What was worse, there were no signs that the tiger had then made its way on or away. She was still around there somewhere. When a tiger wants to hide in the forest, Vadim explained, there is no animal that can secrete itself better among trees. Shaking with fear, he made his way to his first trap. It held a young deer. He killed it and left it for the tigress, begging the tiger spirits not to hurt him. His next trap also contained prey. And the next. As he made his way out of the forest, he collected more meat and skins than he had ever imagined possible on one day. On future visits to the hut, the same thing happened. He would look behind him and occasionally he would catch a glimpse of the orange and black stripes of the tigress, or the green glint of her eyes.

Without fail, if he had signs of the tigress, his hunting yields were better than any of the other hunters. He began to conclude that she was helping him by chasing prey to his traps. He continued to leave some of his bounty for the tiger spirits. Sometimes he came across snares left by poachers, but they were always empty. He began to hear rumours that other hunters had heard of his success and tried to poach on his patch, but they always came away empty-handed. The tigress favoured him. Eventually, someone else got his hunting licence, he said. He and Andrei exchanged those uniquely Russian shrugs and smiles hinting of corruption. So he moved to this part of the forest. He had been told that the hunter after him was scared witless by the snarls of a furious tiger and these days the hut is abandoned once again.

And so, I had to ask. What was the story of Anton? Vadim turned his attention full onto me and, using Andrei's voice, he set about another tale. It turned out that Anton was a motherless brown bear cub that had been adopted by Vadim after his mother had been killed. Without his mother, Anton would have surely died in the forest on his own, a frequent fate for bear cubs in Russia. The other common fate for them is to be captured and sold as circus animals or dancing bears, or kept as pets until they get too big and dangerous for city life and have to be destroyed. Vadim would not countenance either fate. 'It is our responsibility, if the mother has been hunted, to look after the little one until he can look after himself.' So he had taken Anton in and fed him. How, I wanted to know, could he ever look after himself if he was on a chain? 'He is chained because he tips up the *kasha* barrel and causes chaos,' Vadim said. 'When the kitchen goes indoors, soon, he will be free.' During the hot summer months, the hunters cook and eat outside under a wooden rain-shelter and only once it gets colder do they use the stove indoors. Anton, Vadim assured me, had strong instincts to hunt and gather food and he would survive. He told of previous bears that had been befriended and that from time to time would return to the camp to see their comrades (and maybe to raid the food store). 'Anton is not a prisoner,' he assured me. I relented. We toasted to friendship, the *taiga*, the *banya*, peace and the healing wisdom of the forest.

The next morning, I took Anton a water melon. He gurgled with pleasure and stuffed himself until its juice dribbled right down his front. Then, fascinated by my long hair, he raised his paw and pulled his claws gently through it. I tickled his ears and he stroked my curls. A deep Russian voice behind me said 'Friends'. Vadim, typically soundless, had approached and was looking on with approval.

Forest footprints

Stepping silently through the forest, Vadim's impact on it is not so very different from that of a tiger or a bear. The effect on the Russian forests of a person living in a European city is likely to be significantly different.

Environmental organisations such as WWF say that it is time we each took responsibility for our 'forest footprint' on the earth. The first step is to understand just how big those prints are. To make just one day's worth of the world's paper from wood more than twelve million trees would be needed. The paper industry consumes 42 per cent of all the wood felled industrially every year, and its share of the world's cleared forest is an area of about 3 million hectares (7½ million acres) annually. I cannot use the usual measure employed to demonstrate forest loss, 'an area the size of Wales', because, besides it being a cliché, Wales is simply nowhere near big enough to grow sufficient timber to feed the paper industry even for a year. Even if it were 100 per cent covered in forest, the paper industry could use it all by the middle of August.

Tracing the impacts of paper use on forests is a surprisingly complex process because its sources are so diverse. Toilet paper, for instance, is made in a few places in the UK but all of the wood pulp that goes into it comes from abroad and according to the Confederation of Paper Industries it could originate from virtually anywhere on the planet: 'from Scandinavia, North America, South America, the Iberian Peninsula or possibly South Africa'. Bales of dried 'market pulp' are shipped from one end of the earth to the other, with the result that the origins of this tradable commodity are often obscure. Wood pulp is bought by paper-making companies and mixed into the 'furnish' or recipe for a particular paper, which often involves a variety of different pulps from far-flung places. Few people probably realise that a single sheet of toilet roll may have started its existence on several continents, wisps of Africa and threads of Brazil mixed with shreds of Russian *taiga*.

The bulk of the fibres used to make paper come from the trunks of trees, about a third of which are purpose-grown in tree farms, or plantations, but the remainder of which are felled from more or less natural forests. The paper industry exploits forests all over the world, in the tropics, in temperate zones of both the northern and southern hemisphere, and in the vast snowy north, known as the boreal region. Far too much of this exploitation is unsustainable and not welcomed by the local people.

We are more aware than any previous generation of the fact that there are many different indigenous peoples and tribes inhabiting the tropical jungles and finding all they need to survive among their ecosystems. However, there seems to be less understanding that the same is true of the forests of the north. Vadim, the Russian hunter, although at home in the forest, was part of a wave of colonists from only the past century or two. Long before the Russians came to the Far East of the country, indigenous peoples inhabited this land, and they still do: there are more than thirty different indigenous ethnicities in Russia, most in the Far East.

Just over the Sikhote Alin Mountains from Vadim's patch is the traditional territory of the Udege people, in the pristine valley of the Samarga River in northern Primorsky Krai. Many of the Udege of this region live in a village called Agzu. It is extremely remote. From the end of the nearest road, on the coast of the Sea of Japan, it requires a two-hour helicopter flight following the Samarga River upstream. Moscow is seven time zones away.

I spent time in Agzu a few years before the trip when I met Vadim. I camped beside the river, the only means of transport for the local people. In summer they travel by canoes with small outboard motors, and when the river freezes over it becomes the 'ice-highway' and trucks with chains on their tyres can chance the drive up from the coast to bring in fuel and heavy supplies. But most of the time, the people don't travel much, relying on the forest to meet their needs.

The most striking thing about the forest was its diversity of autumn colour due to the many different species of trees, mostly familiar, either because like the crinkly edged leaves of oak, they grow at home, or like the open-hand maples, they are familiar icons of North America. There were hazels, with leathery round leaves twice the size I was used to. The birch leaves too seemed larger than life, their heart shapes littering the path into the forest, signalling that the season was changing. The aspen leaves, the shape of gold sovereign coins, fluttered paper-light on their flexible stalks, catching the breeze, whispering.

Like a tropical jungle the forest was rich with ferns, nestling in crevices between boughs and festooning limbs. Creepers twisted up around trunks, some spiny and laden with berries. But it was so much more colourful than rainforest, which is predominantly green on green.

This Ussuri forest was a gembox of autumn shades: amber, copper, ruby, bronze and jade.

Arkady Kaza, one of the Udege leaders, took me ginseng hunting. He was a slight, brown-eyed man in tough green trousers and jacket, with black rubber boots. There were mushrooms of all shapes, sizes and colours and he pointed out species good to eat. Again, some were familiar from British woods, like the chanterelles that live in association with birches. I asked about a particularly impressive white one and he shrugged and said, 'Dog's fungus', the Russian name for any inedible mushroom. We shared a laugh as I taught him the English expression 'Dog's breakfast'.

The canopy was high, the trees stretched up like cathedral rafters and I could not see the birds that chirped to each other or occasionally called alarm at our invasion. I had a sense of being a tiny creature, snuffling among leaves at ground level, oblivious to the complexities of life in the forest roof. Up there, nearer the blue sky, the important work of the forest went on, photosynthesis capturing the sun's energy, making paper fibres out of sunlight, air and rain. That job was nearly completed for another year and the leaves were tiring, abandoning their branches and drifting to rest on the forest floor.

We feasted on cranberries and tart redcurrants, all the fruits that I had seen on the street-market stalls in Vladivostok and on roadsides, laid out by head-scarved *babushkas*. 'Many people make their livelihoods from these non-timber forest products,' Arkady explained. This is particularly true of indigenous people like him, though this is an economic value not often accounted by industrial foresters. 'We hunt in winter, collect ferns in spring, and mushrooms, berries, herbs and nuts in summer and autumn.' With his shy smile he showed me how he dug up ginseng roots, careful to leave enough so that the plant would recover. The plant was quite large with big leaves, but Arkady explained that it was not very widespread. He knew where all the local plants were and each year was selective, digging roots only from mature plants and leaving some roots in the ground to re-grow. He was steeped in a tradition of managing the forest resources keeping in mind his children, and their children in turn, so as not to jeopardise their future livelihoods. These are the traditions that have sustained these resources for thousands of years. If we want to understand what 'sustainable forest management' really means, it is to people like Arkady that we need to turn.

We walked all day among giant trees, returning with our fingers stained by berries. We had seen deer, smelled the musk of a bear and listened to the drum of woodpeckers in standing dead trees. The next day we spent exploring the river by canoe, carrying the shallow boat over rapids, resting among willows where the water was slack and trailing fingers in reflections of the tapestry of trees.

As evening fell by the camp, mist writhed among the wooded slopes above the riverbank, but the sky was clear. Flurries of leaves danced to the ground and a frost slunk down from the mountains. The earth exhaled the deep, damp fragrance of autumn. The forest smelled fresh, even fruity. Each clean lungful of air seemed to flow more lightly into my chest than any I had breathed before. It tasted nourishing and cleared my brain. I am prepared to believe great things of aromatherapy, but this was a scent that could not be bottled.

The next time I sniffed into a paper tissue, I knew exactly what I was missing.

The call of the conifers

The Far East of Russia is exceptional, as most of the country's forests are dominated by conifer trees, with needles rather than broadleaves and mostly (except larch) evergreen. Russia is so big it takes a week to cross by train and most of the journey is through that coniferous forest. One winter I watched the land unfurl along the long rail-ribbon, letting the images flow past the window. The trees had gobbets of snow on them as if I had just missed a snowball fight for giants. The woods were almost monochrome: white birches, grey aspens and willows, and spruce such a dark shade it barely figured as green. Only the pinebark stood out, fox-pelt red. The textures of bulrush heads, grasses and scrubby bushes were stark and brittle against the smooth matt blanket. Back-lit spruce needles made lacy green fringes. Young birch trunks spotted black like Dalmatian skins and cone-laden alders flanked frozen streams. Footprints criss-crossed among trees. I gazed at the vast and extraordinary *taiga* rolling past, this thickety sea of snow-decked jade. The trees formed billions of vertical lines with birch branches like up-reaching arms and conifer branches slanting down. It became clear to me why northern races invented the alphabet of runes: the white page of this landscape was written all over with them.

The threats to tropical rainforests are well documented and publicised. I harbour a long-standing and no doubt irrational grudge against the tropical forests and their astounding numbers of different species, a numerical biodiversity level with which the northern boreal forests cannot compete, despite their thrilling inhabitants such as bears, wolves and tigers and their seasonal explosions of nesting waterfowl and songbirds. We have, as a global society, been worrying for decades about the survival of the Amazon, while almost totally ignoring the boreal forest of Russia, Canada and Scandinavia, sometimes poetically called 'the forests of the northern lights' but more often known by the Russian term, *taiga*.

Taiga constitutes more than half of the world's forest. Russia, with 26 per cent of the world's forest and Canada, with 25 per cent, are the two great lungs of the world, yet they are being decimated. Logging is the biggest threat, particularly for paper, but they are also being lost to mining and human-induced fires. Not only do they not have so many different species, they also lack some of the resilience of fast-growing tropical forests, spending up to eight months of the year in frozen conditions and thus growing excruciatingly slowly. Often, for example, when areas of forest growing on permafrost are clear-cut, they simply cannot recover as the tree seedlings fail to survive without mature trees to shelter them from wind and snow.

Yet the boreal forests are the biggest carbon stores on the planet and our atmosphere needs that carbon to remain locked up, not released with who-knows-what climatic impacts.

The biggest source of paper imported into the UK is Finland, with Sweden and Germany coming close behind. Germany sources a great deal of its wood from the Baltic States and Russia, as does Finland. The UK's biggest source of pulp is Canada, with another major source being the USA, which itself relies heavily on Canada for wood supply. Europe and North America's footprints therefore step most heavily on the forests of the boreal region.

The most precious of these forests are those that have not been trammelled by industrial logging. Various terms including 'old-growth', 'primary', 'primeval', 'virgin', 'pristine', 'natural' and 'wild', are used to describe them. Some organisations focus their efforts on identifying and protecting 'ancient and endangered' forests; others prioritise those of 'high conservation value'. I call them old-growth.

One of the most wonderful old-growth forests I have been to is in Karelia, the region of western Russia that abuts Finland, about as far away from Samarga as you can go without leaving the country. One of the last remaining forests reserved from exploitation here is in a strictly protected reserve, the fiendishly-named Kostomuksha Zapovednik, reputed to be one of the gems of the province. Zapovednik is one of those Russian words that if you are interested in protecting forests, you just have to learn to get your tongue, teeth and lips around: it means strictly protected reserve.

Boris Kashevarov was an affable, fatherly man, who once adopted two bear cubs and told me an enthralling tale of their decimation of his flat as they grew up. He worked as a scientist for the Kostomuksha Zapovednik and seemed delighted to show me around. Next to Kiitesjärvi Lake, the beautiful boreal woods sparkled in low-angled sun. Among the trees, the snow was waist high, too deep for walking, so Boris headed out onto the lake. I followed his footprints across the frozen expanse, having to trust both him and the layer of ice beneath the knee-high snow. Crusted with glittering frost, jade-green and white trees cradled the lake. Proud pines stood guard around its shores. Behind them, the forest was a thick tangle of branches drenched in white, whole trees bent to hoops by dollops of cream and meringue. My nostril-hairs froze as I breathed in the clear blue light.

Boris pointed out the tracks of wolverine, snow-shoe hare and fox. A jay watched us from a tree. We discussed whether 47,500 hectares (117,000 acres), the size of the Zapovednik, was enough to conserve the large carnivore species. It was much smaller than the territory of the wolves, for example, which roam widely in search of food, following the reindeer on their long migrations. 'There are very strong populations of bears,' said Boris, 'enough to hunt and hunt and hunt.' The area was theoretically big enough for lynx, though they were rarely seen. Wild boar were occasional visitors but Boris thought there was too much snow for them in winter.

I asked Boris to explain why preserving this old-growth forest in reserves was important. What was lost when old-growth forest was clear-cut? He responded with a litany: 'In clear-cuts many birds will not survive. Capercaillie will disappear. Siberian jay and three-toed woodpecker will disappear. Some species of plants, like orchids that grow only in closed forest, will disappear. Capricorn beetles and some other beetle species associated with old trunks will disappear. And lichens that grow on branches, many of these will also disappear.'

Unspoken, the list went on, like a cenotaph.

Bears will disappear.
Wolves will disappear.
Lynx and wildcats will disappear.
Beaver will disappear.
Reindeer and elk will disappear.
Pine marten and polecat will disappear.
Flying squirrels will disappear.

Frogs and toads and newts and salamanders will disappear.

Dragonflies and butterflies will disappear.

Cranberries, blaeberries and bearberries will disappear.

Snowberries and crowberries will disappear.

The honeysuckle and the ivy will disappear.

Obscure fungi and lichen whose names we don't even know yet will disappear.

And all because the trees are cut and the forest made to disappear.

Bleeding Russia

The western side of Russia is increasingly being seen as a resource to supply European paper mills with wood fibre. In particular, Finland is looking to its giant next-door neighbour to keep its mills supplied with trees, importing a staggering 20 million cubic metres (700 million cubic feet) of wood each year, a quarter of its total usage. That's 1,600 truck-loads heading over the border every day, or more than one a minute.

I watched logging trucks being given a check over at one of the border posts between northern Finland and Russia. There was a truck roughly every ten minutes, and as processing my visa took several hours I had plenty of opportunity to spectate. The driver of the bus I was travelling on eventually tired of waiting for me and he dumped my baggage unceremoniously beside passport control and wished me luck; it was the only public transport scheduled to cross the border that day. Fortunately after I eventually got clearance, a passport clerk who was sick of the sight of me commandeered a Russian traveller who drove me at breakneck speed to the nearest town.

As I waited for my passport, I was entertained as, over and over again, customs officials climbed up onto a platform overlooking the muddy juggernauts to scrutinise them from above, as if someone or something might be trying to hide among the bundled logs. It was minus 17 degrees outside; only someone very desperate would use a log truck to smuggle themselves over the border. Most of the lorries were road trains with three trailers. Each had a gripping hoist mechanism for loading and unloading, at rest while in transit, somehow reminiscent of a swan's head, tucked down under its feathers to sleep.

The logs bleeding over the border from Russia into Finland are one of three major causes of forest loss in this great country. The second cause was indicated in Chapter 2: at the eastern side of the country trees are haemorrhaging into Asian countries, particularly China. The third pressure is from within Russia, as paper mills expand production, spurred on by investments and joint enterprise companies formed with multinational corporations. As just one example, International Paper has gained a stake in the Svetogorsk paper mill and the resulting modernisation includes a new paper production line requiring greatly increased timber consumption. Where mills have been established for decades, like the Baikalsk mill in Siberia, they are now draining wood out of forests hundreds of kilometres away.

Russian forests have been logged for centuries, but traditionally not by cutting every tree in an area, a practice known as 'clear-felling', but rather by taking only specifically needed trees, in a process called 'selective logging' or 'continuous cover forestry', which leaves the canopy largely intact. Many Russian foresters and environmentalists speak proudly of their heritage of selective logging that has left many forest environments, like the one I walked in with Vadim, in an almost natural and biodiverse condition. However, in other areas intensive logging of valuable timber trees and elimination of some species has reduced the once-rich forest to a shadow of its former glory. There is a lot of concern that this is happening more and more throughout Russia as a result of a forestry culture becoming more like mining than management.

In Russia's federal system, forest management is largely devolved so the future of its forest is dependent on the regional governments' forest departments. In times gone by there used to be a powerful federal Environmental Protection Agency, which could enforce strong protection of important ecosystems. Unfortunately, this body was an early victim of President Putin's regime. In a move that outraged environmentalists throughout Russia and beyond, in 2000, he dismantled it and handed power over forests to the Ministry of Natural Resources. Ever since, Russian forests have been viewed alongside oil, gas and mining as resources for exploitation, and Putin has made a series of unambiguous edicts and statements urging more money to be made from the forests.

Increasingly, clear-felling is being used as the method to supply paper mills and export markets with the high volumes of timber they demand. In European Russia, central Siberia and the Russian Far East, I have seen clear-felled forests: huge scars on the land, with only a litter of wrecked trees remaining on otherwise bare and eroding hillsides.

Under a new Forest Code, private individuals and companies including foreigners can for the first time gain long-term logging concessions over forests and such leases are being encouraged. In Khabarovsky Krai, the region next to Primorsky Krai in the Russian Far East, a Malaysian timber firm called Rimbunan Hijau, which has a highly controversial history of forest destruction in south-east Asia, has been granted permission to log an area as big as some European countries. To get the timber out to its more southerly markets, it is pushing for a road that will cut a direct route through the previously roadless area of the Samarga river basin, in order to reach the Pacific via the Sea of Japan. Unfortunately the new Forest Code has also made 'mining, road building and development' legitimate forestry activities. The construction of a road through a forest almost guarantees its degradation.

Tragically, since my visit there in 2004 the Samarga forest itself has been handed over for logging to Terneilyes, a joint stock company dominated by Japanese company Sumitomo. The lease was contested by Arkady Kaza and other Udege people of Agzu village who claim that the area is their traditional territory and that under federal law they should have the right to decide how it is used. However this law has never been enacted by the regional government of Primorsky Krai, whose forestry officials have over-ridden the Udege claims, pointing to agreements struck between Terneilyes and Udege leaders in other watersheds. Although environmentalists are lobbying the company to set aside the most precious areas of the river basin and avoid logging in them, the once pristine watershed is destined for heavy industrial exploitation.

The same story is being repeated across the country. The biggest forest in the world is up for sale and its wood is gushing out of the country at the whims of the highest bidders.

Taiga rescue

A snowy morning shortly after meeting Boris found me in the Karelian capital, Petrozavodsk, to meet the Republic's forest campaigning organisation, SPOK, and specifically its bearded, dogged director, Alexander Markovsky, known to all as Sasha. He had set SPOK up a decade before as a student group at Petrozavodsk University, since when it has developed into a professional outfit employing six people and with an enthusiastic band of volunteers.

We travelled across town in Sasha's little red Lada, scrunching through mounds of snow in the middle and edges of the roads. Like many Russians, Sasha hurtled around with no seatbelts, gears crunching, accelerating around corners, wheels sliding on the ice. He was totally nonchalant about the feat of getting a car started at minus 30 degrees. 'No problem,' he said, 'I have prepared it for winter.' This was apparently a matter of thin oil, plenty of antifreeze and petrol rather than diesel. Anyway, it went. At least the engine did. The heating was another matter. When we wanted to see out of the window, we passed an ice-scraper around to try to clear the inside of the glass.

The focus of SPOK's work was on establishing protected areas for old-growth forests. 'The problem is very bad,' Sasha said. 'Since 1997 there has not been a single new protected forest in Karelia.

We have more than two hundred so-called protected areas but in many of them logging is allowed. There are restrictions on hunting or collecting rare plants, yet the government permits logging of the forest where these plants grow. We try to explain to our government that this interpretation of protection is not normal!'

Since *perestroika*, some regional governments with a commitment to forest conservation have good records for protecting forests, but if a regional government has no such value, there is nothing much to stand in the way of forest destruction. Unfortunately Karelia is in the latter category. Sasha gave an example of a proposal for a magnificent area of pristine forest in Pudozh, in the south-east of Karelia, to become a regional protected area, or Zakaznik. This idea has the support of everyone, it seems, except the government. Sasha explained: 'At present we have more or less good contact with business, we have more or less good contact with scientists, we have a more or less joint position on Pudozh that everyone would like to create a Zakaznik, but the forest agency is completely against old-growth forest protection, new protected areas, the development of new forest rules or even changing to sustainable forestry. They are completely against all of it. Their policy is that it is best to do nothing.'

The government seems bent on maximising profits from forests without regard to environmental niceties, Sasha explained, and it seemed to me that the old-growth forests of Karelia must be doomed. But he seemed remarkably cheerful, and it turned out that an extraordinary story is unfolding of forest protection against the odds.

All was revealed when Sasha took me to meet Dmitry Zuev and his deputy Vadim Samylitchev, at Segezha Pulp and Paper's smart, modern office in Petrozavodsk. Dimitry was wearing a black suit, one hand in a bandage and sling, and Vadim acted as his translator. They were an odd double act, both sitting in revolving chairs, constantly swivelling side to side, while Sasha and I sat in an L-shape of sofas, like an audience in front of a comedy duo. It was a friendly meeting.

'We of course support the protection of old-growth forests and we are in constant dialogue about ecological protection areas,' Dmitry said shortly after we sat down, handing over a copy of their ecological policy expressing the company's commitment to refuse to buy wood from old-growth forest areas. 'Do you want us to sign it?' He grinned. 'It's our civil position that we have to do our utmost to protect nature in its existing state.'

I could not believe my ears. Was this someone from the paper industry speaking? I started to understand why Sasha was upbeat about the old-growth situation, saying, 'If you had come a year or more ago, I'd have described a bad situation, but now we are at the beginning of a new era. Some very important changes have happened here in Karelia in the last year.' After negotiations between the NGOs and industry, all the major Karelian paper and sawmills and the biggest Finnish companies that buy wood from the region (UPM, StoraEnso, Metsa and others) have all agreed to a moratorium on logging in old-growth forests identified by NGOs as particularly precious. Throughout an area almost the size of the UK, the industry has promised to fell only in secondary or degraded forests.

Why? There were logistical, pragmatic reasons for staying out of the old-growth areas, explained Dmitry. 'All the old-growth forest areas are places where it is very difficult to get logs out, there's no infrastructure, it's impossible. So cutting in these forests is not the right way to support the forestry industry.' Instead they wanted to focus their efforts on the more accessible forests. His company, he said, had taken a lease on a big area of land that had been intensively logged, where they were involved in intensive reforestation and establishing a forest management system to yield a sustainable source of timber. Meanwhile, he bought timber in from other forest managers and he was convinced that there was sufficient wood to be won from already-exploited forests without the need to log in the remaining old-growth areas. As the government would not enforce forest protection, they had decided to let the environmentalists do it for them.

Industrial logging companies normally say they want to see

environmental considerations loosened, not strengthened. The big North American battles over forests have seen the forest products industry pitted against environmental groups, who have in turn blamed the government for being in industry's pockets. I had never witnessed greens and industry so concerted in their concern for nature conservation and sustainability, and united in damning the government for its failure to protect the environment. Greens and government versus industry, I understood. Government and industry versus greens, I understood. But greens and industry versus government? That was new.

Just before we left Dmitry remarked, 'There is little understanding by the government that the existence of old-growth forests is an advantage for this country. It will help if you can try to educate the government.' I tried to speak to someone at the Karelian state forest department several times, but its officials refused to meet me.

So I was left with the story given to me by environmentalists and industry people, that the Karelian government forest agency actively opposed old-growth forest protection, taking no account of sustainability or the need to protect key habitats in drawing up logging plans and then forcing companies to carry out that logging, even if it was uneconomic, simply because it was in the plan. It stuck to the letter of some aspects of Russian forest law, even when that law was out of step with a modern understanding of sustainable forest management. It was bureaucratic and imposed administrative burdens on the forestry industry, and it seemed totally unwilling to communicate with civil society or interested people in the media.

This appears to be a particular problem in Karelia. Elsewhere in Russia, for example, in Komi or Archangelsk, the forest agencies seem more enlightened and open to negotiation on the detail of how logging plans are implemented, allowing reshaping of forest management along sustainable grounds. Indeed in the Komi republic there has been significant high-level support for a huge model forest project where NGOs such as WWF have worked closely with the forest agency, industry and local communities to achieve Forest

Stewardship Council certification for sustainable management of the Pskov forest.

But in Karelia, as Dmitry put it: 'There is misunderstanding from the Karelian forest agency. It is difficult to explain these things. Normal human logic doesn't apply.' Yet in an inspiring case of poacher turned gamekeeper, the industry has agreed to let environmentalists lay down the laws and has volunteered to police itself. Not only that, the Karelian paper company even made me welcome at their pulp and paper mill (more of which later). Although elsewhere in this book I rail against the paper industry, the Karelian old-growth logging moratorium is a shining example of how this industry can take a lead in leaving forest jewels for future generations, just as Arkady Kaza protects his ginseng roots and Vadim, the Russian hunter, will not shoot a Siberian tiger.

Logged landscapes

The border between Russia and Finland presents a striking view of two very different forest histories and a dramatic picture can be seen by looking down on it from above. I got that perspective by visiting Raimo Heikkila, in the small Finnish town of Kuhmo, close to the border with Russian Karelia. I found him in the office of the Kuhmo Friendship Park, an aptly named collaboration between Finnish and Russian conservationists, which links five small Finnish parks and one big Russian one.

Explaining the historical background of the forests of this borderland region, Raimo pointed at a satellite map on the wall that showed the decimation of the forest on the Finnish side through centuries of intensive exploitation, contrasting with the deep green and blue of the relatively untouched forests and lakes of Karelia in Russia. It was like one of those 'before and after' montages that women's magazines use to show what effect a haircut can have.

On the Russian side, the forests were less intensively used initially due to the Russian practice of selective felling and the low density of population, and latterly due to enforced clearance of the border zone. At the opposite side of Russia, in Primorsky Krai, Vadim and Arkady's forests were similarly protected by the strategic military importance of the border zone with China, Korea and the Sea of Japan. The strict ban on forestry development in that region for much of the twentieth century effectively protected the forest habitat of such endangered species as the Siberian tiger and Amur leopard. In the west of the country, in Karelia, it was wolves and bears that had benefited. It is one of the ironies of history that the high security paranoia of the Soviet era had a big positive impact on nature, at least in the border zones.

By contrast, Finland's forests have been exploited for several centuries and particularly intensively in the post-war period.

The Finnish government makes a big deal of claiming that it is a model of sustainable forest management and the bulk of its forest products come from secondary forest that has been logged in the past and has re-grown, however Otto Miettinen, a Finnish Friends of the Earth activist, describes the effect of these standards on Finnish forests as 'an ecological catastrophe'.

In Finland, in a perfect illustration of the nation's approach to forests, the official definition of forest is determined by the volume of timber that could be harvested per hectare per year without reducing the overall volume of timber: at least 1 m^3/ha/year is forest. Less than this is deemed 'scrub' and not 'productive'. This value reflects the growth rate of the trees rather than the way logging actually takes place; a Finnish forester would not dream of only taking a cubic metre of wood from a hectare of forest and logging is normally done by clear-felling. Woods such as those in the far north of the country, which grow so slowly that it would only be possible to log less than 0.1 m^3/ha/year sustainably, are derisively termed 'wasteland'. In reality, these northern forests are nothing of the sort; many are the home of indigenous Saami people who herd reindeer among the slow-growing trees. It is only after they are logged that they become anything like a wasteland.

In many ways Finland is an ultra-modern society and high-tech industries such as mobile phones dominate its economy, yet forestry is still far more important there than in most European countries. It provides 8.3 per cent of GDP and 4 per cent of the country's jobs, but its cultural and social significance is much deeper than these figures indicate.

When Finland became independent from Russia at the start of the twentieth century a land reform process brought about a radical redistribution of land. As a result, about two-thirds of Finland's forests are owned by individuals or families and the country has 440,000 forest owners with an average of 30 hectares (74 acres) each. (Compare this to Scotland, where half of the land is owned by a mere 343 people with holdings of more than 7,500 hectares/18,500 acres each.) However, in dramatic contrast to the many small forest owners, the Finnish paper industry is dominated by a small number of colossal multinational companies, and the country's huge output of paper is produced from just nineteen pulp mills. This is an extraordinary feat of natural resource consolidation.

Raimo Heikkila explained that recent changes in the paper and forest industries were having negative social impacts. He described how Kuhmo district had been devastated by modernisation in the forest industry. In the 1960s, 2,000 people worked as loggers, but by 2005 only 150 people were employed in forestry. The town's sawmill employed 150 people, down from 2,400 in 1980, and the socio-economic studies pointed to no more growth in forestry.

However, Raimo said, there could be a shift in emphasis happening on the value of forests. Ecotourism employed more than one hundred people in Kuhmo and this sector was growing: nationally ecotourism employed 32,000 people, more than forestry. 'One of the challenges for the forest industry is to see that the forest has values other than timber,' he said.

In Helsinki, I met up with Olli Turunen in the Finnish Nature League office. He was a bundle of energy, passionate about the ecological value of old-growth forests, expert on the arcane science of the rare fungi and lichens that they support, and possessing

a comprehensive knowledge of where, exactly, the precious fragments of such forest remain in Finland. His office was stacked
with maps, and every second sentence seemed to set him rummag-
ing for another colour-coded chart, shifting scales and region in a
bewildering flurry of explanations of precisely where conservation
efforts needed to focus. His work, and that of others in Finland's
active forest conservation community, has helped to transform the
forestry debate in the country, and all their careful mapping work
has led to significant protection of biodiversity in the most important
'hotspots'. More importantly, perhaps, their efforts to do outreach
with their expertise has enabled similar work to go on in the much
bigger and less fragmented old-growth forests of eastern European
countries, and Russia in particular.

Olli had just negotiated an assurance from Metashallitus, the
Finnish state forestry service, that they would protect 1,000 square
kilometres (386 square miles) of the 'Last of the Last' old-growth
forests in central Finland. This was less than the area of greater
London and just a third was what the Finns call 'productive' forest.
Olli conceded that this agreement had not covered all the remaining
old-growth, of which less than 5 per cent remained, but, he said,
'it's as good as it's possible to get'. In Kuhmo, Raimo was delighted
at this breakthrough agreement on old-growth forest protection
and described the amount of land protected as 'better than I could
possibly have imagined'.

So why has the Finnish system of forestry had such a drastic
ecological impact at a landscape level? It all boils down to the creation of clear-cuts, Olli said, and the desire to maximise the yield
that loggers will get per hectare. 'When the industry started this
clear-cut system forty years ago in central Finland, they logged
almost only old-growth forest. Now there are only the last remnants
remaining.' As the efforts to protect the last fragments of old-growth
forests bear fruit, the Finnish timber and paper industry must turn
to other sources for its wood supply, while waiting for cleared
forest to regrow.

After clear-cutting areas of forest, Finnish foresters grow single-species stands of trees. These are thinned twice and then clear-cut when deemed mature (how long this takes depends on how far north they grow). Despite the appearance of dense forest through-out the country (26 million hectares/64 million acres out of a total 33 million hectares/81 million acres land area is forest), it cannot meet its own needs. Olli explained: 'You can imagine if you log the northern forests it takes a very long time for them to regrow, up to one hundred and twenty years. So now we see the age structure is such that we have a lot of very young forest, less than forty years old, and that's the problem.'

As well as age structure, the species composition of Finland's forests is also weak, with a lack of spruce and birch and an excess of pine. This is because pine has been perceived by foresters as a higher value timber tree, so it has been planted in preference to the other species. Birch, perceived by foresters as a weed, was actively cut out of forests to make way for more conifers. But since the paper industry uses more than half of Finland's wood and its preference is for the 'low value' species, demand for spruce in particular, but also birch, far outstrips supply.

I was interested in the extent to which the Finnish paper indus-try could be held directly responsible for old-growth logging. Olli believed that the greatest pressure in fact came from the sawmills. 'Pulp wood comes mostly from final fellings and thinnings, trees of diameter less than fifteen centimetres (six inches) or wood that is twisted or knotted and no good for timber.'

But other activists in the same office disagreed. One said, 'We have large intact areas of old-growth forest in the north of Finland that are being clear-cut and the paper industry is buying wood from it. And in southern Finland there are many very valuable high conservation value forests which are being logged and the wood taken to pulp mills.'

StoraEnso, the world's third biggest paper company, has been a particular target of environmental and indigenous activists because it has been sourcing wood logged in the north from traditional Saami reindeer herding grounds. The Saami's reindeer are utterly dependent on old-growth boreal forests because they feed on a range of lichen species only found there, but the Finnish authorities have failed to respect the Saami's rights to use their traditional pasture lands. Saami herders and environmentalists are allied in long-term and bitter land-rights protests.

Finland's forest activists are a tight-knit community, supported in Parliament by Green Party politicians. When I expressed interest in meeting one of those politicians, I was sent to Greenpeace's office, where a climate change strategy discussion was under way, overlooked by 'Forest Crime Scene' investigators working in goldfish bowl rooms like cop film detectives. There I met Finland's youngest Green parliamentarian, Oras Tynkkynen. Leaning up against shelves full of ropes and carabiners, used for scaling buildings on banner actions, he was clear about what was wrong with the paper industry. 'The Finnish and Scandinavian paper industry has been using its green credentials, portraying itself as a sustainable industry, so not many people are aware that they are using wood from valuable old-growth forests here in Finland. As for imported wood from Russia, we don't always know exactly where it's coming from. The Finnish paper industry should do much more to investigate where it is buying wood from and whether it is actually legally logged.'

The deeper issue from a global perspective is the question of how to stop the landscape-level forest destruction caused by clear-cut logging from spreading elsewhere, for while it waits for European forests to grow back, the paper industry reaches further and further into pristine forests in other parts of the world.

There was one thing all the Finns seemed to agree on. Many different voices in the Finnish Association for Nature Conservation (FANC), Greenpeace Finland and the Nature League repeated a simple message to the industry over and over again: stop making paper from old-growth forests.

Logging the boreal

I got the chance to see modern industrial logging close-up when one of UPM-Kymmene's forest managers, Jukka-Pekka Klemetti, known to everyone as JP, took me to see a harvesting operation in a spruce forest in central Finland. It was late winter and snowing hard. I wore all of my clothes, content to look like a Michelin woman as long as I stayed warm. It turned out I was better dressed for the weather than JP who, with only a waxed jacket and baseball cap, no scarf and no hood, was shivering hard by the time we left the logging site after an hour at minus 18 degrees.

In the course of that hour the big green harvester machine felled a hundred trees. It was a surreal harvest, as if a tiny creature, on the scale of a mouse in a cornfield, was scything down one stalk at a time. The yellow grabber reached for each tree and clasped it around the base of its trunk, causing the tree to shudder and shrug off a shower of sparkling snow. A laser eye measured the tree's height and the computer calculated its volume, determining how many pieces and of what length it should be sectioned into. Then the grab hand's inbuilt chainsaw whined and the tree swung to horizontal, toppling into the snow and thumping up a cloud of glittering white. The grabber stripped the green from the brown, ripping the branches, twigs, leaves and shoots off the tree as it chopped it into bite-size chunks for the forwarder, an articulated truck on caterpillar tracks, to pick up and stack. After a while of watching this it seemed as if the trees were cut flowers snipped and trimmed by an expert florist with an extremely sharp pair of scissors. The operator of the big green machine was a young man called Sammi.

While Sammi worked, JP showed me an area of land nearby where the forest had recently been clear-felled. He pointed out the handful of spindly trees left standing as 'biodiversity trees' to meet the national regulations. Ecologists have long argued that there is no value in leaving a mere five trees standing per hectare (the equivalent of leaving a tree in the goalmouth of every football-pitch-sized area of forest cut) because such a low density of trees cannot function like forest. Back on the logging site, the air smoked with scorched sap and diesel. I clambered into the cab to sit beside Sammi while he showed me the computer system that controlled his movements. I passed on the opportunity to lay waste to some spruces myself, and then watched as he felled every remaining tree bar one, a rather attractive silver birch. JP said he thought it was probably being left for its biodiversity value, but when I later asked Sammi why he had not felled it, we all had a laugh when he said it was because JP's car was parked too close for safety. So much for ecological sustainability.

Environmental activists argue that the industrial forestry system used by companies such as UPM-Kymmene has had devastating impacts on the ecological diversity of the forests of Finland and those of neighbouring paper-producing countries such as Sweden. Industrial forestry has reduced them to monocultures of single-aged trees that provide no habitat for rare species such as flying squirrels and woodpeckers, let alone big furry animals such as wolves and bears. This would be bad enough if they actually provided sufficient wood to meet the needs of the paper industry in these countries, but they do not. Finnish paper companies need to import over 20 per cent of their wood supply, primarily from Russia, where often it is felled from primary or old-growth forest with scant regard for sustainability.

Mechanisation has transformed the industry in recent years. 'The work we see being done by one harvester and one forwarder was done in the past by ten men and five horses,' JP said, admitting that there had been a big shift of people from the region to Helsinki because of the shortage of forestry work.

In recent years, the paper industry has restructured, shedding labour and hiring contractor companies to carry out most off-mill activity. The mill that consumes this timber employs 680 staff directly, but these days more than three times as many people are employed by its subcontractors. The pulp mills exploit every opportunity to save money: for example, it is cheaper for UPM to freeze logs during winter for use in summer than to hire logging contractors all year round. As a result, Sammi may no longer have a job for half of the year, and his boss will have to struggle to cover the capital investment of machinery that must stand idle for months at a time.

The shedding of off-mill work means that paper companies such as UPM no longer need to make capital investment in machinery and employment of people, like Sammi, to work it. Nor do they own the impacts of their business, like damage to soil or emissions from fossil fuels used by trucks. These factors, which should be seen as part of ('internal to') UPM's business, are pushed out ('externalised') to become someone else's problem, i.e. that of the contractors. Economists call this 'externalising the internalities'. This is what corporate capitalism is all about, but its meaning and impact is made clearer by putting a human face on it; Sammi's face.

These days it is the contractors like Sammi's boss who bear the brunt of financial risks in this business, while workers like Sammi bear the social costs. Contractors make all the capital investment in equipment like the harvester and forwarder, and these are not cheap tools, costing upwards of €360,000 each. UPM has no forestry machines of its own, but it sets the price for wood and drives it down as hard as it can, having the same effect on Finland's foresters as many people say that the supermarket giants such as Tesco and Asda are having on farmers in the UK, who bear all the risks and glean only meagre, if any, profits. From the perspective of Sammi, it is not clear that this forestry model is even economically sustainable, quite aside from its environmental impacts.

This Finnish example is actually one of the better models of forestry and the point of this example is to show that even 'good' forestry's claims to be sustainable are questionable. Elsewhere on the planet, from Canada to Russia and from Argentina to Australia, the paper industry clear-cuts ancient forests, logs without consent on indigenous people's tribal lands and establishes pulpwood plantations with no ecological value even in the face of furious local opposition and international condemnation. When they have the audacity to label their products with spurious symbols that proclaim they are 'from sustainable forestry' we, the consumers, should not be daft enough to believe them.

CHAPTER 5: WHOSE TREES ARE THEY ANYWAY?

Illegal logging

The Karelian moratorium shows that there are ways to achieve protection for the most precious pockets of forest, in some parts of the world. Karelia is right on the border with the European Union and has been the target of concerted work by Finnish and Russian environmentalists for the past decade, scrutinising the logging activity in the region and tracing the timber back to particular paper companies and products. The European paper companies using wood from Karelia knew that if they did not agree to keep out of the old-growth forests, they would run the risk of consumer-oriented campaigns like the one that caught Victoria's Secret with its knickers down.

But this kind of pressure can really only work to protect a few forest 'hotspots'. In a country the size of Russia there are plenty of places where destructive forestry companies can hide and there are many other markets that have no scruples about the sources of the wood and paper products being traded. Where governments are weak and environmentalists are not on hand doing ornithological transects and lichen monitoring, there is little to stop those who want cheap timber from heading into the forests and taking it out.

As a result, there is a global epidemic of logging that is completely unregulated and a growing realisation that the world's wood and paper trade is riddled with corruption and illegality.

By its very nature, the global scale of the illegal timber trade is hard to measure, but an estimate by the World Bank puts it at $10–15 billion per year and a more recent report by independent think-tank Chatham House says it is at least that much, and may account for more than half of all logging activities in south-east Asia, South America, Russia and central Africa. There have been various international political initiatives called Forest Law Enforcement Governance and Trade (FLEGT) processes, to tackle the trade in illegal wood in various regions, but they need not take up much space here, since they have restricted all their attention on trade in roundwood, sawnwood and plywood and completely excluded pulp and paper.

Yet, a report by WWF reported that Europe's biggest importer of illegally logged wood and forest products is the UK and that the paper sector is responsible for a quarter (800,000 cubic metres/28,000,000 cubic feet) of those illegal imports. Only China and Japan outstrip the UK for illegal wood imports. It is a lucrative trade, estimated in the UK alone as worth £712 million ($1.4 billion) per year.

Many people's perception of illegal logging is of a tropical problem, but the vast majority of the illegal wood coming into the UK comes from northern forests, specifically from Russia, Estonia and Latvia often via Finland and Sweden. The proportion of Russian wood that is logged illegally and then exported ranges from conservative estimates of a fifth up to an estimate by the USA government of as much as half.

In Karelia in Russia, both environmentalists and industry people confirmed that illegal logging was rife there. When I was there, I asked the team at SPOK if I might be able to witness what was involved. Sasha's response was to nod inscrutably and say, 'It's possible.' Anything's possible in Russia.

The morning we were due to go to the illegal logging site, Sasha called me to say his car had broken down. Eventually he got the old Lada back on the road and we headed out to the periphery of Petrozavodsk. We drove off the main road onto a forest track where the snow seemed infeasibly deep. Sasha, a very determined man, pressed on. The track got more and more difficult, the inclines ever steeper. We were driving in the ruts in the snow made by lorries, but the level in the centre of the track was higher than the car's clearance. Eventually the Lada ground to a halt and would go neither forwards nor backwards. Sasha cut the engine and we piled out into thigh-high white fluff. In the distance was the whine of a chainsaw, so we knew we were close to the loggers. We walked on to the clearing.

Sergei the lumberjack was wearing felt boots like big bedroom slippers, an inch of matted brown wool acting as insulation from the snow, which was so dry there was no risk of the felt becoming soggy. He seemed unperturbed by our arrival and chatted about what he was doing, boasting that he could fell 160 trees a day and brandishing his chainsaw. I asked Sergei if we could watch him in action. He grinned with toothless delight, loped off, wound up his chainsaw and sent a tree plummeting towards us. We scrambled out of the way, showered with snow, laughing.

I want to say that Sergei was cutting trees 'by hand', it was such a humble contrast to the expensive harvesting machines used in industrial logging systems. Contrary to what you might expect, tree-felling is no big drama; there is no shouted 'timber' to warn that a giant will fall after painstaking hours of sawing or axe-work. Sergei was clearing leggy conifers much as you might find in a spruce plantation in the UK and the chainsaw cut them like a knife through a carrot. After he sawed through one side, Sergei held the tree upright with one hand while delivering the final cut, swash-buckling and single-handed, before giving the tree a push to topple it in the direction of his choosing. Then he danced along its length, whipping off the side branches.

They were a small brigade of just four men, two chainsaws and a truck. They manhandled the logs into stacks and burned the brash on a smoky bonfire. The pine trees they were cutting fringed an area that was burned in a fire the year before, probably started by accident by folk out mushroom or berry picking who stopped to brew up some tea. Some of the trees were obviously scorched, not very mature, and I found it hard to build up any outrage at what I was seeing. It was hardly the loss of primeval forest. If this was 'illegal logging' it did not look too bad to me. Sergei even assured me he had a licence to log here, but he would, wouldn't he?

Anyway, it was important to stay on good terms with these guys since our getaway car was up to its hocks in snow, so after we had put a few questions we asked if they could pull us out of the drift. Not surprisingly, they found this absolutely hilarious and leaped into their truck to come to our rescue. The Lada was unceremoniously roped to the truck and dragged free, and then Sasha set off reversing back down the track at a furious pace.

So what exactly was it that was illegal about this logging? I asked Sasha. He explained that it was not so much the activity of men like Sergei that was problematic, but rather the government authority that gave him permission to log. The forest agency was responsible for carrying out forest health operations, removing diseased trees, clearing up after storms or fires, etc., such as we had witnessed. The term for this is 'sanitary logging', or 'rupkiochoda' in Russian. A similar-sounding word, 'rupkidahoda', means 'cash-cropping' or logging for money, and this is often what is really going on. Instead of cutting out diseased or weak trees, the forest agency is accused of 'high-grading', selectively logging high-value timber trees, leaving only the dross. In years past it would actually be state employees who would be out there with the chainsaw, but these days the forest agency does not do the logging itself, having divested itself of equipment and staff after years of under-funding. Instead, independent contractors like Sergei cut the trees, sell the timber and an informal exchange of money happens between the forest agency and these contractors. High-value trees means more money can exchange hands. This hurts industry, as leaseholders find their forests have been ransacked for the best timber under the guise of disease control, and it enrages environmentalists. The whole process is illegal, yet it is carried out by the very body intended to supervise and enforce the forest laws. When the police are the biggest burglars in the street, where do you turn to for the rule of law?

Sasha's accusations were confirmed by Dmitry Zuev of Segezha Pulp and Paper. He said that so-called sanitary logging by the forest agency was 'a big problem nowadays. The under-financing from the government is creating a problem for the future of the forests of this country. There is a process of hidden sales of wood and breaking of forest management rules. It is, of course, illegal.'

This reminded me of a trip I made to the Russian Far East a few years previously, when I stayed for several days in the remote village of Krasno Yar in the Sikote Alin Mountains. It was my first direct experience of the social disintegration that had happened in some parts of Russia since *perestroika*. The local schoolteacher told me that there used to be a phone connection to the village, until it was stolen. 'Stolen?' I asked her. 'How can a phone service be stolen?' She explained that the copper telephone line had been literally taken down from the poles, rolled up, driven away and sold in Khabarovsk, the nearest big city. 'Why did you not complain to the phone company?' I asked. Because it was the phone engineer who took the line down, rolled it up and sold it. 'Surely you could report him to the police?' I ventured. Not when the police car was the vehicle used to transport the cable to Khabarovsk! As one long-time resident of Russia told me then, 'If you want to really understand Russian corruption, you have to live here for two years before you even know which questions to ask.' When corruption is this pervasive the system becomes impregnable, with everyone in any official position caught up in it, leaving no one to turn to with dissent.

I wanted to meet some forest agency officials, even just for a few minutes, to hear their side of the story. I had heard that they were sometimes so short of funds that they needed the revenue from illegal logging simply to pay staff salaries and fuel bills. I made repeated calls to the agency but they refused to meet me, saying that I was SPOK's guest and it was not their responsibility to talk to me.

In Siberia, I had seen the effect of illegal 'high-grading'. Out in a remote Siberian forest with forest policy expert Andrei Laletin, I remember coming across a felled ash tree, its stump more than a metre across. The tree lay near it, intact except for a 4- or 5-metre (13- or 16.5-feet) chunk that had been removed: the rump, the choice cut. Andrei showed how it had probably been hoisted out using a winch attached to a small tractor, equipment easily obtained in rural Russia. Andrei used the term 'tree-poacher' for the person responsible. 'The poachers are paid cash by a trader, probably Chinese, waiting with a truck at the roadside and ready to drive straight over the border,' he said. 'The poachers can earn $150 a night.' That would have been a month's wages for most jobs in Siberia.

Unlike in conventional selective logging, when all the usable wood from the tree is extracted, when timber is poached only the prime wood is taken and the rest of the tree remains in the forest. Andrei and I had a long debate about the ecological impact of leaving this deadwood to rot in the forest; whether it could be a benefit by mimicking a natural tree-fall, or a risk through disease to the trees remaining in the stand. Widespread poaching can lead to the loss of some species and drastically alter the age-structure of the forest. The true impact depends on what proportion of the forest is being logged.

Andrei had been studying the flow of illegal timber from Siberia and the Russian Far East to Asian markets, along with Anatoly Lebedev in Vladivostok and several Chinese activists. It was Anatoly who first opened my eyes to the crucial difference between what can be called 'soft' and 'hard' illegal logging. Soft illegal logging is carried out on a small scale by people who have no legal permission to take and sell wood. Hard illegal logging is carried out on a large scale and is carried out by operators with legal paperwork granting them access to the forest, but either the licence-granting has involved corruption or the actual logging activity on the ground does not correspond to the activity permitted on the licence. Soft illegal logging is like shop-lifting, whereas hard illegal logging is corporate fraud.

When I described to Anatoly the ash tree that Andrei and I had argued over, he listened carefully then laughed. Anatoly is a bouncy radical journalist, and with his silver hair, blue jeans and bomber jacket, and fearless questioning of authority, he's one of the most unconventional Russians I have ever met. 'I would call that community forestry,' he said. 'It's just the local people, trying to make a living from the forest near to their village.' He was outraged by what he saw as the demonising of poor rural Russians who cut a small amount of wood for construction or cash.

Since *perestroika*, the rural economy of the Russian Far East has foundered and people are desperate for money. 'These people have one chainsaw and a little tractor,' said Anatoly. 'They need money to feed their family. They are just the local community. The forests are vast. What damage can they do?'

Anatoly is a passionate advocate of the rights of local people to be allowed to use their local forest resources to make their livelihoods. 'Because the officials will not give local people any licences to use the forests, they are officially illegal,' he said. 'But they should not be treated as criminals. It is the big industrial loggers, who can afford to pay whatever money they need to get legal papers. They are the ones who destroy the forests. They are the criminals.'

The hard stuff

In terms of the paper industry, the soft illegal loggers are effectively irrelevant. The logs they take are mostly hand-picked quality timber for small-scale, high-value use such as furniture making. The paper industry needs huge volumes of cheap wood and it is the hard illegal loggers who are in that market. Anatoly was just the man to help me sniff out what such activity involves.

The smell was the first thing to hit me, and long afterwards it was my most powerful sense memory of the logging site: a scent discord of diesel, resin and wood smoke. Chainsaws spewed hot gas. Exhaust belched from the engine of a forwarder, a rusting monster of a machine that could grab a whole tree as easily as a bird picks up a twig. Diesel had spilled in puddles in the rutted mud where the indestructible once-orange logging trucks churned and growled. Fumes hung heady in the air.

I was there with Anatoly and Alexei, an officer of the since-disbanded Federal Committee for Environmental Protection, the state eco-police. Alexei was chubby and cheerful, with startling blue eyes, an ancient state-issue uniform and an equally ancient chewed pencil.

A scrawny man sat on a stump beside a smoking fire. Fuel wood is the one thing of which there is never a shortage around a logging camp, and a billy can is always on the simmer. The logger was surly, pale and mud-splattered. He looked like he was suffering a bad hangover, and the slag heap of empty vodka bottles behind the battered brown lorry that was clearly home testified that he and the other loggers took the normal Russian approach to tackling stress at work.

He was dressed in tough khaki canvas, paramilitary clothing caked in oil and mud. His gun completed the guerrilla image. He treated us like the enemy. No eye contact. He shifted the gun from horizontal to vertical by his side, then laid it across his lap and looked intently down at it, fiddling with a clasp the function of which I didn't understand. There was no need to speculate whether or not it was loaded.

We asked the whereabouts of his boss, and he shook his head towards the woods and grunted, 'Hunting'. The implication was clear: in the forest was an armed man, ready to shoot. I tried to lighten the atmosphere by asking his name. 'Sergei.' Funny how all the illegal loggers seem to be called Sergei, I thought to myself. He looked at me as if I was a page worth skipping in a pornographic magazine.

We waited, slapping feebly at mosquitoes.

I watched the rainbows on a diesel-lacquered pool, remembering the words of a fat Californian I once met who pointed out how pollution can so often be transmuted to exceptional visual beauty: a sunset in smog; scum on a river.

Cutting through the petro-chemical and wood-smoke fog, there was the sharp tang of pine, the familiar fresh-sweetness, faked the world over for industrial cleaners and public toilets. The fragrance came from the stack of logs, a geometric heap of tree carcasses; their ends an uneven honeycomb of varying diameter. Saw marks showed where the chain had sliced through rings of sapwood, cutting off the flow of sap, cauterising the vessels. Some still oozed their gummy, sugary solution and huge drunken wasps fed, buzzing viciously.

I tottered across the tyre-tracks and clambered across the hazard of balanced rocking logs, wishing I knew more about the science of trees. Among the unmistakable red tortoiseshell bark of Korean pines were others I recognised: the rutted wood of willow, the smooth grey skin of ash, the rough hull of oak, the white papery scale of birch. But of birch alone there were seventeen species out there in this most biodiverse corner of the boreal forest and I had no expertise to begin to identify which ones might be lying here.

There was, ultimately, no need to know. 'The pine alone makes this whole operation illegal,' claimed Anatoly. Protected for its high-value nut crop, this venerable giant of the Ussuri forest, known to all Russians as *kedre* (cedar), can only legally be felled from stands where less than 40 per cent of the trees are of this species. Here, looking up beyond the acre of bulldozed land with its clutter of timber, up to the hillside, it was clear that pine dominated the forest, thronging head and shoulders over a minority of deciduous siblings. 'Pine groves like this are sacred in spirit,' Anatoly said, 'and their protection is written in law.'

Alexei took notes, paced out logs, counted rings, estimated volumes. He frowned, but said little.

I wondered where these logs might go and whether any of them were destined for Chinese pulp factories. It seemed inconceivable that anything so solid could be reduced to tissue paper.

When the foreman returned, taller and stouter than Sergei, but dressed identically and with a similar gun, Alexei murmured questions. The foreman barked back irritated responses, flapping licence papers at him. Alexei shook his head. Sergei toyed with his rifle, but accepted a cigarette. We suffered the whine of biting insects. There were a lot of long, tense pauses between Alexei's questions. The mosquitoes became unbearable. The sun was high and fresh mud crusted on my boots. The camp reeked of corruption.

A tropical tragedy

The next time I witnessed illegal logging was in Indonesia, in Riau Province on the island of Sumatra. An old yellow lorry was parked up on the side of the road and a gang of half-a-dozen young men in jeans and T-shirts were manhandling wood into it from a stack at the edge of the forest. Three wooden props had been placed between the ground and the side of the truck. A log was manoeuvred into position at the bottom of them, parallel with the length of the vehicle. It was a substantial tree trunk, at least 8 metres (26 feet) long and nearly 1 metre (3 feet) in diameter. The men got alongside and put their backs into rolling it up the props. Once it started moving some of them kept pushing from the ground, but as it gained height the only way to keep it rolling was by following it up the props. I held my breath, hardly able to watch their bare feet gripping the smooth timbers as the log slid and teetered. Eventually it neared the lip of the truck and two guys steered it in from inside the back, leaping out of the way as it juddered over the edge. I cheered and clapped with relief and the six grinned and took bows, then started on the next timber.

Dede, my interpreter, and his colleague from Hakiki, a forest campaign organisation, chatted to one of the loggers. He told them they were from the village we had just come from and they were going to sell the wood to a dealer in the next town. He would not say how much it was worth. When Dede asked if they have permits he retorted, 'We don't need permission, this is our community's forest.' Soft illegal logging again. It would be deemed officially illegal, but it was done by local people making a meagre living from wood they perceive to be theirs.

Back in the car, Dede said to me, 'So, you have seen illegal logging.'

I asked him what was the connection between the paper companies and illegal logging. He explained that the Riau mills were so hungry for fibre they would use logs from anywhere they could get them. There are two pulp mills in Riau, one belonging to each of APP and APRIL, two huge multinational companies, which dominate Indonesia's paper industry. Both companies are under investigation by the Indonesian House of Representatives' Environmental Commission over their alleged consumption of illegally logged wood, though both companies vigorously deny such consumption. APP's Vice Director of Sustainability and Stakeholder Engagement, Aida Greenbury, said that APP has implemented a strictly documented and independently verified Chain of Custody (CoC) system, 'to ensure the legality of our wood fibre supply'. Another representative of APP told me that the company has 'a strict wood procurement policy, and has established a rigorous tracking system and procedures to ensure that all wood brought into the mills has a verified legal origin'. He also said 'We support the drive of the Government against illegal logging activities.' Jouko Virta, APRIL's President said that 'No illegal or suspicious wood enters APRIL's wood supply – ever!'.

I asked Dede if he thought the paper companies were concerned about whether their wood came from a legitimate source, an illegally logged protected area or a community forest. 'The dealers who buy this wood are middle men. They can no doubt produce paperwork if the companies want it,' he said.

The paper industry sources its fibre from forests in all regions of the world: boreal, temperate and tropical. Of the tropical countries, Indonesia, in jungly south-east Asia, is one of the biggest producers of paper. The Indonesian paper industry is responsible for clear-felling huge areas of natural forests and it is heavily implicated in illegal logging, but its worst record is its legacy of human rights abuses. In fact the rash of soft illegal logging such as I witnessed is a symptom of much deeper and more outrageous abuses of the law, for which the paper industry is directly responsible.

A tribal elder of the Domo people offered to help me understand the problem. Pak Jafri is chief of Kuntu village, an indigenous community whose land-rights have been ridden roughshod over by the paper industry. He invited me to his home. In Kuntu, the houses are made of rough planks, some with peeling pastel-coloured paint, most with rusty red tin roofs. Around each home is a skirt of swept earth with perhaps a hibiscus bush or some busy Lizzies in old oil cans. Chickens strut and peck among leaves while cats patrol. Dogs flop in the cramped noon-shade of coconut palms.

We drove out of the village, passing *ladangs*, or temporary fields cleared in the forest. In a *ladang* the people grow a colourful variety of crops, some for early harvest, such as rice and vegetables, some such as manioc to produce leaves in the first season maturing later to provide a starchy staple, and others such as bananas, fruit trees and rubber, that will yield over coming years, while the forest regenerates on that ground, restoring its fertility. While this happens, the village will communally clear another *ladang* that has been left in 'forest fallow' for many years or even decades. The result is a slow rotation around the forest, known as 'swidden agriculture' or, derisively, 'slash and burn'. Swidden agriculture has sustained human communities within forest ecosystems of great biodiversity for millennia but it is now, throughout the tropics, under threat from monoculture systems of agribusiness growing crops such as acacia and oil palm.

Not far from Kuntu village its leafy diversity gave way abruptly to tall thin trees, of uniform height, growing in regimented lines. We drove for miles without seeing any other organism; just endless blocks of grey-barked *Acacia crassicarpa*, arrayed across the rolling landscape. Eventually Pak Jafri asked the driver to stop and we got out. A stocky, dignified, nearly old man with a face crumpled into a thousand wrinkles, he stood in the clearing and swept his hand in a wide circle to demonstrate that we were right in the middle of his village's communal land. As the echo of the car engine faded into the cardboard-coloured leaf litter, the most striking sensation was a nagging, eerie lack of noise, as if all sound had been bleached out. In every direction, rows of identical trees pushed skywards, their big leaves like green plastic plates sucking in sunlight, their secret roots pumping for groundwater. Yet all this growth was happening in an aural vacuum. No birds sang. Not even a whirr of a cricket, a blue-bottle buzz or mosquito whine broke the hush. There was no monkey hoot or reptilian hiss. We and the acacia trees were the only living things here.

Jafri walked me towards a sapling taller than both of us. 'This is just eight months old,' he said. 'They grow 3 metres (10 feet) every year, more. In seven years, they are 25 metres (82 feet) tall, and then they are cut. He pointed to a dusty channel and with his finger traced out its route to a stagnant muddy hollow. 'This was a stream.'

'What caused it to dry up?' I asked.

He pointed to a group of taller trees, drew his arm around in an arc as if to implicate them all, and shrugged.

'Does nothing else grow here?' The horror of this landscape began to sink in: other than the ranks of artificial-looking trees, it was as lifeless as desert.

He shook his head. 'Look around. This used to be my community's forest but now – look at it.' To each far horizon, silent trees wobbled in the heat haze. 'We used to fish, but when there's no water in the river there is no fish. We cannot hunt here any more. We lost the animals. We lost our bee trees, so we can't get honey any more. We lost our medicine trees. We lost everything.'

We walked in among the acacia, the fire-dry dead leaf litter crackling, crunching and snapping. It was like stepping through Styrofoam. There was no undergrowth at all.

These trees provide no fruit, no food and no habitat for other life forms. Their roots exude toxic allelopathic chemicals into the soil that prevent other plants from growing near them and they grow so fast and densely that they shade out any potential competition within a few months. Natives of Australia, they are adapted to a tough life in dry conditions, and they have powerful root systems, one of the most efficient water pumps on the planet, lowering the water table and sucking water courses dry. These trees have only one function in Indonesia: as fibre for paper making.

'Who planted them?' I asked Jafri.

'APRIL.' Asia Pacific Resources International Holdings Ltd, one of the two big pulp and paper operations in Sumatra, makes more than 2 million tonnes of pulp from trees felled in Jafri's province. This company, alongside Asia Pulp and Paper (APP), the other big paper corporation, and some timber firms, have clear-cut half of Riau's 6 million hectares (15 million acres) of forest in just twenty years, and everywhere APRIL goes, acacia follows. After cutting down the diverse, native hardwood trees, an invading army of these triffids is marshalled into the moonscape wreckage of what was once forest.

'What happens after they are cut down? Can the land recover?' I asked Jafri. He said he did not know.

'After harvest, APRIL replants. The land use plan of the company is for forty years of this.' No one knows for sure what the long-term impacts of these soil toxins will be, or whether the soils can be restored to support normal forest life again if ever the acacia trees are removed.

In the distance, logging machines scuttled around among the trees like giant cockroaches under the table legs of some seedy bar. We walked on. I started to notice that in any gaps between the maturing trees there were vinyl-green seedlings. I pointed to them, and asked, 'Are these acacia too?'

Jafri nodded, and pointed out more and more of them. 'They spread everywhere they are not wanted. They are becoming a big problem on our fields.' As we made our way back to the village, this invasive behaviour was confirmed when we saw acacia rampaging into a *ladang*. Even APRIL's environmental manager later told me that in forests of up to 70 per cent canopy cover it will out-compete all native vegetation. In other words, it is a virulent and dangerous weed and a major threat to the remaining fragments of natural forest.

The acacia plantations destroy forests, eliminate biodiversity, dry up water courses, leave toxins in the soil and spread invasively; in short, they are an environmental disaster. But this is not the worst of it. The land they are grown on is the indigenous communities' land, and their rights to make free, fair, well-informed choices about how their land is used have been widely abused. Communities like that of Kuntu are involved in legal disputes to get their land back, or at least a fair rent, and meanwhile conflicts between local people and the paper companies and their subsidiaries are raging. Local community livelihoods are damaged as they lose their forest resources, such as honey, fuel wood, hunted meat, medicinal plants and fruits, and they suffer water shortages, loss of fishing and deteriorating health. The pulp mills' demand for wood acts as a spur to illegal logging, exacerbating conflicts and furthering forest loss.

Back in Kuntu, Jafri took me to meet another village elder called Anzam, to learn how the Kuntu villagers lost their land to APRIL. We sat in a ring on the floor of Anzam's house. It was dark inside after the intense sunshine but the shade offered no coolness, though Jafri and Dede, my hyperactive guide and interpreter, seemed unperturbed by the heat. Anzam and Jafri chain-smoked *creteks*, the clove-scented cigarettes so characteristic of Indonesia. I sat on the white-tiled floor, dripping with sweat, thankful that I could hide it under my voluminous long skirt, long-sleeved blouse and the pink scarf that I was using, at Jafri's request, to improvise a *hijab*, wrapping it over my head and around my neck to hide my hair. Gradually more and more family and community members came into the room. Several of them remarked on how much I was sweating, some joking and some enquiring if I was ill. Anzam, a slim, wizened man wearing a round black hat, gave me some water.

'Nine years ago,' Jafri began, 'the government granted APRIL a fibre concession on our land. We did not know anything about it. The first we knew that our land had been assigned to the corporation was when we went as usual to clear a place to plant rubber. The company security arrived, forced us to stop and sent us home. We were very angry. Since then they have taken more and more of our land and we have suffered great economic loss.'

Jafri showed me a document, a list of names down the left, and beside each either a signature or a fingerprint. There were many more thumbs than squiggles. 'All of the men in the village who had land taken for APRIL's plantation were asked to sign this agreement. They did not understand what it meant. They signed to say that this is our land, not to give permission for it to be destroyed. We want our land back, and we want it green, not blank.' Each of the 139 people on the list were given a paltry 150,000 Indonesian rupiah (about £8) in compensation, less than they could earn from one day's rubber tapping. Jafri explained that they have become embroiled in a legal land claim with APRIL. 'We are fighting the company for our rights and our lost livelihoods. We are being offered a share of profits from the trees and support for community development, but really we want recognition that this is our land and a fair rent.'

I wondered whether perhaps there were compensations in the form of jobs, but Anzam denied this, saying: 'They employ mostly people from outside the village, people from all around the country. Local people will not work for APRIL because they pay only 20,000 rupiah (about £1) per day, but you can earn ten times that by rubber tapping.' The fibre plantation had replaced a diverse agro-forestry system that was economically successful with a monoculture that will benefit only the multinational paper industries. As Anzam put it: 'The natural forest gives a lot of life support, but plantations give only profit to the company, nothing to local people.'

Jafri went on to explain the knock-on effect to the village. 'Because of the plantation, there are economic, agricultural and social problems. There is no land for distribution to new families, so, for example, a family with young children can't get land for growing food, and with the loss of natural forest they can't make a business with honey or rattan or dammar (a traditional medicine). Then because of debt, people start illegal logging. People who used to be hunters now become loggers. Some people move away to cities. That's the reality of cultural change in this village.'

'Does the government just look on, indifferent?' I asked.

Jafri scoffed. 'The Indonesian government is no good. They didn't do any survey or research about who lives here before they granted APRIL permission to use our land.' He suggested I go to meet the local government official to ask him direct.

On the other side of the village a little wiry, Dickensian character called Aprianto Agus sat at a desk in an open-fronted stationery shop. Behind him the shelves were stacked with Paper One, APRIL's branded copy paper, selling at 35,000 rupiah (about £2) a pack. He proudly showed off his local produce, seeming oblivious to the irony of selling the very product that was the cause of a major legal land claim. He was remarkably candid about the ill-effects of the plantation. 'Acacia is much different from forest trees,' he said. 'Forest trees keep water, but acacia uses it up. It affects the soil so it is not as fertile as the forest. When there was still forest, there were lots of trees for honey bees, but now the honey they make is horrible, almost black.'

'So if you see that their plantation is a problem, what are you doing to stop APRIL?' I asked.

'We try to take some action, but because we are the smallest form of government we have no power,' he replied. He suddenly looked like a very small man indeed. 'We are only a village government, we cannot do anything. Even the district-level chief can do nothing. The company are more scared of the traditional leaders. They will listen more to them.'

Jafri nodded forlornly. The elected officials had even less power than him.

Community fibre farms

I was curious to find out if Kuntu village was exceptional, so during the next few days I made arrangements to visit two other communities within a few hours' drive of Riau's capital, Pekanbaru, whose land has been taken over by APRIL. The first such was Penarikan village. The road crossed countless tiny narrow metal bridges with the surface on either side worn away by flooding and ground down by the awkward manoeuvres of buses and lorries. The most frequent vehicles we saw apart from motorbikes were trucks piled with oil palm fruits, clusters of orange-red-brown globules like a cross between a bramble and a coconut.

In Penarikan we followed the usual etiquette and went to the home of the chief, Imran. I was surprised to be greeted by a man in his early twenties who invited us into the sparsely furnished living room of what was clearly a brand-new house. The walls were painted bright turquoise. I was wrapped up in my home-made *hijab* and lashing with sweat again. Imran was cool and groomed, in a smart stripy shirt and pressed trousers. There was none of the banter that I had enjoyed watching between my translator Dede and Pak Jafri earlier. Imran seemed discomfited by our presence, though his wife, in a red baggy dress, crawling daughter and a grandmother, with a hare lip and two teeth, all watched with fascination and frequent smiles as I interviewed the man of their house. The story here was very different from that of Kuntu.

'APRIL has recently planted 2,500 hectares (6,000 acres) of acacia on land that belongs to the village,' Imran said. 'Most of that land belonged to individuals. It was empty land, used to cut logs to build houses or trap deer.'

Empty land is how many people describe land that is neither old-growth forest nor actively in cultivation, but in an in-between stage of regenerating secondary forest, normally land that was used as a *ladang* at some time previously.

In Penarikan, APRIL was much more rigorous than in Kuntu about engaging with the local community. 'There is a government regulation that if the company wants to clear our land it must co-operate with the village. So we asked our village co-operative to seek a share in the plantation and they now have a relationship with APRIL. They have an agreement about compensation and will distribute a share of the money when the trees are harvested,' Imran explained. He could not confirm whether it was a written agreement, but he thought so, though my guides later disputed this.

'Have you got a good deal, do you think? Are you happy?' I asked him.

He reeled off the compensation and harvest figures, and then said, 'The people accept it and feel they have got an OK deal. Not happy, but OK.'

The villagers would get about 3 million rupiah (about £170) per hectare at the end of seven years. 'But you could earn that in one month tapping rubber. I don't understand why you go for this deal,' I challenged.

Imran sat back with a beatific smile. 'Because there is no work required. It is effortless.'

I asked Imran's wife what she thought about the conversion of the forest into plantation and she said, 'I am happy. Compared to natural forest, I prefer the plantation, because we will get money from it without having to work. There is no need to do anything but wait for the harvest.'

Once again, no one in Penarikan is employed by APRIL and instead the plantation work is done by an encampment of two hundred workers from Nias and Java, other Indonesian islands.

'Do you have much to do with them?' I asked.

She laughed. 'No! They are mostly not Muslim and we don't allow our children to marry non-Muslims.'

After some more idle chat, we left them, hoping their optimism about how satisfied the villagers will be with their payments at harvest turns out to be well founded.

On the way to the next village, I learned a lot more about the paper industry in Riau. Dede regaled me with horror stories about skin problems and disease caused by river pollution to people living downstream from the pulp mills. Through a flat land of burned tree stumps, the road ran alongside a canal of evil-looking black water. We had reached the Kampar peninsula, a vast swamp that is being ravaged by the paper industry. Visible from space, the patterns of canals mark the industry's incursion into the wet, wild forest of this vast, unique and little-understood peatland ecosystem.

'We must fight to save the Kampar forests,' said Dede, 'because destroying them will be a disaster not just for local people but also for the global climate. They dig canals to take the wood out but also to drain the land for plantations, but if the peat dries out, it will release carbon. Too much carbon, you can't imagine.' (See Chapter 8).

A stream of log trucks passed in the opposite direction, throwing up dense clouds of dust from the dirt road, and shortly after this we arrived at the Kampar River, which we had to cross on a floating barge-ferry. We lined up behind a couple of empty timber lorries and got out to video the bizarre contraption that would transport us across the river, a steel platform tugged by two barge boats. A black-uniformed, heavily armed security guard stormed over and demanded the camera. We refused to hand it over and he shouted at us that no filming was allowed, pointing his gun at us until we retreated to the vehicle. His badge was emblazoned SEAL and Dede said, 'That's APRIL's security firm. They're bastards. They're trained by American marines. They are only supposed to protect company property, but they try to control everything.'

'Why are they here?' I asked. As far as I could see, the only sign of the paper company was the queue of trucks stacked high with stripped acacia timbers waiting on the other side of the river.

'Everything you see belongs to APRIL,' explained Dede. 'The company built the road, they run the ferry, these are their trucks. It's all their property.' This was a paper corporation universe, one where it was best not to get on the wrong side of the police force.

We drew up at a large, brick house that looked to be still under construction and were welcomed by a handsome man in a red-checked sarong, Zainuddin, the chief of Pankalan Gondai.

The village has more than ten years of experience of working with APRIL, the village's land having been involved in fibre plantations since 1995. I was interested to find out whether their experience was more like Kuntu or whether it would justify Imran's optimism in Penarikan.

At first Zainuddin was mild-mannered, explaining how an initial 700-hectare (1,700-acre) plantation had been gradually expanded over the years to the current level of 2,000 hectares (4,900 acres). We talked about the relative pros and cons of rubber, oil palm and acacia for a while and then I asked what condition the land was in after two generations of acacia had grown on it, and could they then use it for other things. 'I don't know what impact it has on the soil,' he said, 'but I am worried about the way it spreads.' We discussed the need for research into this and made comparisons with *Rhododendron ponticum*, the invasive Himalayan plant, originally grown as an ornamental shrub around stately houses in Britain but now devastating native woodlands in Scotland.

Suddenly his body language changed. He spread himself on his sofa, and said, 'You have to realise we are under pressure here. The one thing we hate about APRIL is the security.' He launched into a tirade about SEAL and their heavy-handed tactics, intimidation, aggression and violence. 'They will hurt people,' he said. 'When the first acacia harvest was over, some people in the village, whose land it had been growing on, wanted to get their land back to plant oil palm. But APRIL wanted to put a second planting of acacia on that land and were not prepared to negotiate any other option and they sent SEAL in. They arrived with about a hundred armed security men, five truck loads, to force the villagers to agree.'

'What happened?' I asked.

'I dug up the road.'

'What?'

He was animated now. 'I got an excavator and dug up the road to the village, to stop them getting to us. Then we dug a drainage ditch around the land we wanted to keep and planted oil palm on it. We got to keep the land, and I think that now they are a little bit scared of me. But why could this not have been negotiated without protest action and intimidation by security?'

'I am going to try to meet someone from APRIL,' I told him. 'Is there anything you want me to ask them?'

Zainuddin leaned towards me. 'You ask APRIL why they cannot negotiate directly with us without bringing in their security forces. That's what I want to know.'

A corporate perspective

After months of travel, I was weary. I exchanged polite, defensive emails and text messages with someone called Sara at APRIL and while I waited for her to relent to meeting me, killed time in Pekanbaru, a heartless dump of a place dominated by six-lane roads of rushing 4x4s and motorbikes. An oil town, packed with brand-new Japanese people-carriers, there is no sense of civic life, nowhere to park up and walk, no cluster of civic buildings, just sprawling tentacles of roads and malls and junk-food dens. The heat is desultory, lethargic, as if the sky is a fat thing too heavy to hold itself up, lolling with its elbows propped up on buildings, its belly slumping onto the street.

While I waited for APRIL's gatekeepers to satisfy themselves with protocols and delaying procedures, I tried to take the direct approach of rolling up at their pulp mill, but there were three impenetrable security zones around it and I could not even get close enough to see the buildings. Meanwhile I continued my research, discovering, for example, that APRIL has strong connections to Europe, a partnership with Finnish paper company UPM Kymmene and that European sales of Paper One and other copy paper made by the company are helping to fund the forest destruction and social conflict I had witnessed.

At last I got consent to interview someone from the company. Dressed up in my best skirt and blouse, I made my way to the dining room at one of Pekanbaru's smartest hotels, where I met

Sara, the charming Indonesian woman who had set up the meeting, and her boss, Eliezer P. Lorenzo, a suave, beaming man from the Philippines. I started with easy questions and he bombarded me with statistics and smiles. He confirmed that in Riau alone they are logging at a rate of 9 million cubic metres (318 million cubic feet) per year to supply their production of 2 million tonnes of pulp, and that the bulk of this wood comes from clear-felling native forest. 'We'll pulp almost anything,' he said, 'except quality timber – that would be like converting good steak to hamburger.' But their main thrust is the establishment of acacia plantations on a massive scale: 'We are ramping up to 2009 where we are saying we will have sufficient capacity to produce 2 million tonnes of plantation pulp.'

I nodded benignly as platitudes poured from him. 'I'd like to say that I think we are a driver for positive change in the environmental field,' he drawled, pronouncing 'positive' like a Texan. 'I think we can make a *pasitive* change in the landscape,' he went on, dropping in the names of people I might know at the Centre for International Forestry Research and talking about working with WWF. 'Pressure from consumers has had a very *pasitive* influence on the way we looked internally into our operations.'

The more emphatically *pasitive* he became, the more negative I felt towards him. My head reeled with double-speak: he called the acacia plantations 'community fibre farms' as if they host cuddle-the-animals school trips.

I told him I had been to Kuntu and I knew that they were involved in land-claims and conflicts with indigenous people over their appropriation of community lands.

He clasped his hands together. 'You know, the issuance of licences and concessions is done without the benefit of actual land surveys, they just draw them out on a map in Jakarta. But lo and behold when you go down there, there are already communities! Some of these communities resort to legal land-claim resolution procedures even if legally they are within our concessions.' He was desperate for me to believe that APRIL is really blameless.

'We offer them alternatives,' he said. 'We tell them, if you want to participate in our community fibre farms you may do so.' It was inconceivable that anyone should not be happy with that, surely? 'Most of these are really idle lands,' he said. 'It's unproductive land.' Try telling that to the rubber tappers, the honey gatherers, the rice growers, fruit pickers, fishermen and hunters who have lost their forest lands.

Then his real prejudice emerged. 'Riau is not an agricultural province. We are developing it.' He had an evangelical glint to his eye as he warmed to this theme. 'Compare with Java, where people have maybe three quarters of a hectare or less. Here one family can own ten, maybe twenty, maybe fifty hectares and they can only develop so much. We would like to develop community fibre farms.' But this was proving difficult, he said, 'because the people here are not farmers like the Javanese. There are lots of contracting jobs available for them in our company but they prefer just rubber tapping, maybe one or two hours a day and then that's it. We offer to them to be involved in our community fibre farm, and there are some takers but working in the plantations is strenuous work. The locals, they don't want to work that hard, they just prefer fishing, just tapping rubber.' I wondered if he really thought that farmers were superior to forest-dwelling people, and that the choice of a good forest-based livelihood over low-paid field labour was really a sign of being work-shy.

I raised the issue I had been asked to by Zainuddin: 'One of the tribal leaders I spoke to wants to know why you send security forces into the villages rather than negotiating with them directly. He told us stories about SEAL being aggressive. We were also threatened by SEAL personnel.'

He put his hand in front of his face, blinked hard and laughed with a frown. 'Maybe sometimes these things happen,' he conceded. 'We need security for anti-illegal logging and protection of our property. They are outsourced. Having said that, we have responsibility over contractors and they must follow our procedures.' He went on. 'Sometimes in negotiations not all parties understand.

They expect too much can be done as soon as possible. Some portions of the communities are not patient. And these things do happen, unfortunately. It's really frustrating for us as well – there's a negotiation process going on and, all of a sudden, boom, some party is not patient that there's a process going on. It's an issue.' He gave me puppy-dog eyes. He really wanted me to believe he was a nice guy.

In subsequent correspondence, Jouko Virta, President of APRIL, confirmed that the company have experienced difficulties in managing land conflicts in the past. 'Unfortunately this can result in some unavoidable, but deeply regrettable, physical confrontation between villagers and migrant workers and our security contractors,' he said. Virta firmly denies any wrongdoing on the part of the company.

My interview with Elezier Lorenzo moved on to the ecological impacts of the acacia plantations and the interview reached a level of surreality when he decided to explain the APRIL view of landscape-level conservation. 'Not all forest conversion is detrimental,' he began. 'Our practice is to identify high conservation-level forests then see to it that these are not converted. Our practice actually enhances conservation areas in the landscape!' I could not believe what I was hearing. 'Our mosaic concept for development is similar to the Man/Biosphere concept where you have rings of development around a core area for conservation.' They were promoting this concept through the idea of a 'master plan' for Riau.

'But acacia is an alien species and highly invasive, so if you plant it in the buffer zone around a high conservation value forest, surely this will degrade that value?' I asked.

He smiled. 'We have debated this so much. Acacia is such an intolerant species, that I don't see any imminent danger of having this species replace natural regeneration.'

'But we've seen it next to plantations, in *ladangs*, in new rubber patches, in forest reserves. We've heard it described by local people as a cancer. It looks like a time bomb.'

'No. In open areas, yes, but not in closed-canopy forest.' He shook his head and gave me a 'don't worry your pretty little head' look that made me want to hit him.

And the toxins that the plant exudes? He conceded, 'It has allelopathic effects. Our answer is that we don't grow agricultural crops in the acacia plantations. It's not an issue in the industrial context.'

He seemed to ignore the possibility that the people whose land the trees are planted on might want to grow food on their land. In APRIL's parallel industrial universe, the genuine concerns of the local people appeared not to be an issue.

The landscape level

To simmer down from my fury at the acacia invasion I needed to visit some real forest, a wild environment that had not been trashed by a paper company. I asked Dede to help me out so he hired a car and arranged for me to meet someone who could put what I was learning into perspective. That person was Ahmad Zazaly from the forest campaign network Jikalahari. He spoke softly and slowly, answering my questions with succinct and powerful responses. He was clear that they were fighting for people's lives, sometimes against colleagues or even family who had been co-opted by the paper industry. He said he knew that they were tiny and few against the might of the multinationals, but that they had justice on their side. Here was a true eco-warrior, as gentle and focused a man as I have ever met.

He said, 'If we have natural forest we can show our children a lot of different kinds of flora and fauna, but if we only have acacia plantations we can only show them dryness, dust ... I don't know, only terrible things.' He continued, 'If all the forest in Riau is lost, the low-lying peatlands will become ocean and the mineral soils in the higher land will become desert. Already we see every year more areas flood in the wet season and there is drought in the dry season. It is a disaster happening every year.'

'What can be done?' I wondered out loud.

'The only hope we have is with the buyers of the paper products in Europe, the USA and China,' he said. 'We hope countries
outside can put pressure on the Indonesian companies by asking
about the fibre. Is it illegal or not? Is it from conflict areas or not?
Have there been environmental impact assessments? We also need
campaigns for using less paper: the increasing demand for paper
increases the impacts on these areas.'

The road to the forest wound through a land of low hills, dense
with the lush and varied vegetation of rubber plantations. Tin-roofed
wooden huts were encircled by gardens of banana, mango trees,
paw-paws and palms. We passed through a village with a green-
domed mosque and houses tiled like my mother's bathroom.

I could not wait to get to the forest, to smell it, to listen to the
sound of the insects whirring, that high-pitched bank of violins up
in the canopy of trees, the scratch of a million musical wings hiding
among the big ginger leaves, the climbers clambering up trees, the
creepers tumbling down.

We reached Minas conservation area after little more than an
hour's drive. It was a logged-over forest full of huge tree stumps
and regrowth that was little more than a few years old. I was gutted
not to be somewhere more untouched but at least it was dense and
itchy with insect life, and there was a chatter of birds in the tree
tops. There was a whiff of jasmine, pungent in the heat, and leaves
shaped like hearts, spears, spoons, arrows and hands. I tuned in
to the scratching laugh of grasshoppers, a big zooming bee, the
electric buzzers of beetles, and some insect that sounded like a
samba-band shaker. A breeze rustled and scuffled a gentle round
of applause from the trees.

But even here, in the protected area, acacia was getting a foot-
hold. After a short walk we drove on to where a Caltex oil pipeline
had been driven through the reserve. It was a classic case of a
service road opening up the land for total exploitation. There was
no forest left here at all, just open scrub and acacia everywhere,
seeding into every space.

'I thought we were coming to a protected area,' I moaned.

'I'm sorry.' Dede looked despondent. 'This is as good as we have.'

We got out and took pictures, but Dede wanted us to continue down the road. I was not sure I could take any more and my despair surfaced as petulance. 'Where exactly are we going?' I nagged.

'We want you to see elephants,' said Dede. 'There are only a few hundred Sumatran elephants left and they are suffering very much from the fibre plantations and the forest destruction. It's important for you to see this impact.' I was mollified. I am particularly fond of elephants.

At the end of the road was an elephant sanctuary, where young elephants are taken when their parents are killed by farmers, a frequent occurrence as good elephant habitat is shrinking fast and elephants find themselves encroaching on rubber plantations, farm fields and village land. The director welcomed us and showed us around, encouraging us to pet the tame elephants.

'We train the elephants here to work as guards,' he explained. 'If we hear that elephants are marauding on village land we go there and the trained elephants chase the wild ones back into the forest. This helps to prevent so many being shot by farmers.' He introduced the staff, including two Thai mahouts who train the animals.

'Is the spread of acacia having any impact on the elephants?' I asked.

'Yes, it's very bad,' said the director. 'Elephants don't eat it. The more acacia plantation, the less habitat there is for elephants.' A study revealed that in the twenty years from 1983, the elephant population crashed to a quarter of its previous level, largely due to coming into conflict with farmers because its forest habitat has been destroyed. Today, as few as three hundred Sumatran elephants may remain.

'The elephant is like a symbol,' said Zazaly. 'The same story is true for all the other animals that live in our forests.'

I gave the director of the sanctuary all the rupiah I had with me. I didn't know what else to do.

Back in Pekanbaru, I thought it could not possibly get any worse and then I innocently asked, 'There are two pulp mills here in Riau, right? APRIL's and another belonging to Asia Pulp and Paper.'

'Right,' said Fatra, the round-faced, helpful forest campaigner at Hakiki, one of the grassroots organisations that is part of Jika-lahari's forest campaign network. We were sitting drinking tea in their sweltering front office in a suburb of Pekanbaru, getting a briefing.

'What's Asia Pulp and Paper like? Are they as bad as APRIL?'

'Worse,' Fatra replied.

'Much worse,' confirmed Dede. There was an exchange in Indonesian and nods all around the gathered activists.

'How do you mean?' I asked.

'APP buys much illegal timber and they even log in protected areas. They are responsible for the worst forest destruction, and they pour chlorine pollution into the Siak River, which causes much disease to people downstream.'

'So how come you've been taking me to see only what APRIL is getting up to? Surely I should be on APP's trail too?' I felt somehow cheated. If I was there to see the worst excesses of the industry, I might as well really see the worst.

Fatra looked alarmed. 'No, no, you must not investigate APP.' He checked with Dede to make sure I had properly understood.

'Why not?' I questioned.

He was adamant. 'It's much too dangerous.'

He and the others started talking all at once. Dede struggled to give a coherent account of all their agitated stories. They told of disappearances, threats to their families and children, violent struggles in communities opposing APP's contractors, homes being bulldozed, even people being killed.

I was stunned. 'You mean to say that APRIL are the nice guys in Riau?'

Dede laughed a bleak laugh. 'There are no nice guys in the paper industry here.'

I put the activists' allegations to APP. Canecio Munoz, a representative of APP, said 'The accusation of abductions and threats of intimidation is not true. No company or representative of the company would act or be permitted to act in that fashion.'

Later, I asked Dede a bit more about APP's mill. He had shown it to me on the map, and it looked like a fairly easy drive from Pekanbaru. I was prepared to take a bit of a risk and at least try to catch a glimpse of the worst offender. I wanted to witness timber from natural forest being taken to a paper mill and since I could not get near the APRIL mill at Pangkalan Kerinci, I wondered if there was any chance that we could do a bit of surveillance at APP's plant at Perawang? For once, I was glad that Dede had a reckless streak. He grinned, and after some reassurance that we wouldn't actually try to get into the mill or make our presence felt, he shot off to book us a car.

We endured a blistering hour on the road, passing countless log trucks with teetering loads of trunks. Inexplicably, however, as we approached Perawang, every truck we saw was parked up in a lay-by or next to a roadside eatery. Nothing was moving. We turned left in town and headed towards the pulp mill. Smokestacks belched in the distance, but there was no activity at the gates at all.

We headed back to town and slumped down in a restaurant. Dede stuffed himself with a late lunch. I was not hungry. A strange man, drunk or deranged, hassled us. I drank my tea, regretting the trip. Then without warning, a stream of green Hino and Isuzu lorries came rumbling down the main street, turning left at the junction to the mill. We jumped into the car and fell into line behind a truck with two logs rammed vertically into slots at the back to act as wedges to keep the logs in place. Close-up there did not seem to be any strapping to secure the load, nothing to stop them sliding sideways at all except friction. The logs were clearly from natural forest, not plantations: a mixture of sizes, ranging from thin sticks to buttressed trunks of old giants, and a great diversity of species. This was the product of forest clearance, and the whole lot was heading for one place. The trucks all turned right at the mill gates, now open, and then lined up. We cruised on by. Out of sight we turned round and cruised back the other way, watching truck after truck stacked with a mind-boggling diversity of different kinds of trees. After a few passes I got jumpy about the guards on the gate and decided I had proved the point. Hard illegal logging. Very hard.

Reports by WWF confirm that APP is indeed an even greater threat to the remaining forests of Riau than APRIL. Its unwillingness to make a commitment to protect the remaining high conservation value forest, its ambitions to maintain or increase pulp production and the dire production levels it achieves from its pulp plantations together 'spell doom for Riau's forests', according to a June 2006 report. CIFOR is equally concerned about the pulp industry's effect on Riau's forests, as its 2006 Annual Report made clear. 'Riau province in Indonesia provides a classic example of the damage the pulp industry can do. In 1982, there were 6.4 million hectares of primary forest in Riau. By 1996, almost half of this had gone, and if current cutting rates continue there will be less than half a million hectares of natural forest left by 2015. In just over thirty years, forest cover will have been reduced from 78 per cent to 6 per cent. It is no coincidence that two of the world's largest pulp mills are sited here.'

While global attention is being focused on the role of oil palm production in causing forest loss in Indonesia, including Riau, WWF's view is that the pulp and paper industry 'is the driving force behind this forest loss'. This is because even when forest land is assigned as an oil palm concession, in order to plant the palms, first its trees must be cut. It is the pulp companies and their subsidiaries that benefit from this land clearance. In addition they are clearing land assigned as fibre plantations, the area of which is on a par with the oil palm concessions. The result is destruction of an unprecedented scale and pace. In 1982, 78 per cent of the land area of Riau was natural forest, but by 2005, only 33 per cent was forested. The forest loss in Riau in 2004–5 alone was an area the size of Luxemburg, and this is just one small province of Indonesia. In the past fifteen years, Indonesia has lost more forest than the total area of the UK, New Zealand or Ecuador.

The pattern of this loss is most dramatic when viewed from above. Looking down over the Kampar peninsula from a plane the plantations form a checkerboard with 'corridors' of forest in geometrical strips and a criss-cross of canals. There are no curves to interrupt its engineered appearance. It is like looking down on a circuit board. By contrast the last forested remnant at the heart of the Kampar peninsula is rough-textured with mixed species; a mossy velvet after the corduroy of plantation rows.

Maps of the province are also revealing. Close-in satellite images show geometric patterns of canals, dug in the wet peatlands to extract timber and dry the land for plantations, which look like television aerials etched on land where previously the people left no sign. There are some particularly powerful images on a website called Eyes on the Forest, the result of a joint project between Jika-lahari, Friends of the Earth and WWF, which show the green forests of the past turning year by year into red cleared lands, like a face blushing with shame.

The campaigners I met in Sumatra – Dede, Jazaly, Fatra and others – were not just a bunch of greenies wanting to protect the flying squirrels in a few fragments of old-growth forest. Here paper production is directly responsible for poverty, illness, flooding, even death; for the loss of land, culture and livelihoods of indigenous people; and for massive-scale destruction of virgin forest land.

Is there any way to stop APP and APRIL? If campaigners stop them selling their paper in Europe will their sales simply shift to China, India, where it is harder to get leverage? How can we protect the last areas of Indonesia's pristine forest from the rapacious greed of industry? I don't know the answers to these questions. Nor can I imagine what will be the long-term legacy of these human and land-rights abuses to Riau's forest communities and I don't know whether they will ever recover from the devastation of their forests.

Since my visit, local communities trying to stop the conversion of the Kampar forests have met with violence from industry security forces and, in 2006, clashes between SEAL and the Gading Permai community led to the tragic death of a community member and arrests of activists. I fear the pulp tsunami will be as difficult for Sumatra's southern province to recover from as the natural disaster that wrecked its northern coasts in 2005, even if, somehow, the tide can be turned. For now, this poisoned flood of alien trees moves ever deeper into the Sumatran forests.

Below the surface of this beautiful country, Indonesia is a nightmare, with corruption at the heart of its system of forest governance. It is rotten through and through. The pulp and paper industry has enormous economic power: power to control the forest resources, power to intimidate the people, power to exploit the corruption of the government. It appears unstoppable. Its responses to the campaigns of environmentalists are a matter of fly-swatting; they are an irritant rather than a real threat. To make any real difference, significant political changes have to come from within the country, and they will have to be brought about by Indonesians, within Indonesia's political system.

The main lever available to people outside Indonesia is finance. The paper companies like APP and APRIL must operate within the multinational markets and rely to some extent on international financial backing. People in rich countries can make a difference with campaigns focused on big investors, like the one to prevent financial backing of United Fibre Systems' plan to develop a new pulp mill in Kalimantan (described in Chapter 3). Paper companies with records of corruption, land-rights abuses and illegal logging should have no place in any ethical investment portfolio, and bankers need to get a grip on the risks to their reputations involved in backing these companies. If governments will not do it, then financiers must compel companies to respect and comply with the various international conventions for the protection of human rights: the International Labour Organisation Convention 169 for the Protection of the Rights of Indigenous Peoples; the General Declaration of Human Rights (1948); the United Nations

Convention for the Elimination of all Forms of Racial Discrimination (1966); the International Agreement on Economics, Social and Cultural Rights (1966); the International Agreement on Civil and Political Rights (1966).

The other thing that people in rich countries can do is to be ready to listen to the stories of what is happening in countries such as Indonesia and lend our moral support to the activists trying to bring about change from within. We can act in solidarity with the forest people.

Similar stories to those I have witnessed in Russia and Sumatra can be found in Brazil, Uruguay, Argentina, Chile, South Africa, and even New Zealand and Australia: in all of these countries the land of local and indigenous peoples is licensed by the national government to multinational paper corporations without their consent. Sometimes the results are tragic. On 26 February 2007, Antonio Joaquim dos Santos, a 32-year-old farmer in the north of Minas Gerais, Brazil, was killed while collecting firewood. Local people claim he was murdered by an armed guard of the V&M Florestal Company, which has planted thousands of hectares of eucalyptus for pulp in the area, although no charges were ever brought. A litany of land-rights crises is recorded by the World Rainforest Movement, Robin Wood, Urgewald, Forest Peoples Programme and other NGOs from around the world. The responsibility is heavy on us to hear these stories and to bear witness, even if at times it feels like a back-bending load.

CHAPTER 6: HARRY POTTER AND THE PULPMILLS OF DOOM

The longest blockade

Deforestation, land-rights conflicts and human rights abuses are not restricted to the tropics. Canada, a country with one of the highest standards of living of any on earth, is home to one of the paper industry's most scandalous secrets: the destruction of old-growth forest to make paper. This rich and sparsely populated country has a quarter of the world's forest and all the wealth and freedom to be a model of sustainable forestry, yet it is squandering its forest resources. A staggering 90 per cent of the logging there occurs in ancient forests. This is not forest management, it is forest destruction. And much of this destruction happens on the traditional terrorities and often against the wishes of Canada's indigenous people, the First Nations.

All over the world, indigenous peoples have to fight for their rights to steward their natural resources, particularly forests, because state governments lay claim to them and then license them off to the highest bidder. Like the Saami in Finland, the Udege in Russia and the Domo in Sumatra, First Nations in Canada have had their land-rights abused and their native forests leased out to industrial foresters not the least bit interested in the spiritual or cultural values of the land and driven purely by commercial demands. Right across Canada, First Nations have watched their forests being trashed by multinational paper companies.

One of the worst examples I know of is in Grassy Narrows, Ontario, and the protest against it is now the longest-running blockade in Canadian history. Asubpeeschoseewagong (Grassy Narrows First Nation) is a small community of Anishina'abe people who live in a scatter of wooden houses at the end of a rough road. A modest administration building hosts offices of chiefs and some basic services. The village was once a clearing in the Whiskey Jack forest, a rich environment from which the people made their livelihoods by gathering plants for food and medicine, harvesting bark and grasses for textiles, hunting and fishing. Nowadays it is on the edge of a clear-cut stretching for hundreds of hectares, which has torn the heart out of the forest. Tan hunting dogs loll and lope about, looking bored. The community's traditional hunting zones, known as traplines, have been decimated. Sacred groves of trees have been felled with no thought to the spiritual values of the local people.

Those values are embodied by Judy da Silva, a small woman in her early forties, who was the first person I met from Grassy Narrows and who helped me to go there in 2002, just as the community's struggle against the paper industry was reaching boiling point. Like many people in the community she had health problems and walked with the help of a stick. But though she was delicate in body, her big eyes were full of passion and clarity. In a low, even voice, she told me that she and some of the other women in the village had reached the end of their tether and were about to embark on direct action to try to get the logging to stop. Talking about the horror of seeing her forest home destroyed seemed to cause her physical pain, as if the chainsaws cut her flesh and the clear-cuts scarred her own body. It was humbling to see how strong she had to be to endure the hurt, particularly as I learned more about the history of the community, which has survived generations of abuses. The story of Grassy Narrows was hard to listen to, and I balked to imagine what it must feel like to have lived it.

The community used to inhabit a fertile valley, where they grew wild rice and other crops and lived much more comfortable lives, but in the 1960s their lands were drowned when a hydro-electric dam was built to generate power for the town of Kenora and its saw and pulp mill. The indigenous people were relocated to the site of the current village. Over the next decade the pulp mill polluted water courses with mercury (used in the past to prevent water-transported logs from rotting), contaminating the First Nation's water supply and the fish that made up a significant part of their diet. The result was widespread mercury poisoning causing long-term health problems including cancers, brain illnesses and children born with disabilities. Compounding these insults, Abitibi Consolidated and Weyerhaeuser were granted licences to log the First Nation's traditional territory.

Abitibi, one of the ten biggest paper companies in the world, makes newsprint, on which papers such as the *New York Times* and *Washington Post* are printed. Some of it ends up in Europe. Weyerhaeuser boasts the largest newsprint facility in North America (at Longview, Washington) with the biggest thermo-mechanical pulp mill in the world, churning out enough newsprint every day for a 10-metre-wide (30-foot) sheet stretching from Miami to Seattle. Yet it is packaging paper that Weyerhaeuser majors in. Its own website boasts that each year it makes so much container board (the stuff of brown cardboard boxes) that it would stretch to the moon and back eleven times. And then there are the six billion litre drinks containers it makes each year, not forgetting its factories making brown paper bags, corrugated cardboard and a range of pulps, from absorbent fluffs for sanitary applications to specialist pulps for manufacturing rayon and other textiles. It has been the target of environmental campaigns for years, particularly focused on its North American logging activists.

In Grassy Narrows, Judy introduced me to Steve Fobister, one of the First Nation chiefs. He was frail and prematurely aged as a result of the mercury poisoning, but he agreed to help me try to appreciate the scale and impact of the logging. He drove me out in his truck along a rutted logging track through the wreckage of what was once forest, now just bare earth and scattered brash. We pulled up in a clear-cut that stretched beyond the horizon. Steve pointed to a hillside that had been a special, sacred grove. I tried to imagine it clothed in trees, but couldn't; the brown of scarred soil was too insistent.

Most shocking of all were the huge wood stacks, as big as mansions, rotting by the track. These log piles were the result of a simple failure to follow through the felling of trees with collection and transportation of the timber to somewhere it could be used. Pulp mills do not want timber that has dried out, because it makes their processing too difficult, so logging for paper mills requires careful logistics, clearly not part of these companies' practices. This wasteful excess particularly enrages the native people, proof if any were needed of the industrial loggers' failure to respect the land.

As with Judy, it clearly caused Steve great pain to witness the scene. He said, 'Our primary life-supporting value is our attachment to the land and our ability to enjoy the wildlife, forest, waterways and our traditional way of life – hunting, fishing, harvesting – living off the land as our families have for hundreds of years. Our elders keep telling us we need to focus on the land: it is what sustains us physically, mentally, emotionally and spiritually.'

More than 50 per cent of the Whiskey Jack forest has been clear-cut, destroying the habitats of the plants and animals that form the basis of traditional livelihoods. Where Abitibi has replanted the forest, it has been with a monoculture that is heavily sprayed with chemicals, killing or contaminating the few remaining berries and other plants.

According to an Amnesty International briefing to the United Nations, Grassy Narrows falls within the territory covered by the 1873 treaty between the Canadian state and the chiefs of the Salteaux Tribe of the Ojibway Indians. This treaty, known as Treaty 3, establishes that indigenous peoples have the 'right to pursue their avocations of hunting and fishing throughout the tract'. The

Grassy Narrows First Nation claims that these treaty rights have been violated by the damage caused to their natural resources by forestry. This legal claim is yet to be answered satisfactorily.

'Abitibi should be stripped of their forest licence,' Steve said. 'They are not contributing anything, only taking, depleting and destroying. We can't understand how the provincial government can stand by and allow this to happen and even more so the wilful blindness of the federal government. But they have continued to ignore us so we have no choice but to take direct actions to stop the logging in our territory. The forest should be protected for our children's future. People in this region need to take back what was theirs.'

In December 2002, after years of fruitless negotiation and despite poverty and illness, the Grassy Narrows community decided to take on the two multinational paper giants, David and Goliath style, by trying to impede logging trucks from accessing their land. Judy and her sister set up a blockade on an access road. Through freezing winter conditions, the community held strong. The youth of the community made banners and helped the women through long, cold vigils, keeping a fire burning as a symbol of their commitment.

Five years later, they were still there, making Grassy Narrows the longest-running forest blockade in Canadian history. In recognition of the five-year blockade, Judy and other women from the community posted eviction notices at a logging camp. Their protest meets variously with support, indifference or scorn from the various sectors of Canadian society, but it has drawn international condemnation for the Ontario provincial government, Abitibi and Weyerhaeuser. There are ongoing calls for a moratorium on logging on any First Nation land where there is not free, prior and informed consent of the local community.

There are other conflicts in Canada over land tenure granted to paper companies in breach of traditional land-rights in areas covered by historical treaties and also where no treaties were ever signed. For example, in the Queen Charlotte Islands, British Columbia, the Haida First Nation has protested the failure by the provincial government to consult with them before giving Weyer-haeuser permission to log the land, despite a Supreme Court ruling that they must consult more meaningfully. In 2005, the Haida First Nation blocked roads and harbours and seized timber logged by the company, to demonstrate their outrage that a logging licence on their land, granted by the provincial government without any treaty or consent, was put up for sale by Weyerhaeuser for Can$1.2 billion. A month later the British Columbian government agreed to protect 40,000 hectares (100,000 acres) of the land that the Haida consider most precious. This was an important victory for the Haida, but it needs to be kept in perspective; it covers an area less than 1 per cent of the North American forest that Weyerhaeuser has cleared of trees.

A temperate travesty

Opposition to forestry in Canada is not limited to indigenous land-right conflicts; some of the most heated and dramatic protests have been led by environmentalists. Canada's Pacific seaboard is flanked by a temperate rainforest that is among the most magnificent ecosystems on the planet. This is the home of black and grizzly bears and wolves, which flourish in the shelter of cathedral groves of trees whose lifetimes span millennia. Felling in this extraordinary forest has been getting steadily more and more controversial over recent decades, and efforts to protect it from logging in the early 1990s led to some of the world's highest profile ecological protests.

It all began at Clayoquot Sound on the west coast of Vancouver Island in 1992, when the government announced a land-use plan that would protect 30 per cent of the forest whilst allowing industrial logging (i.e. clear-felling) of the remaining 70 per cent. Environmentalists went apoplectic at the prospect of losing nearly three-quarters of the forest and First Nations were outraged that these decisions were being made over their heads on their traditional lands. As protests erupted, forestry companies went into logging overdrive, determined to get as much timber out as fast as they could.

The result was the biggest civil disobedience Canada has ever known. Thousands of people were arrested for blockading logging roads and other direct actions against the forestry industry resulting in 932 court cases: the largest mass trial in Canadian history. Many of today's forest campaigners cut their teeth on these blockades (a reunion of the alumni of the Clayoquot blockades would make an interesting gathering) and it galvanised Canadians to reconsider what was happening to their forests and to recognise their global significance. Eventually a non-binding logging moratorium was announced. Having apparently saved the Clayoquot Sound forests, environmentalists went on to broker deals to protect the most ecologically important parts of the Great Bear Rainforest, further north in British Columbia, and they are now working Canada-wide, through the Canadian Boreal Initiative, to try to ensure at least half of all the remaining boreal forest remains unlogged.

It is not surprising that forest destruction in Clayoquot Sound should cause outrage. Its forest is one of the wonders of the world. It holds a special place in my heart as it was where I first saw a bear, many years ago. I have returned several times over the years, each time getting lucky with bear-spotting, and I never fail to leave in raptures at the magnificent forest.

On my most recent visit, I camped up under a slate-grey sky where the forest overlooks the Pacific. The sea was petrol blue and portentous. A storm was forecast. It could be dramatic. Fortunately temperate rainforest is especially sumptuous during a downpour. My first sight in the morning was a deep, intense green through the tent door. Dawn light inched its way down the trees, branch by branch, fern by fern. Birds hopped and whistled between splashes of rain. Brief hail gave way to chilly sun, muted and softened by layers of leaf, twig, moss and lichen, layers of life breathing, steaming, dripping and growing. Swaying leaves cast rippling light-shadow dances, like underwater motion. The air was green and smelled sweet, rich and dream-inducing.

In my tent, I listened to the trees' rain drumming on the roof. We don't have a word in English for raindrops that are intercepted by trees, but in Nepali they are called *tapkan*. Trees save rain up to play it again later, at their own speed, in their own way. They hoard leaf-handfuls of it, setting it aside and stuffing it into their lichen pockets and pouches in their trunks. Later, perhaps stimulated by a breeze, they will let it go, plumping it down in fat blobs or drumming in syncopated jazz rhythms.

The Western red cedar trees that dominate this forest live so long they challenge all human conceptions of time and grow so big it is hard to imagine having such presence. Each mighty giant is a garden in its own right, hosting up to 40 metres (130 feet) of epiphytic ferns, creepers, mosses and lichens. Cutting them down to make catalogues and junk mail can surely never be justified.

Out in the forest, I stretched around a cedar to measure its 8-metre (26-feet) girth, but it was far too big to hug. I could only clasp my body against it like a limpet on a craggy weed-hung rock face. Its bark was a deep fox-brown and the texture of flaky chocolate. Its foliage swooped above like feathers on wings of an eagle the size of a whale. The cedars' lifespan is extraordinary: they can live for up to 1,500 years, then die but remain standing for several hundred more years, hosting bears, crows and woodpeckers, before they weaken enough for some storm or rot to send them to the floor. There they can carry on as a discernible form for hundreds of years more. Horizontal, they are known as nursery trees for the nurturing environment they provide to seedlings and saplings, whose roots, helped by fungi and insects, recycle the wood's nutrients back into living structures.

I strolled slowly enough to see into the details of the trees: an old trunk was smoothed by rain as if by a cabinet-maker's lathe; a hollow fallen giant revealed the roots of the next generation of trees hanging inside like a wardrobe of lace dresses. In a nest high up a spruce tree, two ravens serenaded each other with rasps and caws and an occasional operatic 'croop', a complex song compressed into one long, potent tone. Through the heart of the forest a stream of clear water trickled and chuckled along its channel through an overhang of huckleberries, azaleas, roses and ferns. On the swampy ground beside it, skunk cabbages squatted like pot plants with their mad-joy yellow trumpets blasting scent like plastic air fresheners in an over-upholstered living room. I padded along soft leaf-deep paths and across wooden boardwalks letting all this exuberant life soak in.

As I clambered over a 1½-metre-high (5-feet) horizontal russet trunk, spongy and rotting but festooned with a line of saplings and twined with creepers, I reflected that this tree first put down roots into the previous generation nursery tree so long ago that paper making was not even invented. All 27 generations of Cao Zhang's family, and all the generations before then back to Cao Lun's time, would compress into just one twig of this cedar's family tree.

Catface

Although non-binding environmental protection and improved forestry recommendations by Clayoquot Sound Scientific Panel had been adopted in 1996, in 1999, International Forests (known as Inter-for) bulldozers were still ploughing yet another logging road into the pristine forest. My partner Bill and I had just returned from Mears, one of many islands in the Sound, blissed out with images of amber foliage under fern-decked cedars and hemlocks. We were looking for more adventure.

A harassed-looking young man in combats welcomed us into the Friends of Clayoquot Sounds office and indulged us as we raved about the 1,500-year-old giant cedars between whose toes we had been camped for the last few nights. 'You weren't put off by the rain, then?' he smiled. It rains all the time on the west coast of Vancouver Island: they measure rainfall in metres.

Bill shook his head. 'We're from Scotland. We were actually wondering if you could recommend anywhere else we should go. We only came back because we ran out of food.'

Our host looked us up and down, and then grinned. 'Fancy a bit of direct action?'

Bill and I confirmed with a glance. 'If it's in the forest, we're up for anything.'

'You won't be risking arrest. It's just that we're blocking some bulldozers in on Catface Mountain, but two of our activists had to leave this morning. Now there's only Maryjka left on the blockade. It's pretty quiet at the moment, but we don't like only having one person out there, just in case anything goes off.'

'We're all yours.'

We were duly signed up and dashed off to get some provisions. Half an hour later we were in a speedboat hurtling across the sound to the foot of Catface Mountain. Boat is the only way in and out of this spectacular forest. After a long slog up a steep logging track from the jetty we found the blockade: boulders and logs across the track and a huge tarpaulin slung between several trees. Under it, beside a puffing camp stove, sat an elf-like woman. This was Maryjka. Once she realised we were there to support her, she leaped to her feet and launched into a series of stories about Canadian people and organisations we had never heard of. We pointed out that evening was drawing in and we should sling our tent up before it got dark. She showed us to a clearing behind the roadblock and Bill set about pitching the tent, while Maryjka gave me the full tour of the site.

A few minutes later, an engine growled towards us, and Bill came scampering with his camera. 'Er, what's the protocol here on the vehicles? He nearly knocked the tent down with that bucket.' Emerging out of the woods behind Bill was a yellow excavator the size of a house, a bucket swinging on the digger arm big enough to scoop up a car.

'He's just being macho as usual,' said Maryjka. 'They're outrageous, those drivers, they really are. They're always trying to frighten us.'

The digger ground towards us with a check-shirted man glowering inside. Bill approached, took a couple of photographs, and when the metal arm nearly swiped him to the ground, shouted, 'Watch it, we're international monitors. I've come all the way from Scotland to record what's happening here and I've got you on camera.' Bill is good at blustering exaggerations like this, which, combined with our working title of 'worldforests' sometimes leads people to think we aren't just the two-bit organisation (I'm one bit, he's the other) that we really are. Our by-line is 'research, writing and revolution'. I do the research and writing, mostly. Bill takes care of the revolution, mostly; though that day we seemed to be both in it up to our necks.

The big yellow monster's engine roared and its scoop menaced the tarpaulin. We retreated to the far side of the road block. The vehicle pressed on towards it. Then, with a swipe of the digger arm, the driver attacked the heap of logs and rocks, tossing aside the trunk laid across the top, which up-ended and crashed down the slope into the forest. Another smash of the metal arm, a splintering crack, and the edifice started to fall apart.

'Do they do this regularly?' I asked Maryjka.

She responded by cursing vigorously, I'm not sure in what language, and sprinted off to the cellphone to make an emergency call. 'No heroics,' she shouted over her shoulder.

The digger continued dismantling the road block as if it was made of children's building bricks. I looked at Bill. 'What happens if it gets through? Do we lie down in front of it?' I had started the day in a mellow state of forest-induced calm. I had not expected to end it risking my life under caterpillar tracks.

Bill was taking photographs, dodging flying debris and the swooping bucket. I stood in the road, trying to look as if I knew what I was doing there, wondering whether I would have the bottle to lie down when the block was cleared.

Maryjka dashed back just as the excavator was pushing the last of the boulders to the side of the track. 'They're leaving!' she gasped. 'They're heading out.' She tugged me off the road, jumping up and down and whooping with excitement.

Bill caught on faster than I did. 'Do you mean they're pulling off Catface?'

'Yip. They've had orders from Interfor HQ. They're to head down the mountain and they'll be barged off tomorrow.' She gave the driver a queenly wave as the vehicle rumbled past. He scowled back.

Behind the excavator a second orange JCB rolled out from the forest, lights blazing and engine belching. We waved it goodbye and watched its tail lights bump down the hill we had walked up less than two hours before.

'We've won!' Maryjka yelled after it and then turned to us. 'Who are you guys anyway? We've been in deadlock here for weeks. Then you turn up and Interfor's off the mountain before you even get your tent up.'

Bill gave a little bow. 'Worldforests at your service.'

Next morning, we were picked up from Catface and returned to Tofino to a heroes' welcome. It felt great. We had saved the forest, those 2,000-year-old trees sheltering bears and wolves, and we revelled in the victory.

While I blushed in the wholly undeserved glory of that October morning, I knew nothing of Nicole Rycroft, a paper campaigner I was yet to meet, who had spent many days on the blockade and missed the pull-out by about eight hours. Unlike me, she had already worked out that although such actions can keep the chainsaws at bay for a while and help to raise awareness of forest destruction, they are not a long-term solution. The forests will remain threatened until demand reduces for their products, the most pervasive of which is undoubtedly paper.

Interfor happened here

Seven years on, and ten years after the logging moratorium was put in place, I returned to Clayoquot Sound. Ignoring the dubious fumes of a belching pulp factory at Nanaimo, I beavered up the road to Port Alberni, and past another mill, the car juddering in the wind-blasts from passing log trucks. There is no hiding from the paper industry in British Columbia, which supplies half of Canada's pulp. Much of it is exported to other countries, sold around the world as the commodity known as 'market pulp' to be bought by paper factories as one ingredient of the paper furnish. Canada is the biggest source of pulp to the UK, for example, supplying around one-sixth of the pulp imported by paper mills, to make everything from kitchen roll to cheque books. Much of it derives from softwood, such as Sitka spruce, which has long, strong fibres much sought after by the makers of sheets that will need to endure high-speed handling by machines like magazine printers and copiers.

At the Friends of Clayoquot Sounds office I was met this time by a fresh-faced, shiny-complexioned young guy in sports gear, who turned out to be Diego Garcia, a name one might expect to come across in Amazonian, not British, Columbia. He was expecting me. We headed out to the forest, Diego giving directions. As we motored I asked him to fill me in on what had happened in Clayoquot Sound in recent years.

'In the short term,' he said, 'the blockades were a success. Deals were struck on a logging moratorium, and industrial logging rates reduced by eighty to ninety per cent from what they were back in the early 1990s. Then in 2000, Clayoquot Sound was declared a UNESCO biosphere reserve. Hang a left here.'

We piled off the highway onto a dirt track and bumped and juddered our way deep into the forest, pulling to a halt at the brow of a hill beside a wreckage of discarded timber and slash, heaped amid the stumps of huge cedar trees. The whole valley had been clear-cut, leaving the most devastated and impenetrable logging site imaginable, mounds of wood metres high, trees strewn like corpses in a battlefield.

I asked what had happened here.

'Interfor happened here,' Diego said.

International Forests – Interfor – is one of Canada's biggest and most powerful forestry companies and, Diego explained, they had a licence from the provincial government to log here.

'But you just said this is a biosphere reserve.' I had assumed that to achieve such a status from the United Nations Education, Scientific and Cultural Organisation would mean that conservation of biodiversity was paramount, but in reality it has no authority to enforce any such priority.

Diego nodded. 'Each individual tree can be worth up to thirty thousand dollars for its timber. A valley such as the one we are in can be worth billions of dollars. That kind of money talks.'

He spelled out the current situation and as he spoke, my heart sank. Under a new provincial forestry plan the moratorium came to an end in late 2006 with logging due to recommence in many pristine valleys in the sound. Even while the moratorium lasted, the logging had only moved: British Columbia's extraction rate did not reduce and the overall logged area actually increased.

'Because the logging situation in the sound improved over the past decade, this led people to believe that this area is protected, when in fact no new protected areas have been created since the protests,' Diego explained. 'Three-quarters of the productive forest are still available to logging companies, despite the fact that this is a biosphere reserve. Even pristine watersheds like the Sydney Valley and Flores Island aren't protected, yet these forests are the very reason why the area was declared a biosphere reserve in the first place. Most protected forests are in boggy areas where the trees struggle to grow in wet acid soils, so the industry doesn't want them anyway. We are really struggling to protect what the industry sees as productive land, the ancient forests and giant trees.'

'How much of this is down to the paper industry?' I asked.

'The paper industry is one of the major drivers. Without it there would be no industrial-scale logging in Canada. About 50 per cent of what is logged is converted into paper. It's astounding to think that every day people are wiping their noses and using toilet tissue made from these trees, literally, "wiping away ancient forests".' As he said these last four words he gestured to indicate he was quoting the slogan from the Greenpeace Kleercut campaign against Kimberly-Clark, with its clever media jam on the Kleenex brand.

'We passed a couple of pulp mills on the way here; will these trees have gone there?'

'Yeah, probably Port Alberni. They'll be catalogues by now, or market pulp.'

We stood in the clear-cut in driving rain, numbed by the obscenity of the most majestic trees on earth being pulped for junk mail and toilet roll.

As the shock smarted, I tried to focus on detail. Diego pointed out huge mounds of brash stacked up like funeral pyres to hide the massive buttressed stumps of cedar trees that may have been 1,500 years old. 'The industry term for these is "biodiversity enhancement structures",' he said. 'They say it provides habitat for small animals, when in fact it's an easy way for the company to try to cover the evidence that they've taken these ancient cedars.'

In order to extract such timber, the industry deploys huge machinery and to get it to the forest involves a major effort in road building. The access infrastructure just for this logging coup was staggering. Roads are bad news for forests: everywhere in the world, where logging trucks go, hunters follow. The animals and birds endemic to this forest, including the marten cats, Roosevelt elks, marbled murrelets, clouded salamander, pileated woodpecker, northern spotted owl, and of course the bears and wolves, are doubly threatened, first by the loss of habitat and then by the direct attack or indirect disturbance of road users. 'The volume of roads is totally unjustifiable,' agreed Diego, 'but unfortunately there's a subsidy for road building in the stumpage fee system.' For every tree a logging company fells it must pay a government tax called a 'stumpage fee'. By allowing road building costs to be used to reduce this tax liability, the government provides a financial incentive for creating such infrastructure.

Even in Canada, one of the richest countries on earth, where one would expect to find understanding of the value of old-growth forest habitats, the paper industry's greed is destroying ancient forest and government incentives are encouraging them to do so. Despite the fact that in Clayoquot Sound tourism is booming and is worth more to the economy than forestry, somehow the message does not stick that the forest is more valuable intact than reduced to toilet roll.

Wolf man

My Great-Uncle Frank (the husband of my outrageously named relative Agatha Haggith) was a logger all his life, just down the coast from Vancouver Island in Puget Sound, Washington State. He spent decades taking out the biggest trees he could find, using giant saws wielded by two men and dragging the timber out with horses. It took him until he was an old man to shake his head and wonder how he brought himself to do it.

Even harder for me to understand are the First Nations men who turn to logging. In Tofino, one of them was willing to talk to me, as long as I went out with him on his boat. Clayoquot Sound is a watery world of forested islands and inlets, and to get a sense of its grandeur it is essential to see it from the water, said Joe Martin, a Tla-o-qui-aht ex-logger and expert wildlife watcher. It was a calm, grey morning, but Joe knew his climate and wrapped me up in gear that felt like it would survive an Arctic winter.

As we puttered out into the sound, bald eagles perched in trees at the shoreline, diving to scoop fish out of the water as if they came to the surface and asked to fly. Groups of sea-lions gathered, their heads bobbing like balding men chatting together in a swimming pool, but as we approached they ducked and submerged with a flick of a flipper or the curve of a long coursing back.

Joe told me stories about his people. Before Europeans came there were 10,000 First Nation people living in Clayoquot Sound. The forest was intact then; that culture used neither toilet paper nor catalogues. Joe was one of the lucky ones: his great-great-grandmother took the family away from the sound for years to protect them from the epidemics of smallpox and flu, brought by the colonists, that wiped out so many of the First Nations people.

Joe spent twelve years as a logger. 'I felt at the time that if I didn't, someone else would come here and do it,' he explained, taking his leather fleece-lined hat off and fixing me in the full intensity of his stare, 'but I really did feel rotten from it. It made me feel sick to my stomach. When you log, you're scraping away the soil, it's being washed off, and you look down into the river and it's running the same colour as a cup of hot chocolate.'

Joe's big concern with forestry was its impact on salmon, a huge part of the First Nation people's livelihoods in that area. Forestry damage to spawning grounds has been one of the major causes of the decline of Pacific salmon stocks. 'I knew what was happening to the salmon because my father was a fisherman, so I felt really bad about that. In our village we now only have one fishing boat left.'

He described the last place he logged. It was as beautiful as Cathedral Grove, he said, a flat place in the shelter of a mountain with streams meandering through, where salmon fry swam. 'We logged over all that stuff. There was one stream; I left some logs on the other side of it. I just couldn't bring myself to drag them through that stream; I just couldn't do it any more. So they came along and fired me. I said, all right. It was a huge weight off my shoulders.'

The engine idled. The weather was deteriorating. Joe sighed. 'I don't know how much of a difference one person makes, but I began to work against them, to be part of the protests.' He fired up the outboard and swung the boat into motion.

As we explored the sound, scouring the shoreline for bears that might be taking advantage of low tide to gather shellfish, Joe told stories about other First Nations loggers who had had similar experiences of logging. 'Recently, a friend of mind near Port Alberni called me to say he couldn't do it any more,' he said. 'One day he just looked up at this tree and realised, this is crazy: thousands of years to grow and just a few minutes to cut it down.'

He regaled me with profound teachings he learned from his grandparents, about self-esteem and the need for self-respect as the foundation of respect for everything else. Central to Joe's sense of identity was his clan: the wolf. He said that the wolves all but disappeared for years after the logging began but since the moratorium on logging the wolves were coming back again. 'Some people who have heard too many Little Red Riding Hood stories want to hunt them,' Joe said, 'but it's against our traditional law to kill a wolf.'

To shelter us from a squall, he steered his boat into an inlet where, as if on cue, three wolves were padding along the beach. Noticing us, they melted into the forest that blanketed the steep shore. Joe crooned quietly, a little smile on his face. Then he lifted his head and let out a horror-movie wolf howl. The sound echoed around the bay. He repeated it. And then there came a response: not an echo, but a similar call from deep in the forest. He howled back, and a chorus of yowling and yipping returned. There was a whole pack of wolves in there, singing to this voice across the water, the voice of their clansman.

It was a spine-tingling dialogue. Sometimes a single wolf responded to Joe, sometimes a whole family of deep, quavering wails and excited puppy barks. Between the calls, silence. It hailed. The howls got louder, closer, and then retreated. A bald eagle swooped across the bay and perched on a tall spruce. The hail pattered into quietness. Reluctantly, we headed back out into the sound.

Around the headland into the next cove, a bear stood on the rocky strip between sea and forest edge, a black, sleek shadow. He threw us a glance over his shoulder and unhurriedly stepped into the cover of cedars. There is a stroll that only a bear can do: nonchalant but swift, big strides covering a lot of ground in very little time while the body seems to shrug indifference, just stepping out of the limelight, the epitome of cool. I wondered whether both bear and wolves turned, once backstage, and peeked out from the wings, eyeing their audience. Now that logging is back under way throughout the vast ranges that they need, how long will they survive?

On the way back to Tofino, as the hail turned to snow, Joe said, 'It sure is good to hear wolves howlin' in the forest…' He left a telling pause before adding, 'rather'n chainsaws'.

Roaring back to the harbour in driving sleet, Joe shouted about the predicted increases in logging in the area. 'Can they not just leave it alone?' he bawled. 'Is there nothing they'll just leave alone?'

Just before leaving the reserve on my last day, my intention to walk one last trail was diverted by a big black bear loitering at its start. She turned out to be a mum, and up in a nearby tree top was her happy little cub, feasting on the sweet shoots of springtime maple bursting with syrup. With one eye on the mother in the undergrowth, I watched the cub shuffle and clamber about the tree with cute, clumsy-seeming agility. After a repeat performance in a second tree, the mother bear led her young one away. Years ago, First Nation chief Garry Raven told me that a bear signifies courage, steadfastness and commitment. To save their last habitats from the paper industry we will need all this and more.

Reluctantly I tore myself away from the Pacific National Park, struck camp and headed to Port Alberni and then Nanaimo. I was grumpy and outraged at the old-growth logging I had witnessed. At a roadside café a waiter chatted with me and sympathised. 'They're tearing down Canada and trucking the trees to the USA,' he said, putting straightforwardly what the Canadian Forest Products Industry association, Canada Wood, confirms: 80 per cent (by value) of Canada's wood product exports go to the USA.

In fact Canada stands out as a country with a focus on cutting down trees, turning them into paper products and sending them overseas. More than half (51 per cent) of Canada's forest product exports are pulp, paper, paperboard and newsprint.

It dominates the world trade in wood pulp, representing a third of the global export supply, and it is by far the biggest newsprint exporter in the world, accounting for 45 per cent of world trade.

The trashing of old-growth forests is part of a massive system. It angers me and my first instinct is to blame the men with chainsaws. But they have bosses, and the lion's share of my fury must be directed at the industry decision makers who draw the lines on the maps, reduce the forest from a place bursting with life to mere numbers of dead things, those who calculate volumes and profits and hire the contractors. Those contractors are also culpable. Many of the workers are trapped, although ultimately every one of them has choices they can make, just as Joe Martin did. When it comes down to it, so do all the individuals in the industry from the chief executive to the public relations staff, right down to the person who does the deliveries to the staff canteen. We all have the choice as to whether to fund their enterprises by buying their paper products.

It is all one system. And the root problem with old-growth forest destruction by the paper industry is the fact that governments fail to legislate against it. In Canada, and certainly in British Columbia, the vast bulk of the forest land is regulated by the provincial government on behalf of the Crown, who owns the land, the Crown being the ultimate legal authority in Canada, currently held by Queen Elizabeth II. So, she is responsible too, along with the government that carries the can, the queen's servants destroying the forests by issuing permits, making plans, ignoring complaints and being swayed by the industry lobby. The politicians who argue that society is economically dependent on forestry need to be challenged: there are alternative sources of wealth that will have to be found anyway, when all the forest is gone. It is simply not necessary to fell the last 30 per cent of the forest before looking for them. The industry must desist and the politicians and civil servants who do not insist they do are just as culpable in the forest destruction as the men who take chainsaws to those magnificent trees.

Supply and demand

The stereotype of people trying to save forests is of radical tree-huggers who lie down in front of bulldozers or perhaps lobbyists trying to influence forest management. But, in reality, at the forest frontiers there is little that can be achieved in terms of protection. The drivers of forest destruction are not found out among the trees or even in forestry offices in logging towns. The world's forest loss is due to an industry driven by rampant consumerism, powered by the jet-fuel of mass-market capitalism. Neither foresters nor forest researchers can save forests. That is why forest activists such as Nicole Rycroft have turned to the market place for solutions.

I met Nicole in the autumn of 2002, at a conference in Winnipeg called *Forests of the Northern Lights*. Lithe, dressed in sports gear, with dark hair tied back in a business-like bun, she ran a workshop on industrial paper consumption. It was the most serious issue to be addressed at the conference yet we spent the session in fits of laughter.

Once an Olympic rower for her native Australia, then a physiotherapist, in her thirties Nicole became a human rights and environmental campaigner, working for a time for Earth Rights International in Burma. She now lives in Canada.

In a broad Aussie accent, she introduced herself and the organisation she set up. 'I say I'm from the Markets Initiative,' (she pronounced it *maa kits*) 'and folks here say "The what initiative?" and I have to say *marrrrkuts*.' She rolled her eyes along with the 'r's in an exaggerated red-neck American drawl. We giggled and the tone was set. With a self-deprecating grin Nicole confessed how she dressed up to meet top industry CEOs to try to interest them in reducing their paper use, with a campaign style that mixes Australian directness with commercial savvy. 'You just go in there and say, "Look, you guys, you can save money by using less of this stuff." Those folks like hearing that kinda thing.'

Heather Serantis, from ForestEthics, told us how much money the Bank of America saved by simply giving people the option of not getting a receipt from the cash machine – half a million US dollars. Nicole goaded us on. 'Talk about the money. It takes 'em by surprise, you know? They don't expect enviros to care about their bottom line.'

Nicole is a supertanker-turner who chooses her targets strategically, working with industry people rather than against them, lobbying up and down supply and demand chains to help businesses become 'ancient forest friendly'. She reasons that as long as deforestation makes money it will continue, and the reason it makes money is because millions, even billions, of people are paying for it every day. People don't buy forest destruction directly, of course, they buy it indirectly, primarily in the form of paper, and for most paper products, like books, newspapers and magazines, they do not choose the kind of paper they are buying. As Nicole put it, 'If you want to read Margaret Atwood but it's only available on old-growth paper, are you going to stop reading? I don't think so.'

A small number of people in publishing, advertising, packaging and finance corporations make critical decisions as they procure astronomical quantities of paper. Nicole identifies these people and works with them, persuading them to use their buying power to create a market for environmentally friendly alternatives made from recycled and sustainably sourced fibres. She has built her organisation up from a one-woman operation to one of Canada's most effective environmental bodies, winning numerous awards, and she was recently recognised by Canada's forestry industry as one of the most influential people in the business. Markets Initiative has, in a few short years, brought about a sea change in the use of paper by the Canadian book publishing sector and is now helping to clean up the acts of magazine and newspaper publishers. With characteristic modesty, Nicole credited it all to the people she works with. 'As somebody who watches the world going to hell in a handcart, it is so heartening to see business people stepping forward as environmental advocates.'

After my depressing visit to Clayoquot Sound in 2006, I went to see Nicole at her Vancouver office. We exchanged news of mutual friends and before long we were sharing Australian and British misunderstandings of Americans' use of words: the way they call reindeer 'caribou' and confuse us by using 'elk' to mean red deer, when what we know as an elk is what they call a 'moose', a term we in Scotland reserve for small rodents. As editor of the boreal forest activists' magazine *Taiga News*, I infuriated North Americans for years by turning their articles into British English. 'I've lost count of how many times I've had to explain that in British, lumber is the rubbish we store away in the cupboard under the stairs,' I said, 'not something that stairs might be built out of. That's timber. But to an American, timber means a stand of trees destined to be felled.'

'I know someone who called his son Timber,' Nicole replied, 'and I always thought, Jeez, what a weird name, that's like calling him "two-by-four" or something. Once I knew it meant "tree" it seemed a bit better somehow.'

'At least if you're Timber you're doomed but still standing,' I suggested.

'That about sums up the human condition, ay?'

Sitting in front of a bookcase made to look like the buttressed trunk of a giant rainforest tree, she conceded that the situation in Canada was dire. 'The ecological context in Canada is pretty grim,' she said.

'The paper industry here is huge. A hundred million trees from the boreal forest are logged every year to make newsprint and overall 90 per cent of the logging is in old-growth forest. So from an ecological perspective, there are a lot of really devastating stories in Canada, and from a social perspective, what with First Nation lands being destroyed, the trail of depression unfortunately does not stop.'

'I'm not sure I can take any more depression,' I said. 'You must have some good news.'

'Sure,' she grinned. 'What I think is hopeful about Canada is that, firstly, it is home to 25 per cent of the world's intact tracts of ancient forest and that provides this incredible opportunity to help safeguard a global legacy, and secondly, Canada is really quite a rich country so we have the means to do things differently and make paper out of something other than trees that are hundreds of years old. So, there is definitely hope.'

The publishers and printers that Nicole works with make a commitment to be 'ancient forest friendly', which involves three things: firstly, to use recycled paper wherever possible, and only Forest Stewardship Council (FSC) certified tree-fibre paper; secondly, to increase the efficiency of their paper use; and thirdly, to use only paper that is not bleached with chlorine compounds.

I asked Nicole why she gave her blessing to the FSC, even though it had certified some old-growth logging. She nodded thoughtfully and gave me a careful and nuanced response. 'There are so few large tracts of ancient forest left around the world that I don't think we should really be having a conversation about how we log them, the question should really be about whether we're logging them at all, so that's ultimately where I want us to head. At this point the political juggle is that the paper industry is so invested and rooted in liquidating old-growth, we have to allow them a vehicle of transition towards doing something more sustainable whilst we work on some of the longer-term issues. It's part of the social and political reality. The FSC is a vehicle to help shift operations that take place in forests to become more ecologically sustainable, towards the ultimate goal of preserving forest ecosystems around the world. So that's why, for us, in the medium to long term, our priority is that wood fibre that goes into paper should be FSC certified from second-growth forests because there is no need for paper to be coming from old-growth forests no matter how well they're logged. For a piano sounding board or a piece of fine furniture, you may need some selectively logged old-growth pieces but you don't need it for a newspaper, you don't need it for a magazine or even for a coffee table book. There are other options.'

Her point was that FSC certification is a system of traceability. Rather than being a blanket blessing to all forest products bearing the label, it is a tool to enable consumers to make informed decisions about which sources to support.

There are other forest certification systems, including the American Sustainable Forestry Initiative (SFI), the Canadian Standards Association (CSA) and what used to be the Pan-European Forest Certification (PEFC) but now has global aspirations and has renamed itself the Programme for Endorsement of Forestry Certification. These systems have been slow to win the trust of the environmental movement because in the early 2000s they were, in the words of a report by Fern, the European forest watchdog, 'initiated and governed primarily by the forestry industry and forest owners', and failed to impose standards that 'address a comprehensive range of key issues, including, at a minimum: old-growth or high conservation value forests; protection of biological diversity; use of chemicals and genetically modified organisms; recognition of indigenous peoples' rights; soil and water quality; and consistency with laws and international agreements.' They also, crucially, failed to provide a labelling system that involved a credible chain of custody from final product back to its forest of origin and thus, not only did they not ensure a good standard of management and thus risk endorsing bad forestry practice, they were not even useful to the end consumer. In recent years, FEFC has become an umbrella organisation for other certification systems (including SFI and CSA) and has tried to put its house in order, improving its standards and opening up its decision-making system to involve NGOs. However, trust is such improvements is slow to build.

The FSC, on the other hand, is governed by three 'chambers'

representing the three pillars of sustainability: the forest industry corporations are represented by the 'economic chamber'; the forest protection movement by the 'environmental chamber'; and workers, local communities and indigenous peoples by the 'social chamber'. Its standard is agreed by this broad church of participants, and includes compliance with laws and international rights agreements, respect for legal and customary land tenure and indigenous peoples' rights, good health and safety practices and opportunities to local communities as well as a broad range of environmental criteria. No other forest certification system adequately addresses all of these issues, and although it has been used to certify some forest management operations that should never have been given the green label, it is the best of a bad lot and certainly the only system to enable credible traceability of forest origins.

So the little-green-tree label of the FSC is no panacea, but it does indicate that there is a traceable chain of custody from the product back to the forest or plantation where it grew (and, as we have seen, in the case of paper this may involve several chains back to various different sources). The FSC therefore provides forest product consumers with a tool, which they can and should use to satisfy themselves that the source of their product is acceptable. The coding system used by the FSC allows bulk buyers of paper products to choose only sources they are satisfied are sustainable. Although originally devised and still promoted as a guarantee of good forest management, the FSC label, like any eco-label, is in fact at risk from industry players and certifiers who are interested in using it to green-wash bad practice. It should not be treated as an irrefutable stamp of approval; rather it should be used as a traceability device, particularly by big consumers and retailers who sell products carrying the label, to look down the chain of custody with a critical eye. Only if it is used in a discerning way will it do the job it was set up to do, which is to develop trust between consumers and producers of forest products.

Those who believe that consumers cannot cope with anything more complex than a single symbol to convey the environmental impact of their purchases need look no further than the Fair Trade market, in which goods carry labels conveying a rich picture of the places and people involved in production. FSC has the potential to provide the same level of richness of information about forest products and it is to be hoped that it develops in this direction, but it will only do so if consumers ask questions of their suppliers and encourage them in turn to make enquiries right down to the roots of the wood chain.

I asked Nicole if the Markets Initiative was really a success. She punched the air. 'Absolutely! We've really seen dramatic change in the book industry in Canada in the last six years. We've gone from no publishers having a specific vision of what they want their relation-ship to forests to be, to having eighty-five publishers who have made commitments to help to safeguard the world's ancient and endangered forests. That vision and intent is, in itself, a significant step forward. Plus all of those publishers are actually engaged in implementing that commitment. We've saved 210,000 trees in the last four years because millions and millions of books have been printed on ancient forest friendly paper rather than on conventional sheets.'

'The exciting thing,' she went on, 'is that publishers have recognised their impact on forest ecosystems, but they also recognise not just the responsibility but also the opportunity that it provides. Essentially we do live in a supply and demand world and, like it or not, that's the framework within which forests are being destroyed on a daily basis. Large paper consumers have this incredible opportunity to use market leverage for positive change, by actually asking for something that is environmentally responsible.'

'So is that why you are not doing the usual campaign, targeting the general public?' I asked. One of the things that marks out Nicole's campaign is that it is not predicated on the environmental mantra that everyone doing a little bit will make a difference.

Nicole nodded. 'It's difficult for individual consumers or small companies to carry enough leverage to make the fundamental shifts that need to take place in the supply chain for there to be, say, a 20 per cent increase in the amount of environmental papers being produced. But if you get a couple of large corporations to make that commitment they have incredible purchasing leverage: one contract is sometimes millions of dollars, and that carries an influence that would take years to try to harness as focused energy with individual consumers. Once several companies are on board, mills start producing papers for those companies, and then they make them available more widely.'

'So why did you choose to work with the book publishing industry? Why not newspapers, surely they're even bigger?'

'When you look at consumption, book papers in Canada count for probably about 6 per cent whereas newspapers are up around 48 per cent, but when looked at strategically, it made a lot of sense. Essentially when you boil the book publishing industry down to core elements, it is ideas and paper. Frankly, book publishers are in general fairly progressive with their politics so that's really advantageous for us as an environmental organisation just to get things rolling. Book publishers also have iconic spokespeople associated with them who are far more articulate than me as a voice for forests around the world; Margaret Atwood and Alice Munro can definitely phrase things much more eloquently than most environmental activists. When we look at publishing as a whole, printers are really the gatekeepers to so much of the paper that is consumed today: junk packaging, magazines, catalogues, you name it, annual reports, marketing materials; it just goes on and on. We felt with book publishers we had a good entry point to working with printers. Then, once we established a successful model we were able to mobilise on the momentum that was generated with book publishers to help start our work with the magazine publishing industry and then move up to another level of scale with newspaper publishers.'

I quizzed her about the lines of argument she used to persuade publishers to make a commitment. 'You know, you authors are a big help,' Nicole grinned. 'Did I tell you the Alice Munro story?'

I shook my head. I knew Alice Munro was one of Canada's best-loved authors, but not that she had anything to do with saving forests.

'When she found out in 2002 that there was the potential for her book, *Hateship, Friendship, Courtship, Loveship, Marriage*, to be printed on a new recycled book paper, she picked up the phone to the publisher and said, "Stop the presses, I'd really like my book to be printed on ancient forest friendly paper". And, you know, if you get a phone call from Alice Munro, then the presses really do stop. Her book was due to go to print in two days, so it meant quite a bit of fast footwork on a number of people's parts, but sure enough, Alice Munro was the first really big-name author to have a book printed on ancient forest friendly paper. That's a case of a writer being inspired, caring about the environment, picking up the phone and making it happen in an instant.'

The really ground-breaking event in Canada, however, was when Raincoast Books, J. K. Rowling's Canadian publisher, decided to print *Harry Potter and the Order of the Phoenix* on recycled paper. 'What Raincoast books did for forests around the world with that one book, I don't think can be over-stated,' Nicole reflected. 'With that one print run they saved 39,000 trees, but the ripple-effect that it has created with other Potter publishers around the world, with other book publishers and with other big paper consumers, has been phenomenal. That's quite a legacy for just one book.'

The Canadian issue of *Harry Potter and the Order of the Phoenix* was published with a personalised statement from the author, which says, 'The Harry Potter books are helping to save magnificent forests in the muggle world, forests that are home of magical animals such as Orangutans, Wolves and Bears.' The support of J. K. Rowling was very significant, Nicole said. 'By providing that personalised quote that featured in the 2003 edition, she captured the imagination of Potter fans around the world, young and old, as to what is possible. It's sparked this international movement in the book publishing industry.' Since then, several major publishers in the UK, including Random House, HarperCollins, Pearson (who own Penguin) and Egmont Books, have made public commitments to become forest friendly.

Reducing consumption of paper is another major aim of Markets Initiative. Nicole sells this idea to businesses by expressing it in terms of increasing paper efficiency. 'It's a good business move,' she said. 'With the magazine industry in particular, they do massive over-runs. Some magazines end up selling as little as 20 per cent of the volume printed, so that's just a massive waste of resources and time and from a business perspective it's a massive waste of money. So we're looking at incentive programmes they can put in place to help production match the markets a bit more exactly, print-on-demand scenarios and other technology platforms. You're never going to get away from people wanting to sit in their favourite chair turning the pages on a novel, that's not what it's about, but there are a number of publishing realms where electronic media are a really good option and more cost-effective from a business perspective.'

'Our society is not going to stop using paper any day soon, so it's not about closing down the paper industry. It's just about making it work in a fundamentally different way. It's all about changing the system. We need to stop tinkering around the edges and really focus in on creating systemic change.'

To see how the Markets Initiative has worked in practice, Nicole sent me off to meet Dick Kouwenhoven who runs Hemlock Printers in Burnaby, British Columbia, a printing company that serves advertisers, small presses and packaging companies and has an annual turnover of $40 million. With him, I would hear from the horse's mouth what making a commitment to be ancient forest friendly really meant. Waiting in the lobby I took in a dazzling display of certificates and environmental awards. Then Professor Dumbledore appeared, white-haired, balding, with half-moon spectacles and a silvery beard. He ushered me into a boardroom where he failed to muster a cup of tea from the collection of flasks in the corner, so I assured him that water would do fine. He looked relieved and sat down and, with a schoolmasterly air, asked me how he could help me.

I made polite remarks about all the award certificates and comments about leadership, and he shook his head with a self-deprecating smile. 'We see our role as not to carve out an exclusive market position, but to show the industry what is possible.' Like Nicole, he placed a priority on co-operation and bringing about positive change by working with others as a team. Hemlock had signed an agreement with Markets Initiative, committing to support publishers in their efforts to be ancient forest friendly, and to phasing out all papers containing any fibres from ancient or endangered forests by July 2008. He was emphatic that the commitment had been good for his business, in terms of both morale among staff and profits. 'There's a very strong positive response from consumers,' he said. 'It's very rewarding.'

The staff at Hemlock do not wait to be asked to print on forest friendly paper. Rather, the sales team proactively quote for printing on environmental papers as well as on conventional sheets, and on their estimates they not only tally the financial costs but also provide eco-audit results showing how much benefit using an environmental paper would bring in terms of saved trees, water, pollution and greenhouse gas emissions. For example, shifting a print run of a tonne of magazines from virgin paper to 30 per cent recycled content would save 6 trees, 4 million BTUs of energy and 300 kilograms (660 pounds) of CO_2 (thanks to not having to pulp those trees), 10,000 litres (2,000 gallons) of water (because recycling paper uses so much less water than pulping wood) and 160 kilograms (350 pounds) of waste. These figures are worked out using a tool called the Paper Calculator, produced by USA environmental organisation Environmental Defense.

'Most of our competitors are trying to avoid the subject of environmental impacts, but we felt we should do the opposite and it has worked really well. I think it really put us in a good relationship with our clients,' said Dick. 'They say, now we know what it means if we go this way and spend more money.' The active promotion of ancient forest friendly papers has had enormous take-up and most of his customers were happy to pay a premium in order to get the environmental benefits. This stimulus of demand for recycled papers has helped to whittle down the costs; the extra cost of recycled content for many paper grades was now negligible, he said. The upshot of this proactive work is that Hemlock has just walked away with the Most Environmentally Progressive Printer in Canada award.

Bidding the friendly wizard farewell, I felt like hopping on a broomstick to head across town to meet Cindy Connor, the woman responsible for getting all those Harry Potter books published on 100 per cent post-consumer recycled paper.

A diminutive blonde woman with a china-white complexion,

Cindy met me at the front desk of Raincoast Books, where she worked as production manager. We secreted ourselves in a little room just off the corridor. She looked like a schoolgirl, with her sky-blue eyes, matching blue hand-knit V-necked sweater and crisp white shirt, but her soft voice was full of professional passion. She asked about my plans for this book and when she insisted 'the subject matter is so important', I hadn't realised it was possible for a muggle to feel so encouraged. We bitched about the current 'Green Issue' of *Vanity Fair*, full of puff pieces on the environmental credentials of American celebrities, yet not printed on recycled paper. 'It's a big glossy awful clear-cut forest,' she raged, 'I was so livid, I wanted to go and say "Take it off the shelf!"' (Conde Nast, the publisher of *Vanity Fair*, refused to comment on what kind of paper the magazine is printed on when I approached them.).

Cindy outlined the process involved in making the forest friendly publishing breakthrough with *Harry Potter and the Order of the Phoenix*. It was a risk that she admitted cost the company 'a lot of extra money, literally hundreds of thousands of dollars', but the gamble with going recycled paid off. 'The response from readers has been overwhelming. We have the sweetest letters from children and adults saying "because I saw that Raincoast did this, I will look out for other Raincoast titles". Plus the media coverage on it was huge. It has been a little marketing wizardry!'

She explained that her motivation came as a result of a trip that Nicole Rycroft organised, taking a group of publishers and authors to Vancouver Island. They flew over by float plane to get an overview of the scale of forest destruction and then went to see both logged-over and untouched forest close-up on the ground. Having seen the issue with their own eyes, they wanted to make a commitment to try to achieve ancient forest friendly publishing. 'At Raincoast it's something we adhered to with our own personal values very quickly,' Cindy said, literally hand on heart. The experience had totally changed how she felt about signing off a purchase order for a print-run on ordinary book paper. 'It sounds extreme,' she said, 'but it feels like signing a death warrant.'

In Cindy's view the only problem with recycled book paper was that it was still more expensive than virgin. The premium for recycled paper could be 3 to 5 per cent, significant given slim book publishing margins. Cindy said, 'Our long-term goal is to get enough people to use it so the price will come down.' She predicted that as big publishing markets like the USA and the UK made the shift to recycled, there would be a major swing in prices. 'I am really excited to see what happens in the States, because they have the buying power to make a big price difference, and the same in England, for books in particular.'

Unfortunately some printers still resist using recycled paper due to perceptions created when recycling technology was in its infancy, which Cindy found frustrating. 'People think, recycled – it's dirty newspaper. But in fact that's not true any more. Over the years we have pushed and pushed the mills to make it nice and creamy and fluffy. Now,' she said, 'it's fairly close to the perfect paper.'

Although Cindy seemed convinced that every one of us could make a difference by using less paper and shifting to recycled brands, she also acknowledged the power she had as a big consumer to influence the market for paper. When we shook hands to say goodbye, she delivered a simple yet inspiring parting shot. With a big schoolgirl smile, she said, 'It feels good to change the world.'

CHAPTER 7: FRANKENTREE PLANTATIONS

The wrong trees in the wrong place

Half of all the trees in Scotland are of a single species, which is not native to the country. It is known to botanists as *Picea sitchensis*, or more commonly as Sitka spruce. It is at home and grows into splendid trees in Clayoquot Sound, and originally thrived all along the western seaboard of North America, where it forms a natural component of the species mix of the Pacific rainforest. But in the UK it does something completely different.

When I first read *The Hobbit* as a child, I knew exactly the kind of place that Tolkien evoked as Mirkwood. Across the field from my home was the wood where I played whenever I could. It had two parts. On 'our' side of the stream was the open and welcoming shade of oak, ash, elm and beech trees, under which a tangle of hazels, hollies and willows provided endless scope for dens and hidy-holes, not to mention fruiting raspberries, wild strawberries and brambles, sweet-scented flowers like woodruff and primroses and autumn fungi in all their strange colours and forms.

On the other side of the stream was Mirkwood: an impenetrable, scary plantation forest consisting of blocks of trees, all the same species and all the same age. Only the stands of larch trees felt remotely safe; these deciduous conifers would drop their needles each autumn, creating an orange carpet through which the green shoots of bluebells could grow in the spring while the light could still reach in. By contrast, the stands of Sitka spruce seemed seasonless, bleak and dangerous all year round, never allowing a blink of sunshine to reach the floor. As a result the ground was lifeless and dim. Getting in among these trees was only ever done for a dare and it was a physical struggle. The trees grew so close together that their dead lower branches entangled into a harsh, brittle cage-work that caught at hair and clothes and poked into eyes, its sharp needles pricking skin, resisting any hobbit foolish enough to try to make their way through. Any that did would soon find themselves the victim of treacherous ground, as the earth was corrugated with deep, soggy trenches between the lines of trees.

For decades, all kinds of people have bemoaned the conifer plantations that have been planted across the British countryside. One might think that British people just do not like trees; after all, by the end of the Second World War a mere 1 per cent of the native woodland of the country remained: a few corners of once mighty English and Welsh broadleaf woodlands like Sherwood Forest, and in Scotland some fragments of the ancient Caledonian forest that swathed the country from the retreat of the last glaciers until people advanced into it, destroying it with farming and fire. Our history has certainly been one of drastic forest clearance, until in the last century reforestation began on a large scale, covering 12 per cent of England and Wales and 16 per cent of Scotland, mostly with conifers. However, the furious reaction of many people to the resulting plantations is not due to antipathy towards big woody organisms per se, but because they are quite simply the wrong trees in the wrong place. This, in a nutshell, is the problem with plantations all over the world.

Surely tree plantations are better than logging of natural forests? I am often asked this by people who have heard me ranting and raving about the paper industry's destruction of old-growth forest. Indeed the forestry industry, particularly the paper-based end of it, has been arguing consistently for decades that planting trees for harvest later will reduce its need to cut trees from natural forests. If we want the harvesters to stay out of pristine forests and we accept that there is a requirement for trees to be felled in order to provide the fibre for paper making, then they will need to grow somewhere and therefore we are urged to accept intensive 'tree farms' as the answer. We are led to believe that a few hillsides swathed in serried ranks of Sitka spruce plantation is a small price to pay for leaving the great jungles and *taiga* alone. Such cellulose factories may be ugly but they are not as ugly as clear-cuts.

So what is wrong with this argument?

Firstly, our sense of aesthetics can be valid sometimes. We are not wrong to prefer the appearance of natural woodland to the regimented monotone of a conifer plantation. The multiple shades and shapes of mixed woods are visible manifestations of biodiversity; native woodland supports a far richer variety of species of plants and animals, both in the immediate vicinity and also in the wider landscape. Woods provide den sites and seasonal food stores for animals and birds that will roam much more widely, providing valuable services such as eating pests in fields and gardens. They also help to manage water, keeping it clear and fresh and acting as sponges after heavy rainfall, a flood-moderation service that we most certainly need as climate change is making extreme weather events more frequent. The mixture of native tree species was traditionally also a source of materials for a wide range of rural livelihoods, such as charcoal burning and furniture making, which have largely died out with the trees. And let's not forget that a native wood is certainly a nicer place than a spruce plantation in which to walk the dog, build a den or tryst with a lover.

Pulpwood plantations, on the other hand, tend to have three features: they consist of non-native or 'exotic' species, grown in monocultures, on a big scale.

Being non-native, they support very few of our indigenous plants and animals. Indeed many of the trees preferred by foresters, like the acacias in Indonesia and eucalyptus in South Africa and India, actively shun other species by producing toxic chemicals, such as herbicidal exudes from their roots or biocides in their bark, pollen or leaves. Such effects, called allelopathy, make the tree more likely to fight off competition from the natural inhabitants of the area, which in turn makes life easier for foresters. Sitka spruce's sharp pointed needles make it too prickly to eat by deer and sheep, which will eat thistles and holly before hunger would drive them to nibble the conifer. But when these needles die and drop off, they form an acidic, weed-preventing mulch. The effect is that Sitka plantations are far less biodiverse than a native wood.

Growing trees in monocultures, like a giant field of a grain crop, often involves huge interventions with the soil. In many parts of Scotland, where Sitka spruce was to be planted, the ground was ploughed first, usually in a downhill direction to create drainage channels. Sitka, being a native of a high rainfall environment, thrives in wet places but only if its roots are not totally sodden. After the Second World War it was widely planted in bogs and peatlands, by planting between drainage ditches. The result of all these earth movements has been tremendous erosion and degradation of soils, with nutrients washed out and leached away. Until trees are established they are fertilised and weeds suppressed with herbicides, and like any monoculture crop they are at risk of pests and diseases, the usual response to which is also the application of chemical pesticides. Following establishment of the conifers with their acidic needle-fall, the run-off from conifer plantations has caused water courses to become acidic, harming the invertebrate, amphibian and fish populations of streams, rivers and lochs downstream. So, unlike a native wood, which creates a ripple-effect of environmental benefits to the surrounding area, an exotic plantation exudes harm, just as its roots contaminate the soil around them.

A key feature of most exotic monoculture plantations grown for use by the paper industry is that they are large. This is no accident, as it reflects the size of the pulp mills where the trees are destined. Most pulp mills are species specific, involving a large-scale mechanical or chemical process that has been refined to work best to reduce one particular kind of wood to its constituent fibres. Due to the 'economies of scale' beloved of financiers and industrialists, pulp mills have become steadily bigger over the years, and hence the areas of land growing the one species they depend on have needed to become correspondingly larger, along with the extent of their negative impacts.

Sitka spruce is beloved of paper makers because it has very pale-coloured fibres, which are tough and long, and because when heated they can be flattened into ribbon-like shapes that bind tightly together and form a smooth surface, resulting in paper that is supple and strong. The UK's biggest pulper is at the Caledonian mill in Irvine, Scotland, and it makes high-quality magazine paper using exclusively Sitka spruce. Around 1 million tonnes per year of Sitka wood is exported to Finland, where it is made into paper, some of which is then imported back into the UK.

Much of the Sitka was planted after the Second World War, and through the 1960s and 1970s, and it is now reaching harvestable age, leading to a marked increase in the available volume of wood. One of the proposals for using this new flow of timber is a new pulp mill at Invergordon in the Scottish Highlands, which has been promoted in recent years by a band of entrepreneurs calling themselves Forscot, who are linked to UPM Kymmene, the Finnish owner of the Caledonian mill. For a cost of £1 billion, they have proposed to build a new mill that would consume about 40 per cent of the entire timber production of Scotland, mopping up almost all the Sitka spruce into a single, gargantuan pulping machine. Such an investment would mean that every Sitka tree cut down would be replaced with another one to feed the pulp mill in coming years, leading to the hillsides of Scotland remaining covered in Sitka spruce for the foreseeable future. This particular pulp mill proposal is, thankfully, meeting with a cool reception from Scotland's forestry sector, but the business model is one that is being applied all over the world.

Can a tree plantation ever be described as a forest? Some organisations define forest in terms of what proportion of the ground is beneath the canopy of trees. One such is the Food and Agriculture Organisation (FAO) of the United Nations, which is tasked with collating an annual report on the State of the World's Forests, and it counts anything over 10 per cent of tree cover as forest. What this definition completely fails to register, however, is forest degradation: a forest can have been trashed to the extent of being reduced from an intact forest canopy to barely any tree cover at all and yet still show up as green on the FAO map, and of course the FAO figures register the creation of tree plantations as positive contributions to forest cover. Many organisations working on this issue, such as the World Rainforest Movement (WRM), stress that plantations are not forests and that only plantations composed of a diversity of species native to the area can in the long run evolve into true forest ecosystems, including accompanying flora and fauna.

The question of plantations reaches to the heart of the debate about what constitutes sustainable forest management. The FSC's granting of certificates to some pulp plantations, particularly in the global south, has drawn outrage from activists such as Ricardo Carrere of WRM who points to human rights abuses by paper companies and negative environmental impacts of the plantations, arguing that these certificates discredit the FSC and calling on them to cease certifying plantations. The plantation controversy has dogged the forest movement for years, dividing anti-plantation campaigners from those who think they are a necessary evil. What is undeniable is that tree plantations are no panacea.

Frankentrees

One of the things totally ruled out by the FSC is the use of genetically modified (GM) or engineered (GE) trees in forestry. Opponents of GM trees call them Frankentrees, and they share the concerns of campaigners against GM agricultural crops. Many of the modifications are the same, such as resistence to herbicides like Roundup, as are the companies involved in the developments, such as Monsanto.

Many of the biggest names in the GM tree business are paper companies. Weyerhaeuser is involved in trials of fast-growing 'super fir' trees in Washington and Oregon, USA, of which about 4 million have been planted in over 700 sites. International Paper, MeadWestvaco and Rubicon have set up a joint company called ArborGen, which is modifying the genes of eucalyptus trees to enable them to withstand greater temperature variation, so they can be planted more widely. Some companies are engineering trees with low levels of lignin, the substance that makes wood hard and that chemical pulp mills expend so much effort trying to dissolve to get at the cellulose fibres. Millions of genetically modified fast-growing poplar trees have already been planted in China.

GM trees are now being vigorously promoted for use as 'carbon capture' for climate change mitigation, and the low-lignin varieties are promoted as good for making biofuels, but it is pulp and paper companies who are behind much of the research.

Friends of the Earth and the WRM argue that the effects of building things like insecticidal or fungicidal genes into trees are completely unpredictable, as are the risks of them spreading. They point out that forests contain much more than trees, with many insects, fungi and other organisms necessary to the complex web of life. It is irresponsible and misguided to treat trees as independent organisms that can be engineered out of that context.

Soft, strong and very, very wrong

As well as planting trees that are clearly inappropriate to the ecosystem or carry risks of genetic contamination, in other words, planting the wrong trees, the paper industry has a bad reputation for planting them in the wrong places. There are three main ways in which land may be the wrong place for a planted tree: if it is land that belongs to someone who has not given their consent for it to be used in that way; if it is land that would not naturally be covered with trees and supports some non-forest ecosystem; or if it is high-quality forest, which is destroyed to enable the plantation to be established.

In Brazil there has been bitter conflict about the appropriation of land for eucalyptus plantations. Broadleaf trees, including eucalyptus, are known by foresters as hardwoods because their timber tends to be harder under a saw than the wood of coniferous trees. It is one of the paradoxes of the world of paper that hardwoods, when pulped, are most valued for their softness. Just as Sitka spruce pulp is particularly beloved by paper makers for its strength, the fibres of eucalyptus are particularly sought out for their softness, and eucalyptus pulp is widely used for the manufacture of tissue. It is also a very fast-growing tree, with strong allelopathic effects, making it a popular choice for plantation foresters in hot countries.

The world's biggest producer of eucalyptus pulp is a company based in Brazil called Aracruz Cellulose and this company has been at the centre of a huge struggle over land-rights in the state of Espírito Santo that has lasted for almost half a century. In Brazil, there is now more than 5 million hectares (11 million acres) of eucalyptus plantation growing in vast monocultures, termed 'green deserts' by their opponents, who complain that the plantations consume such large quantities of water that they cause rivers to dry up and lead to erosion, deterioration of water quality and loss of fishing and water resources to local communities. They have also resulted in the loss of vegetation and fauna, which provided the livelihoods of local people.

In the 1960s, Aracruz was granted permission to use a large tract of land. It moved in, razing the forests and planting the land with eucalyptus trees. But this land was already inhabited; it was the homeland of the Tupinikin and Guarani people. Fabio Martins Villas, of the Network against the Green Desert, said, 'The replacement of native forests by eucalyptus made their traditional subsistence practices unviable. Rivers and streams dried up and the few left were contaminated by agrochemicals used by the company.'

When the protests of the Tupinikin and Guarani people fell on deaf ears, they decided to take direct action and in 1980 they demarcated and attempted to take back a 6,500-hectare (16,000-acre) section of their land. Some of that land was subsequently clawed back, but they continued to challenge Aracruz and the Brazilian government to recognise their land-rights. Through the 1990s, various government deliberations considered how much land actually belonged to the indigenous peoples, with areas yo-yoing from as little as 2,500 hectares (6,000 acres) up to five times that, but none recognised the 18,027 hectares (44,525 acres) that they claimed.

The late 1990s saw further self-demarcation of land by the unsatisfied indigenous people, followed by scenes of police intimidation and violence in indigenous villages and the arrests of indigenous leaders. An agreement that indigenous leaders were forced to sign with Aracruz was overturned in 2005 when the people once again decided to take direct action. On 17 May 2005, more than three hundred indigenous people went to the site of Olho D´Água and Córrego do Ouro, two of the almost forty villages that were destroyed by Aracruz at the end of the 1960s, and set about rebuilding them and marking out more than 11,000 hectares (27,000 acres) of land that they were determined to take back from the company.

But in January 2006, there was a backlash from the federal police, which stormed Olho D´Água and Córrego do Ouro, destroying them and evicting the village's inhabitants, many of whom sustained injuries. There was international condemnation of the violence and appeals for justice for the Tupinikin and Guarani peoples. Hundreds of women from Via Campesina, a rural women's network, occupied Aracruz's tree nursery in southern Brazil and destroyed millions of eucalyptus seedlings. In September 2006, the indigenous people slashed and burned 100 hectares (250 acres) of eucalyptus plantation. They did this, said Fabio Martins Villas, 'to show that, contrary to accusations, they were not interested in the trees and that the struggle was to recover their lands'. Aracruz launched what was described as a 'defamatory and racist' counter-campaign. Protests and demonstrations against the company continued by a growing movement of Brazilians and supporters around the world, demanding that the Brazilian state and companies must recognise the land-rights of the indigenous peoples and ensure non-violent resolution of land disputes.

The link to Europe has been made by German forest organisation Robin Wood. Aracruz Cellulose's pulp is used by Procter & Gamble to make famous European tissue brands such as Tempo. In a high-profile German 'culture jam' media campaign, Robin Wood recently produced tissue packs with the Tempo brand name replaced by 'Armut', German for 'poverty'. When the German Inter City Express (ICE) train company replaced the recycled toilet paper they used to supply to passengers with Charmin, a Procter & Gamble brand, they too were successfully targeted.

Back in Brazil, on 27 August 2007, Tarso Genro, the Minister of Justice, signed resolutions granting the indigenous peoples their rights to the 18,027 hectares (44,525 acres) they claimed. 'According to the resolutions,' Fabio Martins Villas said, 'the Brazilian Government recognises that the lands have traditionally been occupied by the Tupinikin and Guarani peoples and that, over the past forty years, they had been illegally occupied by Aracruz Cellulose.' This is, he said, 'a victory of indigenous resistance against the economic and political power of the company and its many allies. A victory for life and a defeat, although localised, of monoculture plantations and the green desert.'

It has to be hoped that this victory will give encouragement to the many people with similar complaints in other parts of the world, including Uruguay, Thailand, India and South Africa, where eucalyptus is grown for pulp. These monocultures of trees are described by Plants for a Future as 'an environmental disaster'. They are loathed in North America for their fire risk, in Africa and Latin America for their voracious absorption of water and in Asia for their competition with indigenous species. Yet everywhere in the world they are being planted in increasing quantities by the paper industry.

One of the ways that apologists for eucalyptus and pine plantations try to argue that they are not damaging to forests, is to claim they are grown on 'grasslands'. The key question that must be asked here is whether these grasslands are themselves native ecosystems, in which case they should not be covered in trees. If the land does not naturally support continuous tree cover there is usually a good reason for it.

The savannah lands of Africa are a good example of an environment that is simply not intended to be covered in trees, and where there are drastic negative impacts of swathing it in a tree plantation. One of the worst of these is the theft of scarce water particularly by deep-rooting trees such as eucalyptus, which lower water tables, causing the soil to dry out and leading to water shortages for rural people.

In South Africa, two huge pulp and paper companies, Sappi and Mondi, are among the biggest landowners in the country and lead the way in establishing pine and eucalyptus plantations: more than 1.5 million hectares (3.7 million acres) of grassland has been converted to pulp plantation, of which Sappi owns 465,000 hectares (1.15 million acres) and Mondi controls 430,000 hectares (1 million acres). This has led to a loss of grazing for pastoralist communities, but more drastically it has caused wet land to dry out and water courses to stop running. The loss of wetlands is disastrous for people and animals that depend on them, and causes practical difficulties like wiping out the reeds used for thatching homes. When water courses dry up, agriculture is threatened and people become fearful as the water levels in their wells drop. According to Timberwatch, a coalition of South African non-profit organisations, people who live close to eucalyptus plantations describe themselves as competing with the gum trees for land and for water.

Another way in which tree plantations end up in the wrong place is when they are proposed for an area that currently supports a well-functioning forest ecosystem. Most of the fibre plantations being established in Sumatra, as described in chapter 5, fall into this category. As there is no possibility of an exotic monoculture providing even a fraction of the services to local people and the environment that the natural forest will do, conversion of the forest into plantation has huge social and environmental costs. The experiences of the communities I visited in Riau demonstrated that the economic benefits of this conversion flow only one way, into the pockets of the paper companies, and the costs to local people are poverty and social upheaval.

In their powerful critique of the impact of the pulp and paper industry on people in tropical countries, *Pulping the South*, Ricardo Carrere and Larry Lohmann explained how the conversion of forest to pulpwood plantation leaves a legacy of poverty and conflict. This is because such conversion serves the interests of certain organisations (paper corporations, forestry consultancies and banks, for instance) whilst ignoring the interests of others, notably local people. Whilst recognising that 'plantations result in real gains for real people', they noted that 'these gains seldom "trickle down" to the people who live where the plantations are established, and are accompa- nied by long-term degradation of the land and livelihoods of large numbers of communities.' The impoverishment of local people is not the result of technical failings by foresters; many forest scientists are unashamedly proud of their silvicultural successes in produc- ing high yields from plantations. The problem is a political failing: the negative social impacts on local communities are the result of plantations being established to serve a range of interests other than those of local people.

Dubious plantation developments in countries including Chile, Uruguay, Indonesia, Thailand, the Philippines and Mozambique are even funded by development aid programmes of rich northern coun- tries, notably Sweden, Finland and Japan, whose forestry corporations stand to gain many more benefits than the local people such aid is supposed to support. Chris Lang, whose *Banks, Pulp and People* report offers a scathing analysis of damaging investment in the pulp sector, by both commercial banks and public investors including development aid departments, said, 'Development aid for the pulp and industrial tree plantation sector is not only not leading to poverty alleviation; its net development impact is negative.'

Between 1990 and 2005, the area of tree plantations increased five- fold across the planet, covering an area bigger than Indonesia, but it did so at the cost of local livelihoods and damage or destruction of forests and other natural ecosystems. This is an atrocity that must be recognised as such, condemned and ultimately stopped. We need more healthy forest, not less.

A Vietnamese dilemma

Some of the world's most controversial degraded lands are those parts
of Vietnam that were doused with napalm and Agent Orange by USA
air force aeroplanes during what the Vietnamese call the American War
of the 1970s. The USA troops were trying to limit resistance to their
invasion by Vietnamese soldiers hiding in the country's lush forests,
and their huge aerial bombardment with powerful herbicides was an
attempt to improve visibility. The tragic effects of this spraying are
still being felt today. Where the forest was destroyed the land is still
ecologically degraded. I set out from China to find out if this land is
a good candidate for the establishment of pulp plantations and, if so,
what kind.

Straw burled down the main street of Pingxiang at the end of
the trainline south from Nanning. It looked like the screen set for an
oriental cowboy movie. I tightened my money belt and prepared for
battle. Two hours later, I emerged from the Bank of China victori-
ous, doors swinging behind me, staff casualties mopping their brows
and tending their wounds, vanquished in their efforts to prevent me
changing my remaining yuan back into hard currency. With a pocket
full of greenbacks I whistled for my steed, leaped into the back of the
nearest tuk-tuk and headed for the border.

It was about 20 kilometres (12½ miles) to the crossing and the
moped engine of the tuk-tuk struggled with the hills, so there was
plenty of time to take in the landscape. Grasses stitched down
the edges of ploughed paddy patches. A big grey-brown buffalo
flapped its ears, sitting among sugarcane stubble, and nearby
heaps of sugarcane straw were being burned. I was surprised by
this gratuitous waste of such a valuable resource, known in the
paper-making trade as 'bagass', until I recognised the presence
in the landscape of the plant that had usurped it: ranked stands
of single-age trees swathed the upper hillsides. I had reached
eucalyptus country.

The first toilet I used in Vietnam had no porcelain, just an earth
mound shaped to slope smoothly to the drain, and no paper, only
a big bucket of clean water with a washing dipper. Four blonde

Swedish girls on their first Asia visit took turns to grimace and squeal about how disgusting the experience was. They seemed a bit shocked when I emerged with a cheery grin saying, 'Nice paper-free toilet!' Even after I explained my mission they looked at me as if I was deranged. I failed to convince them of the irony of being in a paper-free toilet culture surrounded by the tree grown to provide the soft, short fibres that make our well-known tissue brands so much 'quiltier' (as Velvet advertisements put it) than Izal.

I took a bus to Hanoi, which was reminiscent of Kathmandu with its narrow streets, courtyard temples and colourful mayhem. I checked into one of the hundreds of cheap hostels in the old part of town and in idle chat with the proprietor, I revealed the purpose of my journey. 'You should meet Hugh,' he said. 'He's into that kind of thing.' They must have another environmentalist staying, I concluded, and thought no more about it.

But a couple of hours later, I was sitting at one of the hostel's computers wading through the daily tide of spam and battering out quick replies to emails, when a soft cough drew my attention to a rather debonair Vietnamese man standing two paces away. He asked me something, but I had to lean towards him to catch what he said. 'You write about paper?' he repeated.

'No,' I replied, 'I mean yes, well, I'm writing a book about it, but not right now.' I gestured at the computer. 'Just email.'

'I am Hieu Vu Huu,' he said shyly. 'I work for Vietnam Pulp and Paper Technology Research Institute. I stay on top floor.'

I was dumbstruck. I could not have been much more taken aback if Dr Who, rather than Dr Hieu, had just appeared before me. 'You live here, in this hostel, and you work for the national Pulp and Paper Research Institute?'

'Yes, I am researcher. You are writing about paper industry, yes? Is there anything you need to know? Perhaps I can help you.'

'What an amazing coincidence.' He smiled, as if this kind of thing happened all the time. I grinned back, scrambling among the thousands of questions that keep me awake at night for one that might be an appropriate starting point right then.

'Is there much paper made here in Vietnam?' I ventured. And so began a tutorial on the small, but according to Huu, very promising, Vietnamese paper industry. Although its annual production would barely keep the UK supplied for a fortnight, the country shared China's ancient paper-making heritage. Its government had ambitious plans to develop the industry: supplying it with wood was a key part of a national strategy to reforest 5 million hectares (11 million acres) of land still denuded from American war napalm.

'What species will be grown?' I asked.

Huu scratched his chin. 'There are two possibilities: bamboo and eucalyptus. They both have strengths and weaknesses and we already use both species. Bamboo is native, ready to harvest in only three or four years and is our traditional source of fibre. But it contains a lot of silicon, so it is difficult to pulp. Eucalyptus is much more desirable for the paper industry, but it is slower yielding.'

'And it's toxic,' I pointed out.

He shook his head. 'I am not expert in the environmental impacts; I just work on technical feasibility of new mills.' So we stuck to discussing the technical side of paper making. The native species, bamboo, had a lot going for it.

The most amazing thing, in his view, was the quality of the traditional bamboo paper. He was insistent that I must visit the museum in Hanoi to see the King's Decrees written on hand-made bamboo paper 1,000 years ago. 'We don't make paper anything like that any more,' he said. 'The paper we make from eucalyptus...' He wiggled his fingers as if to show a sheet disintegrating while searching for the word, then shook his head. 'It disappears!'

Is this real progress? The choice between native and non-native species was coming down to the choice between the finest and most durable paper in the world, and loo-roll. It seemed like a no-brainer, but still, it seems, the paper industry was pushing hard for eucalyptus to be grown rather than bamboo. Rather than modify northern pulp technology to handle the silicon in bamboo, the paper companies were proposing instead that the Vietnamese should modify the vegetation of millions of hectares of their country.

I pressed Huu for more information about the government's plantation programme and he suggested that I should talk to someone who
knew more about the socio-economics and environmental impacts of
the forestry industry. That man was Professor Dr Nguyen van Truong,
at the beguilingly named Eco-Eco Institute. Never one to pass up an
interesting lead, I got in touch and shortly after was in a taxi heading
for the French part of town.

At the door of a Parisian-style tenement flat I was greeted by an
ancient Confucian sage, complete with wispy hair, round face and
bright eyes. The 84-year-old professor spoke excellent English in an old-
French accent. 'Eco-eco is short for Ecological Economics,' he explained,
'and we are trying simultaneously to help the poor and to prove that
these two terms together are not a contradiction in terms.'

He showed me pictures of landscapes still devastated by the chemical poisons that were sprayed from the air during the American War.
'Our focus is the establishment of eco-villages on environmentally
degraded land, like this,' he said. 'I believe there is an opportunity
for us to expand paper production, using this degraded land to grow
fibre.'

'Do you think that bamboo or eucalyptus should be grown on this
land?' I asked him.

'It is an interesting trade-off,' he responded. 'Eucalyptus is easy to
process, but it is not a native species and it is allelopathic, releasing
toxic chemicals into the soil, whereas bamboo is native and fast-
yielding, but less desirable from the paper industry view. Perhaps
there will be techniques developed to ameliorate the toxic effects of
eucalyptus on the soil. It is a difficult choice.'

I asked him about the government's 5-million-hectare (11-million-
acre) reforestation plan and he smiled. 'It is a wonderful dream, though
I am a little sceptical that it will work in practice. But growing trees
for pulp must be part of the solution for poor people: they cannot get
involved in the production process of the pulp and paper industry,
because the capital investment is too large. But they can at least be
involved in the fibre supply.'

The Vietnamese government's vision for the paper industry is unique because it wants to involve many small-scale forest or plantation owners in a landscape mosaic of many different land uses. Unlike in most other parts of the world where plantation development is on the increase, in Vietnam the government claims that the land for growing pulp trees will not be granted to industrial concessions. Instead the state envisages the 5 million hectares of new tree-covered land being achieved by granting land-rights to tens or even hundreds of thousands of small-scale growers. If this works, it would create a land-ownership pattern like that of Finland or Norway but, Professor Nguyen hoped, with more people living on the forested land, leading to a higher ecological diversity. In the south of the country a new mill is being built at Phuong Nam, which will make pulp from kenaf, an agricultural crop, which opens up another potential source of benefit to farmers.

Progress towards the 5-million-hectare reforestation dream is very slow. Millions of dollars of a reforestation fund have been misappropriated, according to the environmental organisation Education for Nature Vietnam. Meanwhile huge investments by Japanese and Chinese companies are being made into new Vietnamese pulp mills that will require eucalyptus or acacia rather than bamboo, and tree plantation developments are being funded by the Asian Development Bank and the German government. Once again we have to ask on what basis such investments are being made.

The right trees in the right place

If the purpose of a fibre plantation is to relieve the pressure on forests, as the paper industry wants us to believe, then the question must be asked as to which forests are reprieved by new plantations. Looking globally, the parts of the planet where natural forests are on the increase are Europe and eastern USA, whereas plantations are expanding primarily in the global south, indicating an insidious trend for the biggest paper-consuming countries to exploit other people's land and forests to meet their fibre needs. Instead, part of the principle of growing trees in the right place must be that their fibre should be processed and used locally.

When the Globetrotter log truck turned left towards the jetty at Ardrishaig in Argyll back in Scotland, I behaved something like a primary schoolboy in my excitement at the prospect of seeing real-life Tonka toys in action. The logs it was carrying were unmistakably the wet fox-brown of Sitka spruce. I sat in the car beside the sign saying 'Dangerous Timber Stack – Keep Off', windscreen wipers going full pelt in stair-rail rain. The red and white TimberLink ship was berthed alongside the jetty, and I squealed with delight as the lorry parked up next to a big yellow crane to be unloaded into the boat. Its grab arm rotated, its two double-clawed jaws open wide, then reached into the back of the truck, closed over thirteen or fourteen logs and lifted them, teetering and precarious, it seemed to me, into the open hold. With remarkable swiftness and fluidity, it swung back and grabbed another dozen timbers, like a fistful of pencils, swooped back to the vessel and nestled the tree trunks down among the cargo.

I have spent a lot of time over the past couple of years, hanging about in the hope of catching sight of movements between logging sites and pulp mills. Whether it is dodgy hardwood harvests in Indonesia, old-growth trees in Canada or train-loads of *taiga* crossing from Russia into China, there have been many days when hours of waiting have eventually yielded up the proof. Such encounters have sometimes left me feeling disgusted, often simply relieved that I can go home, occasionally proud of having fitted another piece of the jigsaw. But I don't think I have ever been as elated as I was seeing Sitka spruce heading out to sea from this Argyll lochside. It was mostly the sheer unexpectedness of the encounter, and of such an impressive display of the operator's handling skill and the machinery's scale, power and mobility. But it was also because this wood was going to the Caledonian paper mill at Irvine, just down the west Scottish coast, and I was fresh from a meeting that had left me optimistic that it had come from a plantation as close to sustainable as I was likely to find.

The British state Forestry Commission owns about half of the wooded land in Argyll, the majority of which is Sitka spruce plantation. They were planted throughout the twentieth century as part of the national strategy to grow some timber resources, to redress the denuded state of the land. Much of what had once been woodland was used as pasture, often with intensive regimes of burning to prevent regeneration of shrubs and trees and high stocking densities. The result was heavily degraded land, onto which tree plantations were established. Sitka spruce was chosen because compared to native trees it grows fast (though nowhere near so fast as the plantations in tropical zones), particularly in high rainfall areas such as Argyll. Much of the first generation of these plantations is now being harvested, mostly as pulpwood.

Nick Purdy, the West Argyll district manager for the Forestry Commission Scotland, has the job of planning how these plantations will be managed into the future, and because of a system called the UK Woodland Assurance Scheme (UKWAS), this plan must deliver environmental and social benefits, as well as economic ones. UKWAS is the national standard for sustainable forestry and it is accredited by the Forest Stewardship Council, one of only two national schemes to be so accredited. The other is Sweden's, though recent dissatisfaction with how it is implemented has meant that it is no longer endorsed by the Swedish Society for Nature Conservation, the biggest Swedish environmental organisation. The UK standard still appears to have a good reputation, due to a large part because the Forestry Commission has embraced the challenge to make dramatic changes to how it manages the national forest estate in order to achieve something closer to sustainability. Friendly and relaxed in his office, Nick Purdy said, 'I see UKWAS as an entirely positive process. We look forward to the assessments. It is very healthy to have an independent perspective on what we do, and it helps us to continually improve our operations.'

All of the state-owned forest land is certified under UKWAS, which has meant an end to the old system of blanketing even-aged monocultures across huge swathes of land, followed by equally enormous clear-cuts. Existing plantations will remain, but they are being restructured to improve biodiversity, enhance benefits to local communities and tackle their sheer ugliness. 'We are redesigning the forest in terms of the landscape,' Nick said. 'We're encouraging restoration of riparian (riverside) zones and thinking in terms of forest habitat networks, connecting up native broadleaf fragments on both public and private land. The percentage of broadleaves is increasing.' In a significant demonstration of their commitment to ecological restoration, they have a management agreement with the Scottish Wildlife Trust and the Royal Zoological Society of Scotland who are seeking to reintroduce the European beaver. This would be the first British mammal reintroduction, beavers having been extinct in the UK since they were hunted out for their fur in the sixteenth century.

There will continue to be a considerable Sitka spruce component in the plantations, and there is an ongoing commitment to supply the Caledonian mill and other paper makers in Finland and Norway with Sitka spruce, but this will be generated within a completely different form of silviculture. 'At the moment, the plantations are relatively even-aged, so large chunks mature at the same time,' explained Nick. 'We are breaking up the age-structure to smooth out production and create more diverse habitats. Clear-fells now average 10 hectares (24½ acres) but this is reducing all the time and we will ultimately move to a maximum of 1 hectare (2½ acres) clear-fell, where continuous cover is not feasible.' The long-term aim is to put as much land under continuous cover forestry as practical, which means that wood is extracted by thinning, rather than creating clear-cuts, and trees can seed into gaps, regenerating naturally. The result is a 'mixed-age class structure', that is, trees of a variety of ages, more like a natural forest. Encouraging natural regeneration also means that the range of species will increase. 'We're very happy if broadleaves will come into thinned areas of Sitka. We're encouraging regeneration and it's very strong,' Nick said.

The other important dimension of sustainability is the social aspect and here again there has been a transformation. Contracts are given to local people by preference and there are several community groups that have taken over the management of their local woods, with income from felling in their area ring-fenced for community management. Local people get firewood, there is a flourishing woodworkers' association that leases land from the state, and a range of paid and volunteer work opportunities from butterfly surveys to major cultural heritage installations. The Forestry Commission has taken the lead on arts, cultural and tourism-oriented projects that are aimed at delivering benefits to the local economy and also to engage a much broader range of people than would normally have anything to do with forestry. The result, Nick said, was that, 'People don't find forestry contentious any more, because so many people have become involved. We reckon that 90 per cent of our budget goes directly into the local economy. It's all about rural development, isn't it?'

It is clear that putting the right trees in the right place is just the start; how they are subsequently managed and by whom is just as important.

Post-plantation restoration

In cases where the wrong trees have been planted in the wrong place, that is also not the end of the story. What goes up can come down, and where planted trees are a mistake they can be cut out. A dramatic example of this happening can be found in the most northerly part of Scotland, in the borderland between the county where I live, Sutherland, and its north-eastern neighbour Caithness, a land known as the Flow Country.

The Flow Country is important because it is the biggest blanket bog in the world, a patchwork of heathers and mosses, pools and streams, and a 400,000 hectare (nearly 1 million acre) breeding ground for wetland birds, such as the rare (and inappropriately named) common scoter and black-throated diver. It has only recently been recognised in Scotland that peatlands like the Flow Country are not only important for biodiversity but also for sequestering carbon from the atmosphere, thereby helping to reduce the build-up of greenhouse gases that cause climate change. This recognition came about as a result of alarming statistics showing 20 per cent of Scotland's greenhouse gas emissions result from damaged bogs; even more than from vehicle emissions. The race to cut emission levels has therefore led to interest in healing the bogs and helping them to return to their natural state as carbon sinks rather than carbon sources. The Flow Country is the biggest experiment in how to do this in the UK, quite possibly anywhere in the world.

In Scotland, damage to bog habitats was (and still is) caused primarily by drainage, either for afforestation, or to attempt to improve the land for agriculture. In the Flow Country, both were the case. In the late 1970s, the Highlands and Islands Development Board gave landowners, including the original owner of the Forsinard Estate at the heart of the Flow Country, grants for draining the bogs to grow barley. When the barley business failed after three years, Forsinard was sold to an international forestry company, Fountain International. They began selling off land in blocks to investors who were able to access grants and tax breaks for afforestation.

In the 1980s there were several high-profile cases of celebrities reducing their tax liabilities by buying up tracts of the Flow Country that were drained and afforested with exotic conifer species, primarily Sitka spruce and lodgepole pine. A bitter and vigorous campaign ensued, together with some highly popular TV programmes that involved the eccentric botanist David Bellamy splodging about almost up to his armpits in bogs, talking non-stop and getting excited about insectivorous plants such as sundews. Awareness gradually grew about the negative impacts of forestry on the wetland ecosystems, and eventually the tax breaks stopped. Some of the undamaged peatland in the Flow Country was protected from further damage, however, forestry's negative influence continued to ripple out into the surrounding ecosystem. The problems included the leaching of fertilisers into the water, and the increased shelter the trees provided for deer, foxes and crows, all usually rare on bogs, which led to steep declines in the wading bird populations.

Draining of the bog when planting trees had also caused the underlying peat to dry out, thus exposing vegetation that had accumulated over long periods of time to air, so that it began to decompose, releasing carbon dioxide and methane. Trees accelerated this process, their roots pumping water from the peat and releasing it through transpiration.

In 1995, the Royal Society for the Protection of Birds (RSPB) bought the Forsinard Estate from Fountain International and ever since it has continued to buy up forestry blocks that Fountain had sold on. More recently, together with Scottish Natural Heritage (SNH), the Scottish government agency responsible for nature protection, the Scottish Forestry Commission, Plantlife and Highlands and Islands Enterprise, RSPB embarked upon a major project, funded by the European LIFE programme, to restore the bog ecosystems to their natural state.

Bog restoration involved two main steps: cutting down the trees; and blocking drainage ditches to allow the bog to re-wet. Norrie Russell, the RSPB's reserve manager, said, 'We are taking emergency action to try to get the trees out before they close canopy, which is when they start to crack the peat, really drawing out the water. The longer you leave it, the more it costs, and the harder it is.'

Some of the tree cutting was done by hand; some by special forwarders with low-pressure treads to cause minimal damage to the ground. Most of the trees were used to fill up the ditches, and dams were constructed to block the main drainage channels. The bog then began to return to wetness, and sphagnum moss soon colonised the tree-blocked ditches. Wetland birds, such as meadow pipits, green-shanks and golden plovers, returned to nest, and hen harriers had good hunting once more.

Part of the aim of the restoration project has been to improve the livelihoods of local people too. All contracts for tree-cutting work went to local contractors, and the local community woodland organisation, North Sutherland Community Forestry Trust (NSCFT) was involved. A large barn, originally built in the barley days and now belonging to the community, was used to house a local chipping and sawmill enterprise, with the best of the timber from the forestry blocks going to NSCFT and lower-grade wood being chipped for biofuel to heat the local swimming pool.

There has been recent talk of getting the area listed as a World Heritage Site. Norrie Russell was keen on the idea but acknowledged that the remaining Sitka plantation blocks could scupper the area's chances. The presence of the paper industry's favourite tree on this biggest of bogs was, he said, 'a bit like having a MacDonald's in the Taj Mahal foyer'.

In other parts of Scotland, the mistakes of the past are also being recognised and corrected. One of the largest and most scenic fragments of the old Caledonian forest is in Glen Affric and tremendous work has been carried out there by the Forestry Commission and private landowners, egged on by a small visionary organisation Trees for Life, which works tirelessly for ecological restoration. Exotic species have been cut out, and the stands of the native Scots pine have been allowed to naturalise and mix with the other natural components of the Caledonian forest.

These examples show that some plantation errors can be reversed and the damage they cause can start to be mitigated, but it is hugely expensive and the process has only just begun. In any case, the UK has many advantages (a strong economy, low rural populations, a temperate climate and good soils come straight to mind), which enable a good stab to be made at the problem. In less fortunate countries, industrial plantations can be far more devastating, as examples in earlier chapters have showed, causing irreversible harm to vulnerable ecosystems and communities. It is crucial therefore that further expensive fastwood plantation mistakes are prevented, so we have to find ways to reduce the demand for the pulp they produce.

CHAPTER 8: THE CLIMATE CONNECTION

A carbon catastrophe

There can be few people who are not now aware of the threat posed by climate change, and of the scientific consensus that global temperatures are rising due to human-induced carbon and other emissions to the atmosphere. Many now acknowledge the connection to their domestic lighting and heating arrangements, holiday flights and car mileage, even if they have not actually done anything to change their behaviour. Yet while a great deal of fuss has been made about light bulbs and 4x4 vehicles, there has been very little spoken about how our use of forest products, and particularly paper, contributes to global warming.

The paper and forestry industries seem to be much better than the electricity and car companies at peddling myths concerning their use of energy and their impact on the global climate. As climate change becomes an ever bigger concern, we can expect their claims to become more vociferous. One such claim is that pulp and paper mills are 'self-sufficient' in energy. Another is that the industry is leading the way in the use of renewable bio-energy. Their core argument is that they are actually helping to solve the climate change problem by planting trees.

The reality is very different. According to the Intergovernmental

Panel on Climate Change, deforestation and forest degradation by forestry is the single biggest source of climate-changing gases after fossil fuels, accounting for more than 17 per cent of global emissions, more than total world transport and almost as much as global food production. Since the paper industry is responsible for almost half of the planet's industrial logging, it must shoulder a significant part of the blame for this. Although the seriousness of the deforestation problem was recognised at the climate change summit in Bali at the end of 2007, unfortunately there were no firm decisions about what to do about it, although a two-year negotiation process has been initiated to come up with an agreement on how to reduce forest-related emissions.

Meanwhile the paper industry is busily chewing its way through the forests of the northern latitudes, despite the fact that these boreal forests are the biggest store of carbon on earth and play a vital role in stabilising the climate. Once cut, they are very slow to regrow, so any carbon they may soak up in future is dwarfed by the carbon released from the disintegrating toilet rolls, incinerated office waste and landfill sites where the trees end up after their short life as paper.

It is not only the trees that store carbon in forests, however. Forest soils are rich in organic matter and also act as an important carbon repository, at least until they are dug up by forestry machinery or ploughed to enable plantations of pulpwood trees to be grown. Peatlands contain the most carbon, so it is a disaster for the global climate when they are decimated by forest extraction to feed pulp mills. Yet this is precisely what is happening on the Kampar peninsula in Sumatra, Indonesia and elsewhere in that country, particularly Kalimantan. This problem is on such a scale that Indonesia's peatland carbon emissions are greater than the total climate change emissions of Germany or Japan.

In fact Indonesia is now one of the major sources of greenhouse gases worldwide: its annual emissions are about 3 billion tonnes, with deforestation and forest degradation accounting for more than 80 per cent of that figure. But if countries in the north, which have already profited from deforesting their own land, now want these emissions to reduce, it is only fair to offer Indonesia something in exchange. Reduced emissions from deforestation and degradation

(REDD) schemes are being set up, mostly by private firms from northern countries, to pay for forest land to remain covered in trees. However there are concerns about the ethics of some of these schemes. As carbon traders scramble for land to devote to a future of carbon absorption, critics such as Robert Oberndorf, of the Asian community forestry training institute RECOFT, complain that insufficient attention is being paid to forest-dependent communities. In a recent report he said, 'Issues such as traditional rights of access and use, the potential role of communities in managing the forest resources in question, and the sharing of any revenue streams created through equitable benefit sharing mechanisms are either being addressed on the periphery of current discussions, analysis and negotiations, or are being completely ignored.' There is always a social dimension when any forest issues are raised and their carbon dimension is no exception.

The carbon released in extracting wood from forests is not the end of the paper industry's emissions. Pulping and paper making both require huge amounts of energy. Globally, the pulp and paper industry's contribution to climate change emissions is one of the largest of all heavy industry. In the USA, for example, it is the third heaviest industrial source of greenhouse gases. In Finland, it is the worst offender. Yet this is a reality the industry tries hard to hide.

Paper disposal is another huge source of emissions. Incineration releases all the carbon contained in paper as CO_2, but paper rotting in dumps is particularly noxious because it produces methane, which is a greenhouse gas 23 times more powerful than CO_2. Paper is the largest component (40 per cent) of the USA's waste stream, and not surprisingly therefore the USA's landfills are the biggest source of methane in the world.

The World Business Council for Sustainable Development will go as far as admitting that 'Direct greenhouse gas (GHG) emissions from fossil fuel combustion in the forest-based industries are approximately 264 million tons of CO_2 per year, which is about 1 per cent of global GHG emissions.' It admits that this figure does not include what it calls 'indirect emissions', from 'purchased power', but it also fails to register emissions from deforestation, soil damage or paper disposal.

A recent study published in the *Journal of Resources, Conservation and Recycling* concluded that paper produces the equivalent of 6.3 tonnes of CO_2 per tonne during its life-cycle from forest to landfill. Given global paper production of 335 million tonnes, this would suggest that paper represents close to 8 per cent of humanity's total carbon emissions, a total of 2.1 billion tonnes of CO_2. A single sheet of copy paper causes emissions equivalent to burning a 40 watt light bulb for an hour. The average person's annual paper consumption causes as much greenhouse gas emissions as a return trans-Atlantic flight. Basically, making paper out of trees takes forest carbon on a fast track to the atmosphere.

Pulp, paper and power

It takes as much energy to make a tonne of paper as it does to make a tonne of steel. If you knock on a wooden table or door and think about it, this is not so surprising. Wood is hard. You know how tough it is to drill into it, so it is not surprising that smashing a tree into smithereens (and to make paper they need to be really small smithereens) takes a lot of power. In the USA statistics for 2002 show that the paper manufacturing industry accounted for more than 15 per cent of the country's manufacturing energy use, consuming more than 2.4 quadrillion BTUs of energy, or 2.5 billion gigajoules, enough to heat more than 18 million homes for the year. The paper industry's energy use is only outstripped by the chemical, oil and steel industries.

Taking a tree's perspective, it becomes clear why this should be. Wood develops to hold aloft a canopy of branches and leaves weighing many tonnes, even in the face of storms and often for hundreds of years, and to withstand armies of insects. It is extremely robust. There are two ways to liquidise it: mechanically and chemically. Mechanical pulp is made by chipping wood and then physically grinding the chips down to individual fibres. Chemical pulp is made by stewing woodchips in strong alkali solutions at high temperatures to separate and bleach the fibres.

Because the chemical stewing process results in a great deal of black waste sludge, chemical pulping requires 2 to 3 tonnes of wood to produce 1 tonne of fibre, whereas mechanical pulping only needs about 1.1 tonnes of wood per tonne of fibre, so it is much more efficient in terms of trees. In chemical mills the sludge waste is incinerated and because there is so much of it, the energy produced is usually enough to power the mill and sometimes enough to produce an excess for a district heating scheme or to generate electricity. In this sense, chemical mills are described as 'self-sufficient' in energy. However these claims ignore all of the gasoline burned in cutting trees and delivering them to the mill, and also their vast consumption of wood: as it takes 3 tonnes of wood to produce 1 tonne of fibres in a chemical mill, two out of every three trees felled is consumed simply in powering the pulping process.

Mechanical pulp mills need some external source of energy. Depending on what is available this may be fossil fuel, nuclear power or hydro-electricity, all of which are environmentally problematic because of the release of greenhouse gases, safety risks or impacts on watersheds, including displacement of people.

I first saw mechanical pulping at the Kajaani mill in Finland, which I visited because it supplies DC Thompson, the publisher that produces my nearest daily newspaper, the *Press and Journal*, Scotland's 'voice of the North', and also publishes some iconic Scottish magazines, notably the glossy little *Scots* magazine and the classic *Beano* comic.

The Kajaani mill is one of many owned by UPM Kymmene, a global giant employing 35,000 people around the world. Like many paper companies, it is part 'vertically integrated', meaning that it owns the whole chain of production from forest to final product. UPM manages 2 million hectares (5 million acres) of forest, half in Finland, the rest in Uruguay, USA, Canada, Russia, the Baltic States, France, Germany and Scotland. It makes 11.7 million tonnes of magazines, catalogues, packaging and mailing paper per year, equivalent to the entire annual UK paper and cardboard consumption. It is the biggest forest owner in Finland. It is also the biggest user and buyer of energy in the country and its biggest water user. It is the biggest printing paper company in the world. It's really big.

At a hundred years old the Kajaani mill is one of UPM's oldest pulp and paper mills. It looks like a child's drawing of a factory: a boxy low-slung building with a couple of tall thin chimneys spouting plumes of vapour. I was shown around by Päivi Lohu, a young blonde pregnant woman. She seemed genuinely pleased to be showing someone around who was actually interested in the paper-making process, rather than her usual diet of tribes of schoolchildren who would rather be somewhere else.

Eighty truckloads of wood arrive at Kajaani mill each day. We watched a monster machine unloading lorries several tonnes at a time and feeding the logs to the gaping, rumbling mouth of the debarker. Päivi said, 'Forests are our green gold,' and I wondered if this was a Finnish national motto.

Between deliveries, the loader, oddly graceful, trundled about the log yard stacking wood, picking up individual sticks as delicately as a hugely outsize elephant, but when it headed in my direction, its long neck raised and swinging, I scampered out of its way: it was suddenly more tyrannosaurus rex than pachyderm.

The mechanical pulping process occurred within a sealed chamber so I could only picture the two enormous grinding stones pulverising the wood into individual fibres. These were then bleached with diothionite and hydrogen peroxide, and the resulting pulp mixed with 'fillers' such as china clay before being diluted to a watery solution.

At Kajaani mill, the paper was made inside a steamy hangar-like building that seemed as long and narrow as a runway with the whole length taken up by a single edifice called the paper machine. This huge, complicated contraption had a warm and sweaty 'wet end' where liquid pulp squirted out onto gauze to make the paper web, a roasting hot middle where the paper was spun on vast heated rollers, and a cool 'dry end' where the paper emerged. It was hard to believe that pulp with 99 per cent water content could, in a matter of seconds, be so transformed, and woven by this enormous loom into dry rolls of paper. It seemed as miraculous as a caterpillar's metamorphosis into butterfly.

The pace of the process was astounding: half of the water was pressed out from the watery pulp within seconds and the machine ran at 80 km/hr (50 miles/hr). In the middle section the web of fibres was dried on steam-heated cylinders, snaking over and under these hot tubes at a speed too fast to see properly. At the dry end, before emerging, the paper was polished by an enormous mangle called the calendar before being wound onto a huge master roll.

I wanted to know how big the roll was so Päivi asked a smiley woman in a blue lab coat, who told us that the 7.6-metre (25-feet) paper roll coming off the dry end of the machine had 50 kilometres (31 miles) of paper on it. Päivi, like me, was visibly impressed and we beamed at each other with the discovery. A back-of-the-envelope calculation revealed that the machine produced enough paper to cover more than two football pitches every minute. Then a slitter-winder spun the paper off the big roll, slicing the sheet and rewinding it into multiple smaller rolls of the widths needed by customers. Finally a sophisticated robot determined what kind and size of paper and packaging to wrap it with.

People sat in a soundproofed box pretending that they made it all work, but really the whole process was computer driven, and all they were doing was watching the monitors hoping that nothing went wrong. 'When there's a breakdown,' Päivi grinned, 'then you should see them run.'

The whole process was deafening, sweltering and on a vast scale. I felt like a Lilliputian creature, a diminutive invader into a world of giants, scuttling about between frothing cauldrons of pulp and huge rolls of paper, like bum-wipe for trolls.

They even dig up the stumps

The high energy consumption of all paper mills is the result of the power needed to pulp wood and then to reconstitute the fibres from liquid form into paper sheets. Together they require so much energy that all pulp and paper mills have their own dedicated power plant. Like most paper companies, UPM claims to be pioneering the use of renewable biofuels in theirs, in order to reduce the use of fossil fuels. The company is changing its forest management to achieve this, extracting not only timber for sawn wood and pulp, but also the brash (branches, twigs, leaves and tips) that results from felling.

Around the back of the Kajaani mill was a mountain of snow-covered tree-roots. The company's forest manager explained to me that after trees are cut to supply the wood for the pulper, their stumps are also dug up and transported by lorry to feed the mill's energy plant. They may be driven more than 100 kilometres (60 miles) to the mill. I wondered how much diesel is burned in order to supply the mill with biomass, and whether, if all of UPM's contractors' fossil fuel consumption was taken into account, this could really make sense in terms of greenhouse gas emissions.

Furthermore, the ecological consequences of not only logging trees but also digging up the forest soils are devastating: apart from all the myriad life-forms they contain, the carbon stored in these soils needs to stay locked up, rather than disturbed and released to the atmosphere, contributing to already soaring levels of greenhouse gases. Even UPM's manager admitted that there had not yet been research into the impacts of digging up tree-roots. It is hard to see how this practice can be any better for climate change than the previous practice of running the energy plant on peat and coal.

Reducing fossil fuel use at mills like Kajaani is not simply a magnanimous gesture on the part of UPM or the result of a commitment to try to address climate change. Finland is dependent on Russian imports of gas; energy prices are rising and supplies have an uncertain future, so there are hard economic reasons to shift to biomass. Economics is also behind the stump-burning; it costs half as much to replant a site if the stumps have been removed than if not, so UPM has sold the practice to landowners on the basis of cheaper replanting costs. UPM pays landowners a fee per tree felled regardless of whether the whole lot, stump and all, is used, so to the company the stump is effectively zero-cost energy.

But what does the extraction of every shred of biomass do to the ecology of the soil left behind? There is no rotting vegetation, no heaps of brash for insects or small mammals. I pursued this issue with ecologist Raimo Heikkila, who said, 'We are worried about the impact of digging up the stumps, and in Helsinki someone is looking at it, but it will take five to ten years to get reliable results and the industry will not wait.' Meanwhile the impacts on the ground will continue.

At the most recent world congress of the International Union of Forest Research Organisations, one of the topics most hotly debated was what will happen when oil and other energy prices reach the point that using wood for energy becomes competitive. In particular, as the user of the cheapest end of the timber spectrum, the pulp industry will be the first to see this competition. The situation will be complicated by carbon credits or taxes: who knows whether they will act as perverse or benign incentives?

The paper industry's efforts to position itself as a leader in the bio-energy field and a progressive developer of renewable energy make much of its 'combined heat and power' systems, yet all of this positive spin downplays the simple fact that the paper industry is one of the most rapacious energy consumers on the planet.

Nine lives

Dramatic reductions in the energy used to produce paper can be achieved by using recycled fibres. There is a myth put around by the most cynical end of the waste management industry that somehow recycling paper uses more energy than making it from trees and land-filling it. Basic intuition should tell us that this is hogwash: if you dump a batch of paper into your bath and leave it for a while it pretty much goes to pulp of its own accord. It flops and squishes without much of a struggle. If you put it in a blender it is pulp within seconds. But try putting a lump of wood in there, goodbye blender. Trust that intuition; it is backed up by hard facts.

In 1998 there was a major American study called the Paper Task Force, involving a range of academics, environmentalists and big companies, which addressed a series of questions about the environmental impacts of paper production. The study collated data from a range of paper-making industries, the forestry industry that supplies the mills and a spectrum of potential destinations where paper could end up, including landfill dumps, incinerators and recycling plants. They carried out what is known as 'life-cycle analysis', totting up the materials and energy used, waste and emissions produced and other impacts of each potential route from the creation of a piece of paper to its disposal (or reincarnation, in the case of a recycled sheet). The study was vast, comprehensive and proved beyond reasonable dispute that recycling paper uses much less energy (between a sixth to a third, depending on what type of paper it is), requires less than half as much water, produces far fewer greenhouse gases, emits a tiny fraction of the toxic chemicals to air and water, and is on all relevant parameters much less damaging to the environment than making paper from virgin fibre.

According to the Paper Task Force, greenhouse gas emissions resulting from virgin paper production going to landfill are up to 2.3 times higher than recycling. For example, to recycle 1 tonne of newsprint produces 1.6 kilograms of greenhouse gas compared to 3.7 kilograms when virgin newsprint is landfilled.

As well as energy and pollution savings, paper recycling also has social and economic benefits and creates more jobs than traditional waste management. A typical landfill employs one person per 34,000 tonnes of waste, whereas paper recycling, according to a study by the US Natural Resource Defense Council, employs one person per 1,375 tonnes, which is 24 times as many jobs. They conclude that 'recycling is a better stimulation of jobs and economic development than is landfilling and incineration'. According to the USA's Environmental Protection Agency, recycling is good for the macro-economy too, by increasing supplies of fibre, thus reducing the likelihood of price inflation, leading to financial stability in the paper sector. Many recycling programmes are models of social inclusion and provide training opportunities for people with learning difficulties and the long-term unemployed.

And, of course, recycling saves forests. To make a tonne of recycled paper requires only 1.1 tonne of recovered paper, compared to up to 3 tonnes of wood used to make a tonne of virgin paper. If each fibre is reused just five times, the impact on forests can be reduced nearly fifteen-fold.

Paper fibres, like cats, can have nine lives if they are treated well. Even the most conservative industry reports say that fibres can be reused five times. However, at present even in Germany, held up as one of the best examples in Europe for its recycling rates, paper fibres survive an average of only two cycles before being disposed of. Only by buying recycled products and then ensuring they go for further recycling after use, can we extend the life-cycle of paper fibres.

The argument that recycling uses more energy than using virgin fibre is based on the claim that a vast amount of fuel is used to transport waste paper to recycling plants. This is fair enough. We certainly need to build more paper-reprocessing facilities closer to the big urban jungles, where the used paper resources are most dense, to cut down on these paper miles. We also definitely need to find renewable sources of energy to power our recycling plants and push for research and development into more efficient processing methods.

'Paper miles' is a concept that deserves more investigation. Huge volumes of transport fuel are used in the forestry industry for logging and delivering timber to pulp mills. A study of Japanese paper estimated that on average the fibres had travelled 6,000 kilometres (3,700 miles) from their forest or plantation of origin.

If paper is not recycled, those big waste trucks also burn a lot of fuel taking it to landfill. In the case of the Scottish Highlands where I live, which exports much of its landfill waste, the scaffy vans (as garbage trucks are known here) are driven about 350 kilometres (220 miles) to a dump in Perth. Paper for recycling goes a bit further south to Croy, about 380 kilometres (240 miles) away, so there is not a great deal to divide them, unless of course, the paper dealer, Scotland's biggest paper recycling firm, Stirling Fibre, sells the paper to a recycling company in China, in which case the paper miles can get a little crazy.

I have grown used to getting a less than ecstatic reception from paper companies so I was somewhat surprised to get straight through on the phone to Forbes Connor, the company head at Stirling Fibre, and even more so to be told that I would be very welcome to visit him and find out exactly what happens to the paper that goes in my local paper bank. It was a murky November morning when I made my way to Croy, one of the company's two paper depots. Forbes Connor was dressed like a businessman but spoke and acted like a normal human being. From the moment he sat down at the boardroom table to the parting handshake two hours later, words tumbled out of him with bright-eyed good humour.

Stirling Fibre is a family business, set up by John Connor, Forbes's father. 'My father says he was the first person in the world to make a recycled manila envelope. You should talk to him,' he said. 'He'd want to write your book for you.'

I was visiting on the last day that waste paper from my neck of the woods would come to Croy. The paper that we put in our recycling bins has been deemed to be good enough quality to go direct to a paper mill. By good quality, what is meant is that not only is there very little contamination with other materials such as plastic, food waste or metals, but the people who put their waste paper in the bins stick by the rules and deposit only newspapers, magazines and the content of junk mail, which are collectively known as 'news and pams' (periodicals and magazines). These are the types of paper needed by the Shotton mill at Flintshire, North Wales (another UPM mill), which recycles them into newsprint.

Under the new arrangement with Stirling Fibre, newspapers put into bins in my area would be taken to Invergordon, where Highland Council gathers recyclable material from around the region. They would then be trucked to Shotton to be pulped and made into newsprint, before being sold to the newspaper publishers who would have them back in a newsagent in a matter of weeks. 'Yesterday you put your Sunday paper in the recycling bin,' Forbes said. 'Today twenty-five tonnes of paper will be collected in the Highlands. Tomorrow it could be in a pulper and by Friday it could be newspaper again.'

This happy arrangement is dependent on the quality of what goes in our bins remaining high. The first threat to quality is people putting unsuitable paper or 'contraries' into the bin, in particular, cardboard, food packaging, fax paper, sticky labels and envelopes (though apparently everything from a zimmer frame and a dead cat to hundreds of pounds of cash have been found in there). Labels and envelopes are problematic because when the paper is mixed with water at the recycling mill the glue forms lumps called stickies, which are the bane of a paper maker's life, causing sheets to be uneven or even gumming up machines. Cardboard and packaging are easily recycled back into board and packaging, but they are not wanted by the newsprint mill.

There used to be a local Scottish market for most of the cardboard collected, but several recycled board mills have recently closed and now almost all the cardboard is also exported. Altogether almost half of the 8.2 million tonnes of waste paper collected in the UK each year is sent abroad to be recycled, mostly to China, whose massive appetite for waste paper and booming economy keeps prices high.

'We could get more money if we exported all the paper to China,' Forbes said, 'but we think our carbon footprint is a big issue and we want to encourage the local market.' He is critical of the government, which has sat back and watched UK paper reprocessing capacity reduce since 2000, despite a fivefold increase in the volume of waste paper collected. While focusing on keeping rubbish out of landfill sites, the carbon emissions from shipping have simply not been taken into the equation. 'We'd rather keep it in the UK and support sustainable businesses here,' he said.

What Stirling Fibre wants, ideally, is for different kinds of paper to be gathered separately. In different areas of the paper depot, various grades of paper are kept apart.

Forbes pointed out some pure white printer offcuts, which would fetch a high price because they can be recycled directly into office paper. Such material makes up about 20 per cent of recovered paper and is classed as 'pre-consumer' waste. Traditionally it was not considered waste at all because it was clean and largely uncontaminated by inks, glues or coatings. According to a report on recycling produced by a consortium of printing industries, pre-consumer recovered paper 'has been used for a long time to replace fresh pulp, often without regarding it as recycled pulp'. It is effectively indistinguishable from paper made from virgin fibres.

The next highest quality is used office paper, which is gathered and shredded and mostly sold to tissue manufacturers. There is something odd about the best-quality waste paper being used to make toilet rolls, but such is our demand for soft, fluffy, white wipes, that the tissue companies give the best price for this paper grade.

In a bizarre twist, following a massive national scandal concerning the loss by the government of personal data about millions of people, awareness of the need for data protection has caused a surge of interest by offices in diverting their waste paper away from landfill. Conscious that many documents have client details printed on them, and facing the daunting prospect of trying to extract such documents from other waste paper, business is booming in companies that collect and shred office waste. Stirling Fibre's security shredding operation has just been bought by PHS, a hygiene services company. In one of the nicest loop-closing cases I know of, PHS now collects paper from offices, shreds it and sells it to tissue manufacturers, who make it into toilet roll and hand towels, which PHS then delivers back to those same offices where it collects the waste paper.

The other important paper grades are 'newspapers and pams' and unbleached (i.e. brown) 'kraft' packaging such as cardboard and paper sacks. When all these different kinds of paper are combined the result is 'mixed paper', which no one seems to want to handle. The main market that is likely to be found for it is in China, where it is largely used to make packaging.

According to Forbes, a big threat to waste paper quality comes when local authorities decide to make recycling easy for people by providing them with a kerbside collection of bins in which all recyclable materials (cans, plastics and paper) are mixed together. These mixed bins, known as 'co-mingle', need to be separated by hand at 'murfs', the name given to Materials Recycling Facilities. This is expensive and although paper may be separated from plastics and metals, the result is mixed paper destined for China, if it finds a market at all. 'When paper is not segregated from other recyclable material, some of it is bound to go into landfill,' Forbes said. 'Segregation is key. It's not rocket science. Separating metal and plastic is feasible, but put paper in the mix, it's a nightmare.'

Unfortunately, local authorities have been set ambitious targets for keeping waste out of landfill with punitive fines if these are not reached. This has led to scaremongering that other council services will need to be cut if recycling levels are not high enough and so councils are cutting corners by collecting a wide range of recyclable materials in single bins. Forbes's recommendation to councils wanting to introduce kerbside recycling is as follows: 'Educate the public to separate paper, plastic, cans and bottles. Use smart bins. It costs a bit more to collect but it will generate more revenue in the end.'

As well as education, one of the key levers that governments have to influence recycling behaviour is to make people pay for using landfill. In New Zealand ordinary citizens have to buy stickers to put on bin bags before they will be uplifted and taken to the dump, which provides a real incentive to keep the volume of such rubbish down. However, in the UK and many other European countries, refuge collection is paid for by a blanket tax, which takes no account of rubbish volumes and gives no reward to people who diligently separate out their recyclable materials.

About 5 million tonnes of paper is still being dumped in landfill each year in the UK, much of it by businesses. Although there is a landfill tax with an annual escalator, its current level is still about a quarter of the equivalent tax in Sweden and is an ineffective barrier, particularly to the producers of relatively small volumes of office waste. If Forbes were in government he would triple landfill tax. 'There is no excuse for any office to send paper to landfill,' he said. Pointing to the solid bales of shredded paper at his depot, he said, 'That's not a waste product, it's a valuable resource.'

CHAPTER 9: THE BIG SOAK

Poisoned by pulp

In Valdivia, Chile in 2005, South America's largest population of black-necked swans was decimated by pollution from a pulp mill, plummeting from a healthy population of five thousand to just four surviving birds in less than a year. The pulp mill, owned by Celco (Celulosa Arauco y Constitución), poured toxic effluent into an internationally significant wetland, causing what WWF called 'an environmental catastrophe'.

The Carlos Anwandter Nature Sanctuary, a 5,000-hectare (12,000-acre) wetland on the Rio Cruces, which was supposed to be protected under the Ramsar Convention, was polluted by toxic mill ash and other waste containing dioxins. This caused die-off of the plant luchecillo (*Egeria densa*), which the swans depend on. Local people described heart-rending sights of swans falling from the sky, so emaciated they were unable to fly.

'This was an area that was once teeming with water birds,' said David Tecklin, WWF's Valdivia eco-region co-ordinator. 'Now, within the space of just months, it has become an empty expanse of brown, polluted water. It is a water desert.'

This was no accident. When the treatment facility at the Valdivia mill failed, Celco decided to continue operating despite knowing that there would be environmental impacts, though presumably even they did not predict the subsequent horror, as the entire swan population, a big attraction to the tourist industry and icon of the region, was wiped out. In a response unprecedented for Chile, the president, Ricardo Lagos, closed down the mill. But a few months later, it was back in operation, with a promise to pipe its filthy effluent out to sea.

The tragedy spurred a groundswell of popular opposition to the pulp mill, and to other developments by Celco. A grassroots group, Accion por los Cisnes (Action for the Swans) formed and set about fighting a new mill at Nueva Aldea, on the Rio Itata, which was granted permission despite an environmental impact assessment recommending against it. In 2006 Celco was fined for breach of the permit conditions, but carried on with construction. In 2007, the company was fined for causing fish deaths with toxic spills from its Lincancel plant into the Mataquito River. Fishers and tourism operators fear contamination of the coastline as so much of the company's waste is poured directly into the sea, but there seems to be no stopping Celco. In 2006 it reported record export earnings of $1.1 billion. Most of its pulp products are for export to China, North America and Europe.

A chemical cocktail

Such pollution incidents are particularly shocking because the paper industry has somehow managed to persuade most of us to believe that paper is a natural material, when the reality is that it is the product of sophisticated chemical engineering. The industry has resolutely and successfully projected an image of clean production, despite a shocking legacy of air, soil and water pollution, particularly from the chemicals used in the pulping process.

Some of the products of chemical pulping are surprising to say the least. Not many people would expect, for example, if they received a glossy box with 'Made in China' on the back, with some lingerie inside, that the whole thing came out of a forest. Such boxes are made of a single sheet of card, known in the trade as paperboard, folded in a complicated origami of corners and overlaps to create a near impregnable rectangular prism. The surface is a laminate, printed on a gloss coating disguising the underlying paperboard. The lingerie is 100 per cent viscose. All of these materials can be gleaned from melted-down wood, if you get the chemistry right. Unfortunately, that chemistry causes all kinds of nasty side-effects.

The most widespread chemical pulping process results in the tough brown paper we use to wrap parcels and from which brown envelopes are made, as well as most cardboard. It is called kraft, the origin of which is the German word for 'force', and it is one of the smelliest industrial processes anyone has ever come up with. Kraft pulp is the result of cooking pine woodchips with sulphurous alkali compounds. These cause an odour of rotten eggs, which notoriously hangs around chemical pulp mills and their nearby towns. They also lead to acid rain.

Brown paper's colour is natural; it is not bleached or dyed. The fibres of pine trees are disliked by the makers of white paper because they are not fair like spruce or eucalyptus. But they are strong, and that is what the kraft paper makers are after. Strength is the special effect of their stinky process.

To experience this scent-fest I went to the pulp and paper mill at Segezha, in north-eastern Karelia, Russia. The Segezha mill makes half a million tonnes each year of kraft paper. It's the world's second biggest producer of brown paper bags (making 500 million per year) with aspirations for the top spot. In the late 1990s, Segezha went bankrupt, a victim of Russia's unstable post-*perestroika* economy. It was briefly taken over and then abandoned by Swedish forestry company Assi Doman. Then, in 2005, a group of Russian entrepreneurs bought the mill and set about the huge task of modernising it. I got a sense of how well the business was doing when one of them proudly showed me a photo of his son, who attends a prestigious private boarding school in England.

I arrived at the mill on a February afternoon. It was already starting to get dark. Vladimir, the mill's wood procurement manager, showed off the timber depot where 1.5 million cubic metres (53 million cubic feet) of wood arrives each year: a volume equivalent to 15,000 double-decker buses, 300,000 elephants or enough for telegraph poles to take a phone line to the moon. Vladimir was responsible for the mill's new traceability system, a database of twenty parameters for every shipment of wood or chips to the mill. He claimed to be able to trace each log back to the logging coup (*kvarttal*, in Russian) where it grew. Most of the wood had arrived at the mill by train from elsewhere in Karelia, Vologda and Archangelsk. As well as logs, the mill bought the waste products of timber production, which also arrived by rail. Wagons of chips had come from sawmills around the region, and were so frozen in their trucks that devices like huge corkscrews were needed to separate them enough to flow.

Segezha is in an inlet of the White Sea and all summer logs had been arriving by ship to be stockpiled for use in winter. When I visited, the port was ossified in ice and looked as desolate as if it had been sleeping for a hundred years. The quiet was exaggerated by a change of shift.

I was watching where the logs were taken into the pulp mill when the next shift started and the action began. A rumble set up from inside the mill, a conveyor belt juddered into motion and a few small logs began to trundle their way past. A digger fired up and started shifting timber from a heap onto a loading ramp.

We followed the logs into the plant, where wood was pouring from belts into the debarker, a huge rotary grater in which logs were tossed like clothes in a giant's tumble dryer, with a deep, rumbling, drumming sound. The logs rolled along another conveyor and down a chute to the chipper, which produced ear-splitting crunching, munching, chomping noises. I imagined a monster chewing the logs between metal-toothed jaws and half expected it to burp after the operator obligingly fed it each mouthful. Instead it spat the split wood out from between its teeth and blew the chips up a chute into three gyrating chip-sorters that shook and shuffled, separating the dust (which goes to be burned) and the big bits of wood (which return to the chipper) from the acceptable flakes destined for the pulping process.

Crossing to the building where the 'cooking' plant was housed, it was dark and snowing. Vapours swilled under orange neon spotlights. There was an overwhelming stench, the gut-turning, putrid stink of a cellar that should never have been opened.

Inside, in belting heat, was a horror scene. Occasional bulbs cast dim pools of light. The fabric of the building was coming to bits, as if it had never seen maintenance since it was built in 1939. Toxic-looking drips sputtered from rusting tubes. The concrete floor was crumbling, patched with deadly metal plates between brown puddles, scummy with yellow froth. There were cracks in the walls where grotesque seepages of ice, crusts of frost from the condensing steam, grew like monstrous moulds. The walls bulged with snow and glassy fingers of terrifying creatures poked in from outside. Ice the colour of battery acid oozed down rusting struts and girders. Creeping through a tangle of pipes and tubes, erosion evident on every surface, my guide talked insistently about modernisation plans. Its pollution record is not particularly bad, as pulp mills go, but, I was assured, it was going to get much better. If this was normal, I was glad I would not be visiting pulp mills on a regular basis.

As we neared the pulping tanks, steam belched and the stench of sulphate was chest-gripping. We ascended in an ancient bird-cage of a lift to the attic where three unfortunate women in blue overalls watched over the delivery belt of woodchips, hiding in a glass box like a wooden greenhouse at a *dacha* holiday home, its wood painted blue and every potential leakage of fumes stuffed with rags. The greenhouse impression was completed by an incongruous collection of pot-plants in hanging baskets, as if, like canaries in a pit, as long as the spider plants lived, work could continue in the furnace-hot, mine-dark pulper.

The woodchips fed a series of 60-metre-tall (200-feet) cooking vats in which they were melted down by various concoctions of 'black and white alkali', powerful sulphate solutions that dissolve the lignin from the wood, releasing the cellulose fibres and the TRS (total reduced sulphur) compounds that make the gaseous emissions so unpleasant. We wove around gargantuan rust-encrusted tubs in the half-dark.

Inside these cauldrons a bizarre brown porridge the texture and colour of buckwheat *kasha* was concocted. We watched it seethe, stinking of hot metal. Then it slurped out of a tube and poured onto a slowly rolling drum to be rinsed.

After hot jets of steaming water had forced a poisonous, tarry liquid out of the pulp, my guide ripped a bit off: it tore rather like thick, soggy cardboard and reminded me of the brown felt boots worn by Russian workers in the snow. This carpet of pulp glooped on into the next vat, where we got a final glimpse of it by peering through a steamy window into what appeared to be a giant washing machine, soap-suds splashing. From here it would be massively diluted before being spellbound into paper.

I emerged, gasping for air, into the snowy night. Clean production? I reeked for weeks.

A dirty business

The pulp and paper industry uses more water per tonne of product than any other industry and 11 per cent of the total water used in industrial countries. Making virgin paper uses up to 40,000 litres per tonne – that's a mugful for every sheet, a bathful for a book. Pulp mills are sited to take advantage of very pure water, but in the course of mixing with the chemicals and additives used in the pulping process, it is not pure for very long. Most mills attempt to recycle large proportions of the water used within the mill. Dealing with the resulting noxious wastewater is a big headache for the industry.

The only time I have ever been invited to see the effluent treatment process at a pulp mill was UPM's mill at Kajaani, Finland, which being a mechanical pulper, does not produce so much chemical pollution to treat. Even so, it was a bubbling witches' brew of shit-coloured sludge-eating bacteria. Kajaani mill takes 4,000 cubic metres (140,000 cubic feet) of water (enough to fill two Olympic-sized swimming pools) every day from Kajaaninjoki, the lake nearby. After use it is cleaned in a biological effluent treatment plant, in which bacteria eat the scraps of fibres. The sludge that results from their feasting sinks to the bottom of a basin and is extracted and burned. UPM has invested 8 million euros into a new biosludge treatment and claims to be a world leader in water cleaning processes. The mill's plumes, I was told, were of pure steam and the water it pumps back into Lake Kajaaninjoki is as clean as it came out. Unfortunately not all mills are so careful, and around the world the emission of toxic chemicals used for pulping and bleaching paper damages the health of many communities close to mills. The following are just a few examples.

Asia Pulp and Paper's Indah Kiat pulp mill, in Perawang, Sumatra, Indonesia, is claimed to pollute the Siak River by flushing untreated or insufficiently treated chlorine effluent from its pulping and bleaching processes into the river, although there is currently no definitive proof for this. When the mill opened in 1984 its waste water treatment facilities were already outdated. Professor Trabani Rab, a medical researcher in the area, has recorded more than five hundred cases of people downriver from the mill with serious skin diseases, which he believes to be attributable to the mill. APP has insisted that the effluents from the Indah Kiat Pulp and Paper Mill are properly treated and even say that 'the quality of the treated wastewater is higher than the quality of the river water drawn into the mill'.

In South Africa in October 2007, the Sappi company was accused by Timberwatch, a local NGO, of polluting the Thukela River, with complaints from fishermen downstream that the outflow from the Tugela mill caused foul smells, filthy foamy water and paper residues that catch on hooks making their fishing tackle look 'like washing lines'. Local people experienced burning sensations if their skin came in contact with river water and fish have declined. Complaints about Sappi's impact on the Mvoti River are even worse, with dioxin levels having caused it to be closed to fishing, washing and bathing since 2005. Sappi says in its 2007 sustainability report, 'At Tugela Mill, there are times when we exceed our emissions limit. Working with the regulators, we have established a plan which allows us to reduce emissions over a period of time.'

China's thousands of pulp mills are notorious for having little in the way of effluent treatment and the result is that they are a big part of its water pollution problems. And those problems are massive.

According to Elizabeth Economy, whose book *The River Runs Black* charts the causes and impacts of China's dirty water, '75 per cent of the water in rivers flowing through China's urban areas is unsuitable for drinking or fishing'.

Although regulations on emissions from pulp and paper mills in North America have meant that many have cleaned up their acts, there are still too many cases of toxic pollution. In Maine, USA, in 2006, the Natural Resources Council of Maine (NRCM) tried to sue Verso Paper for allegedly polluting the Androscoggin River to levels far exceeding what use of the best-available technology would deliver. NRCM lost the lawsuit, but it has subsequently appealed the wastewater discharge terms of Verso's licence. The NRCM claimed that pollution from the company's mill resulted in build-up of phosphorus sludge that has been described by an industry consultant as an 'environmental time bomb', because phosphorous can lead to algal blooms and when algae sink the decay absorbs oxygen, thus threatening the whole ecosystem. Verso says that its emissions are within the bounds of the state regulations.

Many of the toxins emitted into the environment by pulp mills in the past still persist as health risks to present communities. In Ontario, Canada, First Nation communities still suffer the legacies of heavy-metal pollution in water and solid waste, particularly the use of mercury to prevent decomposition of pulp logs stored in water. The Ontario Ministry of the Environment considers mercury contamination, particularly of lakes, to be a 'serious concern, particularly worrisome in the north', because it builds up in fish, which form a large part of northern diets.

Canadian environmental organisation Reach for Unbleached (RfU), states that pulp mill workers face the highest risks on their health, followed by people who eat fish from waters downstream from mills. RfU identifies the main health risks as asthma and other lung diseases, cancers, reproductive and hormone problems, learning disabilities, heart disease, immune system damage and chemical sensitivity. The pollutants they are most concerned about are particulate matter, dioxin, chlorine gas and chlorine dioxide, hydrogen sulphide, acetaldehyde and formaldehyde. What's more, many of these compounds are mobile and persistent, so they are carried by air and water and can eventually be found much further afield.

The bleaching deceit

We associate a blank white page as a fresh start; we reach for a clean white napkin because it seems unsullied. But unfortunately our appetite for bright white paper feeds one of the paper industry's most outrageous scandals, the myth of 'chlorine-free' bleaching.

Even the palest of wood is not white, so to make white paper requires the fibres to be bleached. This is where particularly powerful chemicals come into play, most notably chlorine. Raw chlorine is a powerful bleaching agent that has been routinely used in the paper industry. Unfortunately when the chlorine's job is done in a paper mill and it is emitted into the environment, it goes on to cause some of our most worrying forms of pollution. Chlorine is the key ingredient in a family of molecules known as organo-chlorines, which includes furans and dioxin, some of the most toxic substances on earth. Dioxin is known to cause reproductive problems, including low sperm counts and endometriosis and is implicated in a range of other health problems including diabetes, hyperactivity, allergies, immune system and endocrine system problems.

In some countries, notably in North America and Western Europe, paper companies have made a great play of shifting away from the use of raw chlorine in the bleaching process, declaring themselves to be 'elemental chlorine free' (ECF). This phrase is used by the paper industry to encourage the belief that it is effectively 'chlorine free' and therefore safe, but this is not true. Most of the mills that have stopped using elemental chlorine have simply shifted to using chlorine dioxide, which means that the effluent and the bleached paper still contain the basic building blocks of organo-chlorines. Although chlorine dioxide is much more stable than raw chlorine so dioxins and related compounds do not form so readily, it still presents a risk, particularly if the paper or mill waste is incinerated.

There can be no denying that the shift to ECF bleaching has been beneficial. For example, in the USA, Environmental Protection Agency rules on chlorine bleaching have led to a 94 per cent reduction in dioxin emissions. However, the EPA's own rules point out that there is no safe level of dioxin and the 6 per cent remaining is still a concern.

The paper industry argues that they are simply responding to consumer pressure: consumers demand bright white paper, so they are obliged to bleach ever more intensively. Yet Judy Rodrigues at Greenpeace International compares paper with bread, suggesting that 'just as we have come to understand that brown bread is healthier and better for us, consumers need to learn that bright white paper is not necessary and less-bleached paper is actually much less dangerous'.

Cleaning up the act

The risk from organo-chlorines will not be eliminated until chlorine is no longer used at all and instead alternatives are adopted, such as hydrogen peroxide, which is much safer and is the basis of 'processed chlorine free' (PCF) or 'totally chlorine free' (TCF) bleaching. As the Kajaani mill showed, it is possible for mechanical mills to avoid pollution by investing in state of the art emission controls to minimise impacts on air and water. Swedish company Södra Cell has pioneered totally chlorine-free processes for chemical pulping and bleaching, its Värö mill becoming in 1993 the first totally chlorine-free chemical pulp mill. By the end of the 1990s it was the biggest producer of chlorine-free pulp in the world, and as demand for its product was strong, despite a global downturn in profitability of the industry, it seemed set to be a trendsetter.

In the 1990s pressure from environmental groups led to an increased use of PCF and TCF processes but paper industry representatives responded by vigorously promoting ECF as the industry standard, despite protests from environmentalists that it is a lie to claim that paper bleached with chlorine dioxide is 'chlorine free'. In Germany there has recently been a row about a national standard (DIN Norm 6730), which allowed paper made by both ECF and TCF processes to be described by the general term 'chlorine-free paper'. Environmental organisations and companies that have invested in TCF technology are horrified that ECF, in which chlorine dioxide and other chlorine compounds are used, can be fobbed off to the public as 'chlorine free', and claim that the standard authority was put under pressure by the dirty end of the paper industry. The German decision leaves fears that similar moves may be made at the European level, thus giving no incentive for European paper companies to shift to less harmful bleaching technologies.

The industry clean-ups that have happened have been at least partly driven by governments tightening up environmental regulations, and enforcing them. Both enforcement and penalties for breaches are needed; otherwise companies find it cheaper simply to pay fines if they are caught than to invest in cleaner practices.

Recycling is another important part of the clean-up solution for the paper industry. Recycling saves huge amounts of water, reducing water consumption to just 20 per cent in the case of paperboard and corrugated packaging, and by half in the case of office papers.

The difference in toxic pollution from recycled and virgin production processes is dramatic. The American research study called the Paper Task Force found that making corrugated packaging from virgin fibres results in more than 2 kilograms (4½ pounds) of hazardous air pollutants per tonne, whereas recycling the same material produces none. The task force also found that air emissions of nitrous oxides, particulates, volatile organic chemicals and sulphur compounds are all less for recycled paper production than virgin, and recycled manufacture produces none of the hazardous organic halogens (AOX) that result from the use of chlorinated compounds for bleaching.

Recycling also prevents the pollution caused by landfilling and incineration. Landfills, according to the USA's Environmental Protection Agency, release a cocktail of dangerous pollutants into the environment and incinerating mixed waste paper produces a wide range of toxic air pollutants, including dioxins, furans and heavy metals such as mercury, cadmium, lead and acid gases.

According to the USA International Institute of Environment and Development, the cost of reducing worldwide hazardous paper mill discharges to safe levels would be $27 million. The reduction in pollution brought about by recycling thus makes huge economic as well as environmental sense.

Chlorinated crumble

Although recycling paper produces only a fraction of the dangerous substances that pulping wood involves, it is by no means a pristine process as I discovered on my own doorstep. When I began to investigate the industries behind our most common paper brands I began with toilet paper, partly because it is such a good symbol of our paper use – pretty well everyone in northern societies handles a toilet roll once or several times a day – but also because I have a particular childhood connection to it. I grew up in Northumberland, England, a couple of miles downstream on the River Tyne from a Kimberly-Clark tissue mill. One of my most vivid childhood memories is of the river turning lurid shades of pink, blue or green, depending on what colour toilet rolls were being made that day.

It turned out that the Prudhoe mill is still the nearest toilet roll factory to my current home in north-west Scotland, although it has since changed hands and now belongs to SCA (Svenska Cellulosa Aktiebolaget), a Swedish-based multinational company and the biggest tissue producer in Europe. These days the mill produces Velvet toilet rolls, marketed using the slogan 'Love your bum', and also supplies the own-brand tissue to many major supermarket chains, including Tesco and Asda. I wanted to visit.

I phoned and explained to a receptionist that I wanted to arrange a tour of the mill and I was advised to speak to their public relations man, Mike Thompson, who was unfortunately not available. I tried again later, but he still could not come to the phone. Next day, he was in meetings. Finally, he phoned back and left a message to say that a tour would not be possible. I called again and eventually managed to speak to him in person. We had a strange conversation in which he used a lot of emotive phrases including 'industrial espionage'. I tried, in vain, to explain that I was a writer rather than a spy and that I would not be able to recognise a tissue-industry trade secret even if it were handed to me in a plastic-wrapped four-pack marked 'Love your bum'. But Mr Thompson would not budge. 'The drawbridge is up,' he insisted. I eventually managed to get him to agree to answer some questions by email and he promised to send me lots of information about the factory. What he actually sent was a two-year-old 'Environmental and Social Report', which did not contain a single page about the Prudhoe mill. My suspicions were raised. I decided to pay SCA a visit.

Next to the mill, a huge crane hung over the shiny skeleton of a new seven-storey incinerator building. At the main entrance, a security guard sat in his box operating the huge gates. When he saw me peering through the fence he lumbered up. 'What yeez deen?' I could feel myself looking embarrassed. I told him I was interested in the mill and asked if I could have a look around. 'Got an appointment?' he retorted. I had to admit I did not. He looked me up and down and, with a terse, single clipped syllable, 'Na,' shook his head, turned his back and waddled back into his box. I was not prepared to pick a fight.

Despite not being allowed into the mill, I crossed the road and watched Velvet toilet roll lorries with 'Do you love your bum?' emblazoned on their grimy back ends driving in and out and lurking beside the factory. White plumes of vapour belched out of the cubic structure. Around the back of the mill the solvent smell from the plume was much more marked and a stagnant little burn sat forlornly under a tan-coloured scum. A few hundred metres from the mill, a drumming noise drew me to a brick construction, half-hidden among trees close to the river and heavily fortified by railings. Peering through them, it was possible to make out two open tanks of brown swirling water where the mill's run-off was swapped for fresh river water. Clearly the mill's treatment of run-off was vastly improved since I had last been there as a child.

I strolled back to Wylam along the riverbank, through a scene of almost miraculous post-industrial environmental recovery. This part of Tynedale was intensively mined for coal, and during the eighteenth and nineteenth centuries it was a hotbed of engineering enterprise and heavy industry. The legacy is permanent, with the landscape reshaped into bings and denes, bings being the hills formed of the discarded mine waste, and denes being the narrow valleys that were once natural streambeds, straightened and used as the routes of railtracks to transport coal from the mine shafts down to the river. Now the bings are growing over with trees and shrubs and the denes are dense with brambles. River pollution has reduced to the extent that salmon are running up the river again for the first time in hundreds of years, and otters, cormorants, herons and goosanders have followed them. I had hoped that I might be able to credit the paper mill with some of this recovery of the riverine habitat, but their refusal to communicate gave me no chance.

I continued to ponder their secrecy as I researched this book, in the course of which I was welcomed into paper mills making everything from newsprint to top-security bank paper, and even into some of the most notoriously dubious paper factories in the world. Nowhere, except in my home town, was I actually refused entry, and as time went on my suspicions about SCA's Prudhoe mill festered. There are so many environmental and social issues a paper factory could conceivably be failing on (air and water pollution, chemical and energy use, workers' conditions, unsustainable wood sources, etc.), that there was plenty to feed the imagination about why SCA did not want me to see inside their factory. I found it extraordinary that a PR professional would risk my speculation about what aspects of the mill are dubious, rather than simply allowing me in and feeding me the company line.

I did eventually get to see inside the Prudhoe toilet roll factory, for a whistle-stop tour. The mill does not pulp wood; it makes tissue from imported bales of pulp and recycled paper. I was forbidden from seeing the process of returning paper to a pulp, which is much like putting old paper in your bath and squidging it until it falls apart and the ink washes out, only on a much bigger scale, but I watched the resulting pulp being reconstituted into paper on a surprisingly small machine. SCA announced a few years ago the installation of new 'fluffing technology', which was presumably what made Velvet tissue 'now even quiltier', but I was whisked so quickly through on my tour that its wonders remain, as I had promised they would, an industrial secret.

But in Wylam, downstream and downwind of the SCA factory at Prudhoe, a bitter dispute has erupted concerning the recycling plant, which provides about half of the fibre the mill uses to make toilet roll. The problem is a new incineration system at the mill, which is intended to generate energy by burning a side-product of the recycling process, the delightfully named 'paper crumble'. This is the waste matter left at the bottom of the tub when the paper has been squished, washed and the usable pulp removed. It consists mostly of fibres too short to be reconstituted back into paper. Although it sounds good enough to eat, unfortunately because paper makers elsewhere have bleached these fibres with chlorine compounds, burning the paper crumble incurs a risk of release of organo-chlorines including dioxin. The villages downwind of the mill, such as Wylam, are not surprisingly unhappy with this prospect.

There is a general lesson here, that recycling a product can only be as environmentally benign as the original production process. Paper made by dirty technologies using dangerous chemicals cannot be easily recycled without continued risk from those chemicals. This means that if we want to have safe recycled toilet paper, we must ensure that all the paper put into recycling bins is unbleached or made white by a bleaching process that is chlorine free. The price of handling the bright white bleaching toxins must be paid each time the fibres are recycled. How much better it would be if they were designed right out of the system.

A trip to Baikalsk

One of the most controversial pulp mills in the world is found on the southern shore of Lake Baikal, Siberia, Russia. Baikal is the most ancient, the biggest and by far the most amazing body of fresh water on earth. The average lifetime for a lake on earth is 40,000 years, but Baikal is 25 million years old. It is so huge it acts like a sea, with currents that keep the water oxygenated right down to its 1,600-metre (5,000-feet) depths. It contains 20 per cent of the world's liquid drinking water and the only population of freshwater seals, called Nerpa. There can be no more powerful a symbol of fresh water than this lake, nor of the impact that the pulp and paper industry worldwide is having on our water resources, either by flushing toxic effluent out of mills or belching poisons out of chimneys to be washed down from the sky in acid rains and dioxin clouds.

Jennie Sutton is a small, energetic English woman, who has lived in Siberia for decades and is part of a campaigning outfit in Irkutsk called Baikal Environmental Wave. She has studied the impacts of the paper industry on Lake Baikal. I arrived at her office still rocking from the motion of the four-day train journey from Europe. With her purple corduroy trousers and slippers, Jennie looked thoroughly British, but I soon discovered how Siberian she had become, when after a conversation with a colleague she turned back to me and continued speaking in Russian. Eventually she noticed that she had lost me and apologised that her 'stream of consciousness' is Russian.

Jennie has encyclopaedic knowledge of the notorious Baikalsk Pulp and Paper Mill, with its dreadful record of more than thirty years of dumping chlorine in Lake Baikal. She promised to try to gain permission for me to visit the mill, and began an extended process of faxes and phone calls.

Meanwhile, she filled me in on the background. 'The mill is almost certainly the main source of negative impact in the lake and it's a very serious source,' she began. 'The mill's impact is felt on the floor of the lake over a significant area that is now incomparable with the rest of the lake in terms of damage and disappearance of species. It is mostly endemic species that have suffered.'

The Baikalsk mill was built in the 1960s and was controversial right from the start, with scientists warning that its pollution risks were unacceptable. 'The turning point for the mill was in the late 1980s,' Jennie said, 'because of the seal epidemic.' This was the breakout of canine distemper that decimated seal populations throughout the Baltic and North Sea as well as in Baikal. 'The question of the mill and of Lake Baikal's protection was raised at the national level and the communist party produced a document that basically called for the "reprofiling" of the mill. In those days the Irkutsk legislature was more radical than now and there were demands to turn the mill into something quite different, like a furniture factory, which would not produce waste water. This was the beginning of a fight that has continued throughout the 1990s and into the twenty-first century as to whether the mill should be closed down or modernised.'

In the late 1980s, because of the epidemic, the mill became a target for social protest. The official plan was to build a pipeline to take the waste waters of the mill out of the Baikal watershed. 'Can you imagine?' exclaimed Jennie. 'This would have meant pumping it up over the mountains to the Irkut River and on to the Angarra.' The proposal was heavily attacked by the public and there were big demonstrations against the pipeline. 'Many people think that the environmental movement in the Soviet Union arose here at Baikal because of the pulp and paper mill, though I believe there are also other pretenders to this glory.' She chuckled. 'Anyway, the pipeline was never built. It was a harebrained idea from the start.'

Over lunch, she explained how UNESCO got involved in plans to modernise the Baikalsk mill, after Lake Baikal became a World Heritage Site in 1996. UNESCO, said Jennie, 'were prepared to support the modernisation process on condition that it involved an eventual phase-out, beginning with a shift to a closed-loop production and a stop to using chlorine for bleaching. But this shift has not happened yet.'

Instead there were years of wrangling and planning how to clean up the mill. In the early 1990s, the UN Industrial Development Organisation, the European Union and the Finnish government all said that the mill should be modernised and Jaakko Pöyry, the world's biggest forestry consultancy firm, these days just known as Pöyry, devised a modernisation project for the company. The World Bank declared its support for the plan of action but after years of serious work with the company during which the pulp and paper mill changed hands (in 2003) and was bought by Oleg Deripaska, an aluminium tycoon, the Bank eventually pulled out because the mill's management was not fulfilling the agreed plan.

Meanwhile the mill continued to pollute the lake, pouring the effluent from its chlorine bleaching process into the water.

Jennie said, 'Over the past four or five years the question has been standing of whether Lake Baikal as a World Heritage Site should be transferred to the list of World Heritage Sites in Danger, for a number of reasons, one of the main ones being the mill.' This would be a scandal for the Russian government, but, Jennie wondered, 'It has endured so many scandals, would another really make any difference?' Now that Western nations want Russian gas and oil, perhaps they would be ready to forget minor questions like World Heritage Sites. As she pointed out, UNESCO had shown itself to be helpless in the face of power politics, and power politics is all about energy.

The timber source for the mill was 90 per cent pine, from Irkutsk, Krasnoyarsk, Chita and even further north. The wood came entirely by rail since transportation by water had been banned. In the past, many logs were accidentally dumped into the lake when rafts of larch and pine being transported across the lake broke up in storms: pine floats but larch is dense and sinks to the bottom where the logs rot, using up oxygen from the water. Jennie said, 'the cost of transporting wood to the mill is increasing and supply is a big issue: areas closer to the mill are logged out, or in the lake's close watershed or national parks.' Pöyry estimates that wood will need to travel 500 kilometres (300 miles) to keep the mill supplied.

'Logging for the mills is all in virgin forest, and here it takes up to a hundred years just to regenerate the timber and two hundred or more to properly restore the ecosystem after logging,' Jennie said. 'There doesn't seem to be any systematic approach to sustainable use of forests. The pulp and paper industry is expanding all the time and basically they're destroying Siberia.'

There were also reports of the Baikalsk and Serenginsk mills being involved in illegal logging. Baikal Environmental Wave recently took legal action against the Serenginsk mill for logging in the buffer zone of the Baikalsk Zapovednik, but unfortunately the President of Buryatia had shares in the mill and backdated legal agreements between mill and state were hurriedly drawn up. According to Jennie, corruption like this was rife, with collusion between criminal business operators (colloquially known as 'mafia'), that evaded prosecution by bribery of police or judiciary. A business that achieved such protection from the law was said to 'have a roof over its head'.

Jennie told of a public prosecutor in Buryatia who took issue with gas prospecting that broke environmental regulations, and who as a result was moved on to work in another area, and moved again when he still tried to uphold the law there. 'Such men of principle can be counted on the fingers of one hand,' she sighed.

After several days of phone and fax exchanges with the paper company, I was ready to pay a visit to Baikalsk Pulp and Paper Mill. It was in a glorious location. Dramatic, snow-covered, *taiga*-forested mountains reared up from the lake shore. Immediately to the east was the Baikalsk Zapovednik: not only inadequately protected from logging but also fumigated by the mill's plumes.

I arrived at the mill by local workers' bus, which reeked alarmingly of diesel and went to what looked like the only building that could be anything akin to a 'front entrance'. Natasha, my interpreter for the day and a Baikal Environmental Wave employee, looked scared stiff. From her perspective we were entering enemy territory. I was seeking Alexei Nayaram, the mill's PR man. Although I had not exactly managed to achieve a welcoming invitation to the mill, he knew I was on my way. A blank-faced security guard sent us off to 'the red brick building' with a gesture across the snowy compound.

Huge red-and-white striped chimneys puffed out plumes of steam and a thinner, blacker chimneystack spewed sulphurous grey fumes into the air-stream over the lake. I was tempted simply to wander around and look about, but as a foreign guest, I was at the mercy of my guide. Natasha was anxious to find the office and bustled towards the only brick building in sight. I followed meekly behind. Several nondescript, crudely painted metal doors presented themselves, none obviously the 'PR' office. We chose the director's door. A scruffy staircase of cracked tiles led up. Natasha questioned the middle-aged woman washing the stairs, and she directed us back out to another door. In every industrial building in Russia there always seemed to be a grim-faced woman, mop in hand, on the staircase. I wondered if their job included taking note of all those who passed and, if so, who those notes were for.

Two flights up an even more unprepossessing staircase, like a small Glasgow tenement, Natasha tentatively opened a door onto a corridor. Around a tight corner we reached an office where a woman droned to a young man in a grey sweater sitting behind a computer monitor far too big for his minuscule desk. We stood in the corridor perusing the company newspaper, and eventually got our turn in the tiny PR office, where we were told to sit on the rickety chairs, while the young man scrutinised my correspondence. After a long silence, he announced emphatically that the company was 'not a monster', as if I would ever suggest such a thing. Then he gave a charming smile and assured me that he did not have the authority to answer my questions.

We set off for the director's staircase again, passing the quizzical cleaning lady, and found the head office, only to be told by the secretary that the director was 'busy' and that we should go away. Now. A taxi was called for us and within minutes we were off-premises and being hurtled towards the centre of Baikalsk town.

We ate lunch at the shopping centre: deep-fried battered dumplings stuffed with potatoes and cabbage, a greasy vegetarian staple in meat-crazed Russia, which, I am sure, would catch on in Scottish chip shops or bakeries. The toilet rolls here were small, brown or sludgy peach, slightly stretchy or crisp, badly perforated, single-ply, unbleached and most definitely not 'quilty'. It had clearly not yet reached the fetish levels of the West. But just ten years ago the shelves of Russian stores were home to piles of tinned sardines, bread, perhaps butter (perhaps *nyet*), cheese, noodles, and not much more. I remember visiting in the mid-1990s, and what was provided beside the drop-toilet at the bottom of the garden was a few sheets of an old child's schoolbook, or some scraps of newspaper. I suspect for most Russians the days of wiping their bum on a page of young Fyodor's maths homework or essay about last summer holiday are long gone and, given the radical change and the swiftness of the spread of olives, Carlsberg, Pedigree Chum and Britpop, I assume Russian toilet roll will soon be 'quiltier' than thou.

We sat and watched life in Baikalsk go by and Natasha related what she knew about the place. The town had around 16,000 inhabitants,

3,000 of whom worked at the mill and most of the rest of whom were dependent upon it. It had a flourishing ski resort, but that belonged to the mill, as did the taxis and most of the shops. Natasha explained that Baikal Environmental Wave had been supporting a local business incubator, but invariably successful new business start-ups ended up being bought out by the mill. The mill ran the buses, funded the school and, most controversially, handled the town's sewerage and other waste. The dependence of the town on the mill for its municipal waste water treatment was one of the factors that made the mill's impact on Lake Baikal so intractable. The chlorine from the mill limited the efficacy of the biological treatment process, resulting in *E. coli* pollution. But close the mill and the town would pump raw sewage into this precious ecosystem. An independent municipal waste treatment plant for the town was desperately needed.

After lunch we took a taxi back to the mill and returned to the director's office. We stood outside in the corridor, floor newly tiled, walls freshly plastered. It was warm. The secretary stalwartly ignored us. Outside, two dramatic chimneys fumed, stark grey against the fresh fall of snow. The sensitive question of whether I was to be made welcome or not still hung in the air. After fifteen minutes or so, the secretary phoned the director and then told us to wait. We sat in the antechamber for an age before being told that the chief technician of the mill would come and answer my questions.

After a while she arrived. I was surprised that she was female and wondered how many Western European paper mills' chief engineers are women. Her name was Elizivieta Pavlovana Tarakanovskaya. She wore a substantial blue hat like a big cornflower on her head and she kept it on throughout the interview, which took place in the director's office. The floor and walls were tiled with big, gleaming bathroom tiles. We sat on padded plastic chairs. The room felt more kitchen than boardroom.

Ms Tarakanovskaya explained that the mill made 200,000 tonnes per year of unbleached pulp for producing viscose textiles. These were what she mystifyingly called 'strategically important varieties of cellulose', which were originally destined for aircraft applications (parachutes, I learned later), but soon after the mill was built in 1964, synthetic alternative materials became available. Now most of this viscose was sold to China, through the mill's Moscow-based parent company Continental Management. Waste from the primary product was used to make paperboard packaging.

The mill took 90,000 cubic metres (m^3) (3 million cubic feet) of water from the lake every day and produced a similar volume of effluent. A closed-loop project was promised by 2007 to recycle water and return none of it to the lake, though this would reduce consumption only to 50,000 m^3 (1½ million cubic feet) (less than a 50 per cent saving) and all of the current liquid emissions would be steamed off as air pollution. The new plant would, I was told, include a separate municipal waste system. When I asked who would pay for this, Ms Tarakanovskaya said, 'I don't know. I just make pulp.'

Ms Tarakanovskaya grew annoyed when I sought an explanation of the pulping process. She was fractious about water treatment. When I asked if we could tour the plant she pointed furiously at my letter of introduction and said that it did not mention seeing anything or taking pictures. We made a narrow escape before she lost her temper, fearing what might happen to the blue cornflower hat in such an eventuality.

The secretary told us to return to Alexei, the PR man, as he had someone for us to meet. This turned out to be an ecological toxicologist, Elena Grosheva, a balding woman wearing dark glasses, pale face-powder and a turquoise Paisley shawl. She spoke some English and was in a suspicious rush to explain how the mill's waste did no harm at all to Baikal. When she claimed that life at the end of the outflow (which she called 'the tube') actually flourished on the warm effluent I grew sceptical of what I was hearing. She proudly showed us photographs of an endemic species of shrimp, *Epishura Baikalensis*. 'This shrimp is living on the tube, because you know the water of Lake Baikal has a very low concentration of organics, and on the tube they can obtain these organics, and eating, eating!' She chuckled.

Before the shrimps got to feast on the pulp sludge, it was cleaned in a process that she claimed was the first ever usage of such a system in Russia. This involved the use of even more chemical reagents to lighten the liquid (at least the shrimps got to eat pale-coloured pollution), then bacteria and micro-organisms consumed contaminants, and finally the effluent was pumped into two sludge ponds, where sediments settled out. The remaining liquid was pumped out into the lake and the solids were burned for energy. Ash was 'recultivated' for use as a tree fertiliser. 'It is very efficient and there is no serious pollution,' she said, but she admitted that 'sometimes on the bottom we have some points of polluted sludge'.

The effluent of suspended solids of sulphur, chlorine and sodium compounds is discharged at 11 to 14°C, 100 metres out into the lake at a depth of 40 metres. I asked Ms Grosheva outright if the chlorine bleaching could cause any problems, and she confessed that this was 'a hard question' and that 'bleaching is the most dangerous part of this industry. Peroxide is better ecologically, but the viscose requires chlorine compounds because peroxide reduces the quality of the product.'

On further questioning she revealed that the planned closed-loop system may simply shift the problem of chlorine pollution of the water to the more dangerous one of air pollution by dioxins. 'This residue they are planning to burn, it must be at more than 1,000°C otherwise it is very dangerous,' she confided. At the moment, however, she claimed that dioxin levels were lower in the region than in parts of Germany and the USA, and she denied that Baikalsk mill had anything to do with the levels of dioxins and other organo-chlorines that had been found accumulated in the fat of the Nerpa seals. Instead she blamed these levels on forest fires, coal-burning power stations and chemical works.

Jennie Sutton disagreed. 'There is very significant organo-chlorine (like dioxins and polychlorinated biphenyls, or PCB) pollution of the wood web of the lake. This can be seen by the presence of organo-chlorines in fish and seals up to levels comparable with the Baltic in the 1980s and 1990s. The latest scientific literature shows that human mothers' milk in a lakeside village was found to be very high indeed in PCBs because the people there eat a lot of fish from the lake. The mill is obviously one of the sources of these.'

Jennie asserted the precautionary principle, saying, 'If you compare the changes over these forty years with the lake's twenty-million-year history, we should be afraid of the impact we can make.'

Ms Grosheva was still bullish about the lake's resilience. 'Lake Baikal is very big and very stable,' she said. 'It has a very good in-built water treatment mechanism. For forty years this mill has been working and we have a very good experience of monitoring and investigating the ecological impact. It's a very good ecological experiment.' But what if that experiment goes wrong? There is only one Lake Baikal.

Baikal breathing

Bolshoi Galo'ustnaya is a village on the shore of Lake Baikal. Throughout the two-hour bus journey there from Irkutsk the new *King Kong* movie played on the video at ear-splitting volume. The gorilla had just climbed up the Empire State Building when the bus pulled to a halt and disgorged its passengers into a scene that could not have been a greater contrast to Manhattan: a cluster of little wooden houses on two unlit streets, separated by hayfields, backed by mountains and fronting onto the snow dunes of the shore of the lake.

I found a place to stay with an indigenous Buryat couple, Misha and Faina. We spoke very little of each others' language but I received a warm welcome and after a simple supper of bread and cheese went to bed. It was a starry night, and in the stillness and quiet, I had a tantalising sense of the vast frozen expanse of lake nearby, waiting.

The morning was clear and sunny. From the huge haystack in the yard, Misha fed his cow and calf, two horses and several sheep, watered them from buckets hauled from the shared well and let them out of their shed for the day. After a huge breakfast of rice porridge and tea, Faina packed me off to walk on the lake.

Strolling down through the village, cattle and horses breathed dragon clouds through wooden fences. I scuffed through snowy dunes towards the jetty, where boats sat frozen like nuts in chocolate, and then tip-toed out onto the ice. The lake was stunning: it glittered to the horizon, where mountains stood, hazy in the far distance, snow-covered and majestic, over 2 kilometres (1¼ miles) high. Between them and me stretched 60 kilometres (37 miles) of ice. Close to the shore it was calm and smooth. A dinghy rested in a blanket of snow.

As I left the land behind, the only sounds were the groans and whispers of the dialogue between wind and lake, interrupted by crunching footfalls. Powdery snow blew like icing sugar, lifting into little whirling dervishes, settling like sand, filling my boot-prints behind me and wiping out my traces.

The frozen lake creaked where silent currents welled up from below and I juddered to a halt, breathing hard. In front of me was a crack, a wound of broken ice fragments. It took all my courage to step across. I knew it was irrational to fear the cracks. I knew that people drive trucks on the frozen lake. But I also knew that the lake is the deepest in the world. Beneath my feet was water to a depth of 1,642 metres, a mile of water. It was terrifying.

But the cracks were everywhere, like membranes of a multi-celled skin. Light refracted at the seams, like holograms casting rainbows and kaleidoscopes of colour. Below the wrinkled white snow was black ice, more than half a metre thick. Below the ice, weird green shapes lurked in the gloom, blurry signs of the endemic fish and other animals that make up two-thirds of the species found in the lake.

The currents keeping that life alive, circulating oxygen through their deep underworld, meant that the ice was imperceptibly in perpetual motion and its surface was thus no smooth skating rink. Great blocks were scattered like dice, their blue an odd shade, paler than sky, lighter than sapphire, glassier than turquoise, reminiscent of copper-sulphate crystals. Translucent plates and shark fins reared up or lay buckled and shattered into heaps. Far out, as if a huge breaker snap-froze, a wave of ice crashed silently, a visual echo of a storm months ago. Ice-flakes and wedges crumpled where ice-plate edges joined and crushed together, making little ranges of snow-capped peaks, mimicking the formations of the distant pyramidal mountains. Valleys wove among them, meandering and glistening in the sunshine.

At the crack I stepped over, the ice surface was pulling apart more slowly than I could see. On a planetary scale, Baikal is also growing as the continental fault widens, like a smile broadening 2 centimetres (¾ inch) a year.

Most intriguing were the bubbles, globes of gas frozen into the ice, perfect spheres of white hanging under the black surface and wee vertical streaks eking their way out, slowly pressing upwards. When I got back to the house, I searched for the Russian word for 'bubbles' in a dictionary and said to Faina, *'poozheer'*.

She understood instantly. 'Baikal breathing,' she nodded. 'Baikal organism.'

I was thrilled to be with someone who saw the lake as alive. We beamed at each other. I looked up 'cracks' and mimed the way the bubbles came squeezing up through them. She laughed with me, sharing the joy of discovering that the lake was not only beautiful, but full of life.

'And the wind?' she asked. Did I hear the wind? *'Vyetyer'* – her voice.

To the indigenous people who have lived around the banks of this beautiful lake for generations, Baikal is a living being. No wonder I walked tentatively on her skin. To poison her with chlorine is a sin.

CHAPTER 10: WHAT WE CAN ALL DO TO MAKE A DIFFERENCE

Paper is problematic

It should now be quite clear that paper is not a natural, benign product. Paper is an enormously useful material that can bring a diverse range of benefits but its manufacture has wide-ranging and problematic impacts. The sheer scale of consumption, particularly among the affluent people of European and North American countries, is out of all proportion to our real needs and is achieved only by using up more than our fair share of the earth's resources. Far too much paper is wasted.

This book has only been able to take a snapshot of what is a rapidly changing industry, but even a brief consideration of the history of paper making and the path that this material has taken within the culture of China, from ancient times to the present, shows that the current shape of the paper industry in North America and Europe is by no means the only way it could be. How China responds to its new pressures of increasing consumption will be key to the future shape and impacts of the paper industry.

China's future and that of the USA are intricately related, as much of the direction of paper industry development is decided in financial institutions and the headquarters of multinational industries based in

America. Having led the way in paper consumption and production for decades, it remains to be seen if it can lead the industry towards a more sustainable way of working, one which is good for the environment, for society and for the economy.

Change is sorely needed, because there is not an unlimited supply of the basic raw material of the modern paper industry: wood. Although the forests of the world, and particularly those of the north, are vast, they are not so huge that they can survive if they continue to be decimated to feed pulp mills at the current alarming rate. Indiscriminate logging, sanctioned and even aided and abetted by governments, can have no justification, yet the sheer scale of modern pulp mills creates a hunger for timber that is ravaging forests around the world.

The worst scandals around the paper industry happen when companies do not even stop to enquire whose trees they are cutting for pulp. Land-rights abuses, social conflicts and impoverished communities are the result. Illegal logging is rife and the paper industry is culpable. The most shocking impacts of the paper industry's misdemeanours are not so much environmental as social. When forests are trashed, people suffer. Where the paper industry appropriates natural resources, like land, forests and water, livelihoods dependent on them are lost. Paper making is thus directly linked to poverty.

Even in rich countries like Canada, the greed of the paper industry for trees means that a blind eye is turned both to the abuse of human rights, particularly of indigenous people, and to the environmental travesty of old-growth logging.

The paper industry argues that by planting trees it will reduce its future need for forest timber, and so all around the world plantations for fibre are being established. But these are no panacea, particularly when they are monocultures of non-native or, worse, genetically modified species or when they are planted without the local people's free and informed consent. The paper industry is competing with a wide range of other, prior resource users and unfortunately that means that pulpwood production uses land and water that might otherwise have provided food.

Once cut, smashing wood to smithereens to make paper takes as much energy as making steel. Between production, and the losses of carbon from forests and their soils, the paper industry is responsible for more climate change emissions than most countries, and more than three times global aviation.

Its threat to the planet does not end there. Making a single sheet of A4 paper not only causes as much greenhouse gas emissions as burning a lightbulb for an hour, it also uses a mugful of water. In the thirty most industrialised countries, paper making uses more water than any other industry and, unfortunately, too much of the water that goes into a pulp or paper mill comes out polluted with dangerous chemicals that threaten the health of people and wildlife unlucky enough to live downstream from a mill. The dirtiest mills are found in Asia, Latin America and Africa, so it is the poorest people whose environment is worst polluted and effluent treatments to clean up water outflows sometimes simply transfer the problem to air pollution or toxic solid wastes. The primary culprit for the most harmful pollution is our obsession with bright, white paper. We need to unlearn our perception of a blank page as clean, safe and natural and see it for what it really is: chemically bleached tree-mash.

A new leaf

The problems caused by the pulp consumption of the global north are not intractable and they can be tackled on a range of fronts. There are many things that we can do to reduce our paper footprint. The first step is simply to stop taking this material for granted and, by becoming conscious of its value, to encourage decisions to be made about what use of it is appropriate. A simple example is the choice of toilet paper: it is up to each of us whether to wipe our bums with the products of forest destruction or to use 100 per cent recycled tissue, thus giving a valuable material one last use before flushing it away.

Unlike steel, which needs to be made from iron ore, paper can be made from a huge variety of raw materials. China still retains a rich heritage of paper production from a variety of agricultural residues and could teach the rest of the world a huge amount by sharing expertise about how to use these waste fibres. Straw is an important part of China's rural economy, and as farmers are squeezed in North America and Europe, perhaps they too could benefit from baling it up for sale to paper mills instead of burning it in the field.

The paper industry is undergoing massive structural changes as the market prices for its raw materials, and the demand for its products, make global shifts. Huge amounts of money lubricate these changes, and investors in new paper industry developments need to invest in a more ethical manner and become much more aware of the hidden price paid by those who suffer the negative impacts of the industry. Financiers can and should demand full, independent social and environmental impact assessments, corporate social responsibility reports and social audits, and be prepared to see through company greenwash. Almost everyone in Europe and North America is a bank customer or has financial investments, and it is becoming ever easier for us to shift our accounts to institutions that are committed to ethical investments and prepared to use their leverage to force the paper industry to plan for a fairer and much more sustainable future.

Part of that future must involve large tracts of forest being protected. Across the globe, environmental campaigners are lobbying for precious forest ecosystems to be guaranteed to remain unlogged for future generations of people to enjoy them, for the plants and animals that depend on them to survive, and for the services they provide to stabilise climate and provide fresh water to continue. There is no doubt that we can and must set aside much more of the remaining old-growth forest. Where governments are weak, the paper industry can make its own commitments to stay out of the areas of forest that ecologists consider most precious.

Governments all over the world need to be strong in upholding the human rights of forest people and the communities who are adversely impacted by paper and pulp mill developments, including unwanted tree plantations. All forests are inhabited, and the local people who live in them are most likely to know how they can be managed sustainably. The paper industry should respect and support local economies and businesses, reversing the trend towards ever-larger industrial units and promoting community ownership and a diversity of small- and medium-sized enterprises in the paper sector. Production systems must not hinder local food production or jeopardise environmental services or ecosystem assets, such as water quality, and their equitable use. Much more space needs to be made to listen to the voices of indigenous people and forest communities and to respect what they have to say. What has been gained if the wrapper on a fair trade bar of chocolate, or the packet on a fair trade brand of tea, has caused the loss of livelihoods in a forest-dependent community?

In consumer countries, we all have many opportunities to make more ethical and environmentally sensitive choices about the paper we buy: we can choose recycled toilet paper and greetings cards, or opt for a lighter weight copy paper or a hand-made notebook. However, a lot of paper products are acquired as a side-effect of buying something else, like the package on food, the statement from a financial service or the content of a magazine. Within big packaging and publishing corporations, there are small numbers of individuals who make decisions to purchase huge volumes of paper. If they could be persuaded to make more forest-friendly, ethical decisions, they would change the face of the paper industry. If we can inspire these people to buy paper responsibly (by choosing recycled and totally chlorine-free sheets) they will create a level of demand that is bound to make a huge difference.

A key tool for such people is the ability to trace the origin of the fibre used in a piece of paper all the way from the paper mill back to the forest where it grew. Credible certification systems like the Forest Stewardship Council provide that traceability, and allow the chain of custody of every paper fibre to be determined (while other certification systems are little more than industry badges of allegiance). In the FSC system, whether the forest of origin has been sustainably managed is assessed by an independent third party, but more importantly, the chain of custody allows responsible purchasers to check for themselves if they are happy to buy that product.

The best way to reduce pressure on forests, however, is to use paper that is made not from virgin tree fibres but from recycled fibres. Recycling paper uses a fraction of the energy that pulping wood requires and thus it emits much less greenhouse gas. It also prevents paper from going to landfill, and rotting down to release methane, a powerful climate change agent. Recycling paper has a plethora of other benefits, including using less water and causing much less pollution and creating more jobs and wider economic benefits than making tree-based paper. Recycling is also good for our souls. Committing to recycling involves not only ensuring our waste is recovered as a useful resource, but also making use of paper products that have been made from recovered waste, thereby extending the life-cycle of the tree fibres within them. Using recycled paper and then sending it for recycling helps us to cultivate awareness of our relationship to others and our responsibilities to them; it is a practical way of recognising our interdependence with each other and with the forests and other ecosystems where the fibres in paper originate.

The biggest problem with recycled paper is that if toxic chemicals, particularly chlorine compounds, are used to bleach the original tree fibres, then their legacy will remain in the recycled product. Even the strongest tree fibres cannot last for ever, and so some paper will continue to need to be made from virgin fibres, hopefully increasingly from a range of agricultural crops, but realistically also for the foreseeable future from trees. It is crucial that the pulp industry should phase out the use of any chlorine compounds for bleaching and switch to totally chlorine-free technology and big buyers should avoid anything but genuinely chlorine-free paper.

We must not forget that though recycled paper is certainly better than virgin, its production is not impact-free. The biggest reduction in environmental footprint is achieved by not wasting paper. Ultimately, the best way that each of us can help to reduce the negative impacts of the paper industry is simply to use less of its product.

Some future speculations

It is difficult, possibly risky, to try to predict the future, particularly of anything as vast and diverse as the paper industry, but there do seem to be three broad and worrying trends.

The first is that paper consumption seems to be set to continue rising globally, and even in Western countries where we are already awash with the stuff, every year new applications, technologies and gizmos are devised that make our environmental footprints a bit bigger. In Europe, there seems no end to the inexorable rise in office printing and both the tissue and packaging sectors are bullish about their ability to persuade consumers to continue transporting paper and board from supermarket shelves to rubbish bins in the service of hygiene fetishes and corporate branding.

The second trend that looks unavoidable is for increasing areas of land, particularly in the global south, to be converted into tree plantations for fibre production. This is because the cost of growing wood in a country like Brazil is much less than in most northern countries. In the north, the paper and board industry currently mops up the cheapest wood on the market, but as governments try to tackle climate change by promoting renewable energy, paper companies will face increasing competition from the energy sector for use of that wood as biofuel. They will therefore turn, as they are already doing, to countries in the global south to promote the establishment of increasing areas of fast-growing tree plantations. There is already a growing movement to fight this expansion, particularly in Latin America, where the 'green desert' movement champions the rights of peasant farmers and indigenous peoples with whom the paper industry is competing for land. As pulpwood spreads, so will conflict.

The third trend will be for increasing consolidation in the industry. Pulp and paper corporations are becoming ever larger: new pulp mills are being built that are even bigger than the current generation of mega-mills, while small mills and companies are absorbed or eliminated with consequent losses of jobs. The concentration of production in a few giant units also concentrates the problems of mill pollution, energy and water demand, and increases the need for transport. All of this happens due to an international financial regime dominated by a few huge investment banks, along with an elite posse of paper industry development consultants, which claim that this is the best way to maximise economic returns. As long as their world view dominates, promoting profit for shareholders at the expense of any other issues of sustainability, such as the impacts on forests or local communities, the result will be an ever greater concentration of the power and resources of the industry in fewer and fewer hands.

I hope I am proved wrong on even one of these predictions.

An alternative future

So what future do the paper industry's critics want instead? In Europe, a network of environmental organisations, including all the big names like Greenpeace, WWF and Friends of the Earth plus lots of smaller more locally focused groups, came together to draw up a shared vision for transforming the paper industry. Writing the vision involved an eight-month process to agree a text, at the end of which, consensus was reached at a meeting of the Forest Movement Europe (FME) in Brussels in late 2005. The result was a four-page document entitled 'A Vision for Transforming the European Paper Industry' and it was signed by 50 NGOs from 21 countries. Its opening gambit was a long-term vision:

> We, the undersigned, want to see a future Europe that consumes dramatically less paper than at present, with all that paper made by an industry that is less reliant on virgin tree fibres, maximises use of recycled materials, respects local people's land-rights, provides employment and has social impacts that are beneficial, conflict-free and fair. We want to see all of Europe's paper being made from responsibly- and sustainably-sourced fibres, using entirely renewable energy, with water that is as clean after paper production as before, producing zero waste and zero emissions.

The document then laid out an agenda for the transformation of the industry within the next ten years, acknowledging the cultural benefits of paper in our lives, and challenging the industry to commit to sustainability. Calling on the paper industry to open up about all its environmental and social impacts, the vision was expressed as five pillars: to reduce consumption; shift from virgin to recycled fibre; source all wood fibre responsibly; clean up production; and ensure social responsibility. Each pillar was set out as a series of specific goals. Its biggest challenge was the need for Europe to cut its paper consumption by half, justified on the basis of the unsustainable ecological footprint of the European Union.

The creation of this shared vision was a landmark in environmental work in Europe, drawing together forest campaigners with activists working on other issues affected by the paper industry: water pollution, air pollution, climate change, energy efficiency, waste recycling and human rights. The many groups with paper-related interests have tended to work alone, or occasionally in small partnerships, focused on their local industries or consumers and each with their own campaign or advocacy style and approach. However, the multinational nature of the industry created a realisation that civil society needed both to think and work globally in order to convince the industry to reform, and that in order to do so alliances and co-operation were needed between organisations in different countries, with different constituencies, big and small, radical and mainstream. A similar alliance and common vision to that in Europe has also been developed in North America. The Environmental Paper Network is burgeoning, with a membership of more than a hundred organisations from all continents.

The launch of the European vision took place in a conference suite in a building above Frankfurt's Central Station, as a parallel event to Paperworld, a huge international pulp and paper industry congress held in Frankfurt every year. Industry representatives flocked to listen to a panel of some of the world's most experienced environmental paper activists, who told them in no uncertain terms that 'the paper industry must act now to address the crisis of over-consumption of resources and irreversible negative impacts on the lives of people all around the world and on our environment.'

On the platform were campaigners from global environmental organisations including Greenpeace and WWF and German groups

Robin Wood and Urgewald. Otto Miettenen was representing Friends of the Earth, whose network of chapters all around Europe, and as far afield as Indonesia, were vocal, inspiring and highly effective in strengthening the text of the vision. Otto was dressed in combat gear and fresh from the battle to prevent the Finnish paper industry's assault on the last remaining fragments of old-growth forest. 'Nothing falls in the forest in Finland without the involvement of the paper industry, so this vision means everything for Finland, everything, really,' he said. 'Few natural forests are left in Europe. The paper industry and governments need to commit to protecting our valuable forests while there's still something to save.'

The turn-out was good, with a lot of suited industry representatives curious to learn what was in the vision, and also some perhaps keen to be seen to be networking at an event run by environmentalists, in the hope that some green might rub off on them. I was amused to see that SCA, the company that runs the Prudhoe tissue mill in Northumberland, had sent along a representative. During the question and answer session he remarked: 'We must tackle human behaviour with paper and educate people. We use paper every moment of our lives, but no one knows where it comes from. We have to start in schools, so children will know.' I wanted to ask him why, in that case, his company was so cagey about allowing me into their mill to document where their toilet roll came from, but although I sidled up several times to ask him, he shrugged me off, preferring the conversation of potential customers.

The only aspect of the vision that gained a negative response from the audience, perhaps not surprisingly, was the call to reduce paper consumption. It fell to Otto to explain why Europe should cut its paper usage by 50 per cent. 'Consumption is the ultimate cause of all the problems with paper,' he said, 'and this means reducing consumption is the ultimate means of tackling the impacts of paper production and disposal. Paper consumption is unsustainably high and much of it is unnecessary. It has doubled in the last twenty years and our ecological footprint is now twice our biological capacity. Industry must play a part in reducing this unnecessary consumption.'

An Italian paper industry representative stood up and challenged Otto: 'Who wants to say how much toilet roll we can use? We can't create a new kind of police to control consumption. We have to recognise the human element of greed.' The biggest challenge we face is to persuade the paper industry that ever-increasing production is not necessarily its only viable future, and that a more sustainable option is to use paper resources more efficiently to meet the real needs of consumers.

Using less paper

The simplest solution is to consume less, but most of us use considerable quantities of paper that companies buy on our behalf when we pay them for some other service, for example, when we bank our money, use a restaurant, use transport or buy packaged goods. For most of us, genuine paper purchasing decisions, when we buy only paper and can choose what kind, are a tiny fraction of our actual paper consumption: toilet roll is one example, notebooks another. Normally we get paper as a side-effect of wanting something else, like news, information, or whatever is inside the cardboard box. In those cases, it is the decisions of corporate paper purchasers that need to be influenced to develop better paper policies.

There are some key people in the paper market who make procurement decisions and sign purchasing orders for enormous quantities of paper. They work for major magazine publishers, catalogue producers, governments, banks etc. By understanding how these people make their decisions and helping them to make savings, large changes to paper consumption patterns could be achieved. Unfortunately people in the paper industry often react to the language of 'reducing consumption' as anti-business. But if we turn the language on its head, and think of it as 'increasing resource efficiency', the concept is much less threatening. Saving paper is a way of making bottom-line gains by cutting the expense of unnecessary wastage and making more effective use of fewer resources. It is perfectly possible in most offices to make a 20 to 30 per cent cut in paper consumption by eliminating wasteful and unnecessary paper use through simple tricks like double-sided printing that in no way cause inconvenience or discomfort; indeed getting rid of some paper, like junk mail and pointless bureaucracy, is positively helpful. We need to think 'travelling light' rather than 'going on a diet'.

Some assessments of levels of waste are astronomical. For example, totting up mill waste, printing waste, over-runs and returns, up to 75 per cent of the paper used in magazine production may never be seen by a reader. Yet, there are massive financial as well as environmental benefits to be gained by using paper more efficiently: Bank of America saved a packet just by making money teller printouts optional, smaller and lighter; Hewlett Packard reduced printer breakages by wrapping them in clingfilm instead of thick cardboard, so they look fragile and are treated gently; Tullis Russell has increased the security features on cheques, increasing profit margins despite volumes steadily decreasing year on year.

We need to begin a dialogue about the benefits of saving paper, and to help industry to recognise that end-consumers can continue to enjoy services such as hygiene, information or entertainment, while the supply chains are transformed to be more resource efficient, making savings that are both good for business and for social justice and the environment. Packaging design courses are needed that emphasise the benefits of resource efficiency. Introducing the idea of using just our 'fair share' of the world's paper can add an ethical dimension to paper saving, and gifting some of the money saved to a good cause can help paper buyers feel less like Scrooge and more like Santa.

There is a widespread belief that paper use is correlated with literacy rates, but this is a myth most starkly demonstrated by the USA and Vietnam, which have similar literacy rates (roughly 95 per cent) yet Vietnam's paper consumption is less than 2 per cent of America's. Japan and Bulgaria both have almost 100 per cent literacy rates, yet Bulgaria manages this with less than a tenth as much paper as Japan. Paper use is a better indicator of wealth, as it correlates well with national disposable income. A study in the UK showed that income is a prime determinant of paper use, with wealthy households using up to three times as much as poor ones. According to Susan Kinsella, of Conservatree, a USA-based specialist in recycled papers, 90 per cent of the world's printing paper is consumed by less than 20 per cent of the world's population, the wealthiest fifth. A United Nations Environment Programme estimate is that 30 to 40 kilograms (66 to 88 pounds) of paper is all that is required for good communications and education, but in rich countries the average use is much higher than this. It seems that the more money a society has, the more it can afford to spend on paper. It also means that those of us living in the wealthy paper-consuming nations are causing a disproportionate share of the impacts of its production.

As individuals we can all commit to breaking bad habits. In Europe and North America most people use many kinds of paper with great frequency, from toilet roll to catalogues to newspapers to computer printouts. We need to learn to identify our bad little paper wastage habits and give them up.

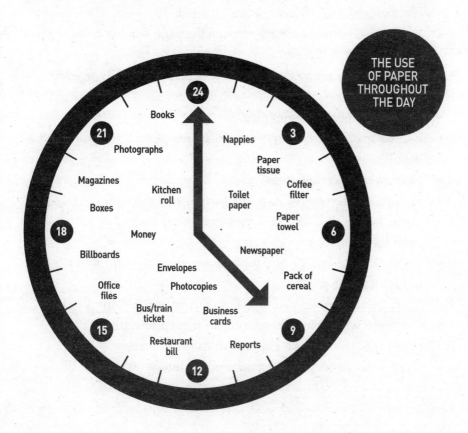

There are many decisions we can make to avoid paper completely: not buying the newspaper, sharing someone else's; not picking up the napkin, using a handkerchief; not collecting the leaflet, reading it and putting it back; not printing, reading it on screen; not pulling that hand-towel, letting hands dry naturally; not accepting the bag, the flyer, the free magazine, the conference advertising, the seminar handout, whatever. Each day we have dozens of such opportunities to crack our paper addiction.

Even where paper use seems essential, we can almost always find ways to use less. Here are some more examples:

- Think before printing, and if you must, always print double sided.
- Forget paper archives; electronic ones are easier to search, lighter, cheaper and take up less space.
- Learn some tricks for fitting more on the page: smaller fonts, thinner margins, better layout.
- Question how many copies of a document are really needed.
- Reuse envelopes.
- Read news online sometimes.
- Use scraps of waste paper or old envelopes for notes instead of Post-its.
- Hold paper-free meetings.
- Sign up not to receive junk mail from the Post Office.
- Write to people who send you junk mail asking to be removed from their database.
- Don't tick the box on the form saying you would like to receive more information.
- Carry a fabric, washable handkerchief to avoid using tissues.
- Get some washable kitchen cloths for mopping up.
- Resist the urge to take napkins in cafés.
- Use fewer sheets of toilet paper every time.

Pulp or people?

My interest in paper began as a result of the paradox of being a writer (and thus wanting huge amounts of this material to come pouring off the presses with my name on it), whilst also being passionate about forests and horrified by their destruction to feed pulp mills. My interest became obsession, however, when I was taken in Indonesia by Pak Jafri out into the pulpwood wasteland that was once his community's forest, garden, food store, DIY emporium, pharmacy and temple. This was not just about deforestation. The impacts of the paper industry, I realised then, were rooted in injustice: pollution, loss of livelihoods and theft of land that is better used for food, shelter and wildlife than for faxes and direct mail.

Yet paper is a fundamentally important material for cultural development and freedom of expression. In the words of Palestinian refugee writer Iyad Hayatleh:

> When paper becomes scarce,
> for it I would offer my skin.
> When ink becomes scarce,
> for it I would offer my veins
> And the sea of my blood.

Paper is a potent and necessary part of society, but the rampant consumption in Europe and North America becomes obscene when set against the millions of African children who do not have books to learn from in school or the authors imprisoned without writing implements by oppressive regimes.

Paper making can be an art form in itself, as Cai Zhang showed me in China. Support for the artisans and small-scale paper makers of the world can also keep alive the knowledge of how to make paper from something other than wood and perhaps help the paper industry to advance towards a more diverse and sustainable range of fibre sources.

In the meantime, I am not so naïve as to suggest that we can give up making paper out of trees altogether. Indeed, as a forest product it has supported the livelihood of lumberjacks like my Great Uncle Frank, and will continue to support people like Sammi, the Finnish logger, and all the other forestry workers around the world, in making their living from the woods. But those people deserve fairer treatment from the paper industry than they are getting at present.

So do Arkady Kaza, Pak Jafri, Steve Fobister, Judy da Silva, Joe Martin and all the other indigenous peoples whose forest lands have been appropriated by the paper industry, pulping sacred trees and trashing traditional hunting and fishing grounds. Their protesting voices sing the same tunes as ecologists like Boris Kashevarov, Raimo Heikkila and Olly Turunen. They would all agree with Faina when she listens to the song of Lake Baikal and concludes that we are all part of one living, breathing planet, upon which we depend for our cultural, as well as physical, survival.

I am, ultimately, optimistic. I have heard paper tycoon Dmitry Zuev of Segezha Pulp and Paper commit to saving old-growth forest, and I believe such commitment can spread throughout the industry. I have touched the bales of paper that Forbes Connor has chosen to recycle in the UK rather than make a fast buck by selling them to China, thus leaving a smaller carbon footprint and helping to grow a sustainable market for recovered paper, and I am confident that his way of doing business can prevail. I have seen the pride in Cindy Connor's eyes when she printed Harry Potter books on recycled paper and I am sure that every other paper buyer will feel just as good when they make a similar choice.

When we realise that the cost of runaway paper consumption is social conflict, ill health and poverty, we will want to use less. When we decide that we want to create the opportunity for poor countries to get the benefits of a bit more paper, we will think about how to use less. When we come to see that by wasting so much paper we are not just causing environmental harm but are actually taking more than our fair share of a finite resource; when we see that, we will decide to take action. Everyone who wants a fairer world will use less paper.

POSTSCRIPT

If you look closely you will see that the leaves of this book (unless you're reading an eBook version) are made of tree fibres. The paper is sufficiently pale so that the ink of the words shows clearly, but without being brashly bleached. It is textured so that the pages are pleasant to touch and turn, smoothed to respond to your fingers with an ear-enticing swish, and firm enough so if you flick the sheets they will patter like little footsteps.

Fortunately, because this paper is recycled, each of the fibres within it has already served some other function since being cut from the forest, hopefully more than one. Rescuing them and giving them another life has prevented them rotting to climate-wrecking methane and clogging up a bit of landfill space, avoided the felling of more trees to make fresh paper, used less energy and water than would have been needed to pulp those trees, and emitted minimal pollution.

In the woods, shoots of green nudge aside last year's crumbled undergrowth with promises of flowers. Great tits are twittering about territories, chaffinches chirp their snippets of spring and a robin is sitting on the highest twig of a rowan tree improvising love songs. Inside the tree trunks, just underneath the bark, cylinders of cambium are beginning to weave a new generation of cells, a new ring of fibrous tubes to suck sap up to swelling buds, living fibres tough enough to withstand gales, forest fibres just like the ones in your hands.

Postscript

If you want to do just one thing having read this book, please make a pledge to use less paper. You can do so at the European Environmental Paper Network's website on reducing paper use, part of their project called Shrink: Addressing the Madness of Over-Consumption of Paper. Visit www.shrinkpaper.org for more details.

BIBLIOGRAPHY

The following list contains some of the most important sources and inspirations for *Paper Trails* and some suggestions for related further reading.

Chapter 1

World Resources Institute Earth Trends website (earthtrends.wri.org)

Food and Agriculture Organization (FAO) of the United Nations statistics (*FAOSTAT*) (faostat.fao.org)

Abramovitz, Janet N. and Ashley T. Mattoon, *Paper Cuts: Recovering the Paper Landscape*, Editor Jane A. Peterson. Worldwatch paper 149, December 1999. (www.worldwatch.org/system/files/EWP149.pdf)

Chapter 2

Gifford, Rob, *China Road: A Journey into the Future of a Rising Power*, Bloomsbury, 2007

Needham, Joseph, *Science and Civilization in China: Volume 5, Part 1.* Taipei: Caves Books Ltd, 1986

Dequan He, Christopher Barr and Steve Rhee, *China's Paper and Paperboard Industry: Supply and Demand Trends and Projections to 2010*, Center for International Forestry Research (CIFOR),

2005. (www.cifor.cgiar.org/publications/pdf_files/research/ governance/foresttrade/briefs/PolicyBrief_01.pdf)

Zakreski, Sheldon, *Crouching fiber, paper dragon: China and the global paper market*, Metafore, 2004

Economy, Elizabeth C. , *The River Runs Black: The Environmental Challenge to China's Future*, Cornell University Press, 2004

Lines, Clifford and Graham Booth, *Paper Matters: Today's Paper and Board Industry Unfolded*, Paper Publications Ltd, 1990

Evans, Joan, *The Endless Web: John Dickinson & Co Ltd, 1804–1954*, Jonathan Cape, 1955

Chapter 3

Tio Minar, Betty, *No Chip Mill Without Wood, A Study of UFS Projects to Develop Wood Chip and Paper Pulp Mills in Kalimantan, Indonesia*, Down to Earth, August 2006. (dte.gn.apc.org/cskal06.pdf)

Spek, Masya, *Financing Pulp Mills: An Appraisal of Risk Assessment and Safeguard Procedures*, CIFOR, 2006

Lohmann, Larry, *Pulp, Paper and Power: How an Industry Reshapes its Social Environment*, The Corner House, 1995. (www.thecornerhouse.org.uk/item.shtml?x=52196)

Lang, Chris, *Banks, Pulp and Paper*, Urgewald, 2007. (www.pulpmillwatch.org)

Greenpeace's Kleercut campaign site (kleercut.net/en/, particularly www.kleercut.net/en/files/ChainofLies_final.pdf)

WWF European Forest Programme, *Scoring of the Tissue Giants*, November 2005. (www.panda.org/about_wwf/what_we_do/ forests/our_solutions/responsible_forestry/forest_conversion_ agriculture/tissue_issue/scores_tissue_giants/index.cfm)

Victoria's Dirty Secret campaign (www.victoriasdirtysecret.net)

ForestEthics catalogue campaign (forestethics.org and catalogcutdown.org)

Imhoff, Daniel, *Paper or Plastic: Searching for Solutions for an Overpackaged World*, Sierra Club Books, 2005

Chapter 4

Harrison, Robert Pogue, *Forests: The Shadow of Civilisation*, University of Chicago Press, 1992

Kuchli, Christian, *Forests of Hope: Stories of Regeneration*, Earthscan, 1997

Lynch, Wayne, *The Great Northern Kingdom: Life in the Boreal Forest*, Fitzhenry and Whiteside, 2001

Newell, Josh, *The Russian Far East: A Reference Guide for Conservation and Development*, Daniel and Daniel, 2004

Raffan, James, *The Boreal Forest: Rendezvous with the Wild*, Boston Mills Press, 2004

Tudge, Colin, *The Secret Life of Trees: How they Live and Why they Matter*, Penguin Books, 2006

Paper Loop (www.pulp-paper.com)

Pulp Universe (www.pulpuniverse.com/onlinemagazine.asp)

Chapter 5

Carrere, Ricardo, *Pulp Mills: From Monocultures to Industrial Pollution*, World Rainforest Movement, 2005

Hurst, Philip, *Rainforest Politics: Ecological Destruction in South-East Asia*, Zed Books, 1990

Chatham House briefing paper on illegal logging (www.illegal-logging.info/uploads/BP0806illegallogging.pdf)

Friends of the Earth, *APRIL Fools* (www.foe.co.uk/resource/reports/april_fools.pdf)

Friends of the Earth, *APP – Paper Tiger, Hidden Dragons* (www.foe.co.uk/resource/reports/paper_tiger_hidden_dragons.pdf)

Eyes on the Forest, a coalition of Indonesian NGOs (www.eyesontheforests.org)

Chapter 6

The Markets Initiative (www.marketsinitiative.org)

Global Forest Watch Canada (www.globalforestwatch.ca)

Rowling, J K, *Harry Potter and the Order of the Phoenix*, Raincoast Books, 2003. Printed on recycled paper. (www.raincoast.com/harrypotter/forest.html)

Bibliography

Chapter 7

The World Rainforest Movement bulletin (www.wrm.org.uy/ bulletin)

Carrere, Ricardo and Larry Lohmann, *Pulping the South. Industrial Tree Plantations in the World Paper Economy*, Zed Books, 1996

World Rainforest Movement, *Plantations are not Forests*, 2003

World Rainforest Movement report on impacts of pulp plantations (www.wrm.org.uy/plantations/pulp.html#bulletin)

Chris Lang's blogs (chrislang.org and pulpinc.wordpress.com)

Lang, Chris, *Genetically Modified Trees: The Ultimate Threat to Forests*, WRM and Friends of the Earth International, 2004

Sampson, Viola and Larry Lohmann, *Genetic Dialectic: The Biological Politics of Genetically Modified Trees*, The Corner House, 2000

Chapter 8

Counsell, Thomas A.M. and Julian M. Allwood, 'Reducing climate change gas emissions by cutting out stages in the life-cycle of office paper', *Journal of Resources, Conservation and Recycling*, 49(4): 340–352, 2007. (dx.doi.org/10.1016/j.resconrec.2006.03.018)

Paper Task Force (consisting of Duke University, Environmental Defense Fund, Johnson & Johnson, McDonald, The Prudential Insurance Company of America, Time Inc), *Lifecycle Environmental Comparison: Virgin Paper and Recycled Paper-Based Systems*, White Paper No.3, February 2002 (www.environmentaldefense.org/documents/1618_WP3.pdf)

Natural Resources Defense Council, *Too Good To Throw Away*, February 1997. (www.nrdc.org/cities/recycling/recyc/recyinx.asp)

Hershkowitz, A., *Bronx Ecology: Blueprint for a New Environmentalism*, Island Press, 2002

Lifset, R., M. Grieg-Gran, M. Smith, R. Denison, 'Roundtable on the industrial ecology of pulp and paper', *Journal of Industrial Ecology*, 1(3), 1998

Chapter 9

Reach for Unbleached (www.rfu.org)

Pollution Watch (www.pollutionwatch.org)

Pulp Mill Watch (www.pulpmillwatch.org)

The Battle for Baikal by Baikal Environmental Wave
(www.baikalwave.eu.org/Oldsitebew/battle.html)

Chapter 10

The Environmental Paper Network (www.environmentalpaper.org)

Hawkins, Paul, Amory Lovins and L. Hunter Lovins, *Natural Capitalism: Creating the Next Industrial Revolution*, Back Bay Books, 2000

von Wiezsacker, A.B., Lovins and L.H. Lovins, *Factor Four: Doubling Wealth, Halving Resource Use*, Earthscan, 1997

Robins, N, and S Roberts, *Rethinking Paper Consumption*, International Institute of Environment and Development, 1996. (www.poptel.org.uk/iied/smg/pubs/rethink.html)

McDonough,William and Michael Braungart, *Cradle to Cradle: Remaking the Way we Make Things*, North Point Press, 2002

ACKNOWLEDGEMENTS

I am grateful to my many colleagues and fellow activists, too numerous to mention individually, in the Environmental Paper Network, the European Environmental Paper Network and the Taiga Rescue Network, for sharing a love of the forests and an interest in their most ubiquitous product. Particular thanks to Helma Brandlmaier, Jim Ford, Judy Rodrigues, Joshua Martin, Feja Lesniewska, Chris Lang, Ricardo Carrere, Katy Harris, Mandy Meikle, John Bolland, Jane Alexander, Jason Donald, Felix Boon, Hannah Ritchie, Jenn McCartney, Kate Orson, Ashley Lennon and members of the North West Highland Writers for reading or commenting helpfully on drafts of this manuscript. Thanks also to Gregor Milne, Forbes Connor, Nick Purdy, Peter Gerhardt, Maggis Renstrom, Duncan Pollard, Lydia Bartz, Otto Miettinen, Olli Turunen, Raimo Heikkila, Otto and Ammima and all at FNL, Paivi Lohi, Jukka-Pekka Klemetti and others at UPM-Kymmene, Anatoly Lebedev, Andrei Laletin, Fyodor Kronokovsky, Arkady Kaza, Sasha Markovsky, Olga Il'ina, Boris Kashevarov, Dmitry Zuev and all at Segezha Pulp and Paper, Jennie Sutton, Natasha and all at Baikal Wave, Cai Zhang, Tamara Stark, Liu Bing, Xiao Na and Chris, Professor Dr Nguyen van Truong, Hieu Vu Huu,

Dede Kunaifi, Pak Jafri, Pak Anzam, Imran, Zainudin, Ahmad Zazaly, Rivani Noor, Fatra and all at Jikalahari, Hakiki and CAPPA, Sara and Eliezer P. Lorenzo at APRIL, Nicole Rycroft, Maryjka Mychajlowycz, Diego Garcia, Joe Martin, Steve Fobister, Judy da Silva, Frank Locantore, Scot Quaranda, Stephanie Fried, Heather Serantis, Pete Kazanjy, Dick Koenhowen and Cindy Connor for sharing your knowledge and experience with me. Thanks to everyone else who I have overlooked who helped me on my travels.

Thanks to Channel 4 whose WriteAway travel writing competition got me started on dreaming up this project, and particularly to Margaret Blythe at Dogtooth Media who has mentored me throughout, and to Margaret Elphinstone, one of the competition judges who has provided endless encouragement to bring the book to fruition. Thanks to Hi-Arts for financial support for my journey in 2006, to Eleanor Scott for allowing me to take a 'sabbatical' for the journey and to the Scottish Arts Council for a writer's bursary enabling me to focus on developing the book on my return. Professor Tom Leonard helped me to become a better writer with two years of tuition in Glasgow and has supported my efforts ever since.

Thanks to the editors of Am Bratach, Resurgence, Mslexia, Pulp and Paper International, Clean Slate, Reforesting Scotland Journal, Parks International and Taiga News for publishing my paper-related writings during the course of my research for this book. The audiences at the various slide-shows and presentations I have given in Lochinver, Golspie, Ullapool, Falkland, Edinburgh and Falkirk also helped me to hone the story.

Thanks to my agent, Laetitia Rutherford, for her many insights and encouragement in developing and promoting the book, to Ed Faulkner and Davina Russell for their editorial guidance and enthusiasm, to Claire Pierotti for leading the publicity work and to the rest of the team at Virgin Books who have 'walked the talk' by helping to get this book out into the world in paper-free form and on recycled paper.

Acknowledgements

I am grateful for the encouragement and humour of my family and friends as they have seen me go paper mad over the past few years.

Last and most heartfelt, thanks to Bill Ritchie for camera-work, cuddles and camaraderie. Your help shows on every page of this book.

INDEX

Index

Index

corporations 34, 37–41 *see also under individual corporation name*; paper production 29, 34; paper waste 174; pulp mill projects 34, 37–41
UPM-Kymmene 30, 36, 71, 79, 80, 81, 103, 152, 176–7, 178–9, 183, 192, 193
Urgewald 40, 222
Ussuri forest, Russia 61, 90

Valdivia, Chile 187–8
Van Truong, Professor Dr Nguyen 163, 164
Verso Paper 194
Via Campesina 156
Victoria's Secret 52, 82
Vietnam 160–4, 224
Villas, Fabio Martins 155, 156, 157
Virta, Jouko 92, 106
Vu Huu, Hieu 161–3

waste, paper 13–16; branding and bills 49–51; cash machine receipts 42, 44, 136; junk mail/catalogues 51–2, 224; levels of 224; packaging 48–9; paper saving initiatives 223–4; printers and 44; publishers and 138–9, 141–7, 223; reducing 42–5, 224–6; toilet roll, kitchen roll 45–7; use of internet and computers, effect upon 2, 14, 42–5
Weyerhaeuser 36, 118, 120, 121, 154
Whiskey Jack forest 117, 119
wildlife, effect of paper industry upon 41, 65–6, 74, 76, 77–8, 80, 96, 109, 130, 150
World Bank 32, 38, 39, 41, 83, 203
World Business Council for Sustainable Development 174
World Rainforest Movement 153
WWF (Worldwide Fund for Nature) 40, 47, 58, 72–3, 83, 104, 113, 187, 220, 221

Xaxys 50
Xuan paper 23, 24–5

Zazaly, Ahmad 107, 109
Zhang, Cai 24, 25–7, 30, 124, 227
Zuev, Dmitry 70–1, 72, 73, 86, 228